To Place Our Deeds

THE GEORGE GUND FOUNDATION
IMPRINT IN AFRICAN AMERICAN STUDIES

The George Gund Foundation has endowed
this imprint to advance understanding of
the history, culture and current issues
concerning African Americans.

To Place Our Deeds

The African American Community
in Richmond, California, 1910–1963

Shirley Ann Wilson Moore

UNIVERSITY OF CALIFORNIA PRESS

Berkeley / Los Angeles / London

The publisher gratefully acknowledges the generous contribution to this book provided by the George Gund Foundation.

Portions of this book, used here with permission, were previously published in slightly different forms as follows: "Traditions from Home: African Americans in Wartime Richmond, California," in Lewis A. Erenberg and Susan E. Hirsch, eds., *The War in American Culture: Society and Consciousness During World War II* (Chicago: University of Chicago Press, 1996), 263–283, Copyright © 1996 by the University of Chicago; "Not in Somebody's Kitchen: African American Women Workers in Richmond, California, and the Impact of World War II," in Elizabeth Jameson and Susan Armitage, eds., *Writing the Range: Race, Class, and Culture in the Women's West* (Norman: University of Oklahoma Press, 1997), 517–532, Copyright © 1997 by the University of Oklahoma Press.

University of California Press
Berkeley and Los Angeles, California

University of California Press, Ltd.
London, England

Library of Congress Cataloging-in-Publication Data

Moore, Shirley Ann Wilson, 1947–
    To place our deeds : the African American community in Richmond, California, 1910–1963 / Shirley Ann Wilson Moore.
        p.   cm.
    ISBN 0-520-21565-6 (alk. paper)
        1. Afro-Americans—California—Richmond—History—20th century.
    2. Afro-Americans—California—Richmond—Social conditions—20th century.   3. Richmond (Calif.)—Race relations.   I. Title.
    F869.R5M66   1999
    979.4'63—dc21   99-15209
                                                                        CIP

Manufactured in the United States of America
08 07 06 05 04 03 02 01 00   9 8 7 6 5 4 3 2 1

To my parents, John L. Wilson and Rosa Mae Lewis Wilson, whose migration from Oklahoma to California started me down this path, and to my husband, Joe Louis Moore, whose encouragement, support, and love have kept me on it.

Contents

LIST OF ILLUSTRATIONS   ix

LIST OF TABLES   xi

ACKNOWLEDGMENTS   xiii

Introduction   1

1.
Richmond before the War: A "Slow, Gradual and
Comforting" Change   7

2.
Shipyards and Shipbuilders   40

3.
Boomtown   71

4.
Demobilization, Rising Expectations, and Postwar
Realities   94

5.
Traditions from Home   127

6.
Epilogue: Community, Success, and Unfulfilled Promise   147

NOTES   151

BIBLIOGRAPHY   203

INDEX   219

Illustrations

Figures *(following page 70)*

1. The Freeman family, North Richmond, ca. 1919
2. Santa Fe Railroad workers, ca. 1920
3. Walter and Jessie Freeman with the family dairy cows in North Richmond, ca. 1920
4. The Joseph Griffin family and their new Durant car, ca. 1930
5. Richmond High School shop class, Walter Freeman Jr., ca. 1928
6. North Richmond Missionary Baptist Church, ca. 1940
7. The Slocum family, North Richmond, ca. 1939
8. Sunday morning, North Richmond, ca. 1940
9. Jessie Freeman displaying one of her quilts in front of her North Richmond home, ca. 1925
10. Mr. and Mrs. Joseph Malbrough, North Richmond, 1985
11. Ida and George Johnson, ca. 1937
12. Louis Bonaparte, Richmond Yard 2, ca. 1943
13. Black women workers in the Richmond shipyards, ca. 1943
14. Launching the S.S. *George Washington Carver,* 1943
15. Shipyard workers in downtown Richmond, 1942
16. Richmond shipyard workers end shift, 1942
17. Former Arkansas sharecropper at her North Richmond trailer home, 1942
18. Shipyard worker on her day off, Richmond Cafe, ca. 1943
19. Richmond wartime housing project, ca. 1944

20. Parchester Village Improvement Association,
ca. 1950
21. Well-baby clinic staff, ca. 1943
22. Advertisement for Tappers Inn, ca. 1945
23. Opening night at Minnie Lue's, North Richmond,
ca. 1950
24. Minnie Lue Nichols and assistant, ca. 1950
25. The Spiderettes, ca. 1945

Maps

1. The City of Richmond, 1917   10
2. Richmond Shipyards, 1944   42
3. The Black Crescent   112

Tables

1. Race, Gender, and Nativity in Richmond,
   by Decade, 1910–1940   12
2. Employee Weekly Budget, Kaiser Shipyards,
   Richmond, 1944   44
3. Yearly Incidence of Selected Crimes and Total
   Arrests in Richmond, 1940–1943   76
4. Unemployment Rates in Richmond, by Color
   and Sex, 1950   96
5. Race and Sex Distribution in Richmond,
   1950 and 1960   101

Acknowledgments

Many people have helped me complete this book, and I am indebted to them all. Lawrence Levine, Earl Lewis, and Olly Wilson were my advisors when this project was a doctoral dissertation at the University of California, Berkeley. Their invaluable scholarship and encouragement have strengthened the present work. Thanks also to Waldo Martin, Albert Broussard, Joe William Trotter Jr., Charles Wollenberg, Susan Hirsch, Quintard Taylor, Madelon Powers, Opal Nations, and Lee Hildebrand. Special thanks to Joe Louis Moore for copying and restoring the photographs.

I am grateful to individuals and staffs at numerous institutions. Heartfelt thanks go to the Honorable George Livingston, former mayor of Richmond; Emma Clark and the staff at the Richmond Public Library; Kathleen Rupley and the staff at the Richmond Museum; Robert Haynes, senior curator for the African American Museum and Library at Oakland; the staff at the Oakland Museum of California; Dr. Richard Boyden of the National Archives in San Bruno; Willa Baum, the director of the Regional Oral History Office at the University of California, Berkeley; Michael McCone and the staff at the California Historical Society; Lynn Bonfield and the staff at the Labor Archives and Research Center at San Francisco State University; and the faculty and staff of the history department at California State University, Sacramento. I am indebted to the editorial staff at the University of California Press for their support, and patience. Finally, I extend my warmest thanks to all the women and men who lived, worked, and played in Richmond and who opened their doors and hearts to me.

Introduction

*So many things we were doing no one ever gives [us] credit.
No one wants to place our deeds in the right light. But we were
there and did it.*

Margaret Starks, 1988

Richmond, a sleepy backwater on the San Francisco Bay in Northern California, was transformed into the quintessential war boomtown when Henry J. Kaiser and other defense contractors located four shipyards and numerous war industries there in 1940. Although the war is an important part of the story of that transformation, the history of African Americans in Richmond begins long before World War II brought hundreds of thousands of black people west.[1] Decades before the war the small black community, operating under visible and invisible constraints and stigmatized by other Bay Area blacks as unsophisticated and "primitive," was busy raising families, establishing institutions, and building economic structures. The influx of hopeful, determined black newcomers from the South in the 1940s only rejuvenated processes that had already been set in motion. Black wartime newcomers, determined not to be "Jim Crowed" in California, helped shatter racial barriers that had marginalized African Americans for decades. The war was only one phase of this transformation, however. This book examines the history of the African American community in Richmond during the critical transitional years of the first half of the twentieth century. It places the activities of black working-class men and women, regarded by some as unlettered peasants who were spatially and intellectually isolated from larger social currents, at the center of the nation's most profound, transformative events.

In the past two decades a number of works have begun to explore African American history from a new perspective. These works have liberated blacks from their role as passive victims in history. They have examined black agency using a model that recognizes the impact of internal as well as external forces on the lives of African Americans. However, most of these works have limited their analyses to African American communities east of the Mississippi River.[2]

In recent years, a number of works have begun to examine the history of African Americans in the West, and several have explored the impact of World War II on blacks in the San Francisco Bay Area.[3] This book, however, moves beyond the eastern focus to look at the experiences of African Americans in what is now the country's largest and most influential state. This work is the first to examine the historical development—including migration, the rise of a black urban industrial workforce, and the dynamics of community development—of one black working-class community in California over a fifty-year period. This work affords the opportunity for studying a western black community in which middle-class and professional blacks were among the last to arrive.

The study of black Richmondites allows us to examine the role of culture in the process of black entry into the industrial proletariat. Moreover, it offers an opportunity to analyze the function of culture among working-class blacks who also interacted in a culturally diverse general population. Black working-class cultural expressions prevailed in Richmond despite their lower-class connotations. Even though thousands of black newcomers brought with them a panoply of sustaining cultural traditions that took root in new soil, black community building in Richmond involved more than the simple transplantation of southern black folk culture to the Golden State. The experience of black Richmondites suggests that men and women were equally responsible for bearing and preserving culture. This important duty was not relegated to the realm of women, but was part of the community-building process that occupied black Richmondites of both sexes.[4]

The experiences of black Richmondites suggest that, in California at least, the cultural traditions of black migrants were not isolated or immutable. Their "traditions from home," while critical to the emergence of their political, economic, and social voice, were distinct, malleable, and inextricably linked to forces within and external to the black population. Black Richmondites' cultural traditions were introduced into the diverse threads that comprised California's (and the Bay Area's) cultural fabric even before the second Great Migration brought in thousands of blacks from Texas, Louisiana, Arkansas, Mississippi, and other southern states. Black Richmondites lived, worked, and interacted on a daily (and sometimes intimate) basis with whites and other ethnic groups including the Mexicans, Portuguese, Chinese, Japanese, and Italians who made up a large part of Richmond's population. The possibility of life in a diverse, tolerant environment represented what some black Richmondites called the "California lifestyle." This possibility was, in part, the California equivalent of the "promised land" that led millions of African Americans to eastern industrial cities during the first Great Migration. Their hope is what historian Quintard Taylor has identified as black expectations of Seattle's "free air" in that Pacific Coast city.[5]

The California lifestyle held out the promise of social freedom as well as economic advancement and stood in marked contrast to the Jim Crow existence that many had known in the South. This promise motivated and sustained black Richmondites before, during, and after the war. Black newcomers to Richmond wanted the opportunity to "mix and mingle and get along" in California.[6] The history of black Richmondites suggests that unlike the larger eastern and midwestern urban black communities that were defined almost from the outset by rigid boundaries, small black communities in California, and perhaps in other western states, were formed and functioned within broader spatial and cultural parameters.

In addition to exploring the role of culture, this book examines the impact of racial solidarity and intraracial conflict. For black Richmondites voluntary racial congregation was not merely a reaction against exclusion and denial; it was at the heart of community formation. Racial congregation, like culture, was another manifestation of black agency and positive self-perception. Even before the civil rights and black power movements called upon African Americans to unify against segregation and discrimination, black Richmondites expressed racial solidarity in the founding of their churches, in their educational endeavors, and in their clubs, mutual aid societies, and other institutions. This process of unification was accelerated during the war and in the postwar period as black Richmondites struggled to retain their wartime gains.

Voluntary racial congregation did not, however, preclude intraracial conflict. The study of African Americans in Richmond provides an opportunity to analyze the internal divisions and variations in a black population that was generally regarded as ideologically monolithic, unsophisticated, and intellectually inferior. Political orientation, length of residency, and gender generated internal divisions in the community even though the small size of Richmond's black population, the comparatively late influx of black migrants, and its truncated class structure tended to compress and blur these distinctions. While newcomer/oldtimer animosities flared during the war and conflict over political radicalism became pronounced in the postwar chill of the McCarthy era, gender was the most enduring of the intraracial divisions.

The experience of black Richmondites suggests that although black men and women shared an economic, social, and cultural interdependence, black women, clinging to the bottom rung of the economic ladder with their male counterparts, nevertheless experienced discrimination on two fronts. Although the black community's economic survival was greatly dependent on female labor, black women in Richmond were constrained by male notions of a woman's place until World War II opened up new options. During the war some women, utilizing traditionally sanctioned female work skills, moved beyond the kitchen and shipyards to carve out convention-shattering avenues of economic autonomy in the blues clubs and after hours clubs that proliferated in North Richmond.

Despite their struggles and achievements, African Americans who lived and worked in Richmond never saw the full fruition of the city's economic and social promise. The city's prewar dynamics had been permanently altered, and the black wartime shift upward could not be sustained. The study of black Richmondites provides an opportunity to explore what historian Earl Lewis has called the "culture of expectation."[7] Black migration to California, entry into the industrial workforce, and wartime prosperity heightened blacks' anticipation of advancement in the workplace and on the home front. The formation of the Richmond branch of the NAACP (the most active branch on the West Coast) in 1944 underscored black expectations of life in the Golden State. The NAACP's bold campaigns against workplace and residential discrimination in the 1940s and 1950s were manifestations of community aspirations that lasted long after the shipyards pulled out of the city, substantially eroding the economic underpinnings of their culture of expectation.

These events suggest another variation in the eastern and midwestern pattern of black industrialization and economic development. The meatpacking, tanning, steel, automobile, and mining industries of eastern urban centers provided relatively steady albeit low-paying employment for millions of African Americans before World War II and endured past the end of the war boom. In Richmond, black prewar industrial employment was precarious, despite the town's aspirations to becoming the "Pittsburgh of the West." With the demise of the Kaiser shipyards after the war, black Richmondites lost their tenuous foothold on the employment ladder.

The history of black Richmondites should prompt more inquiries into the activities of other black working-class communities in California and the West. This study suggests that small black western populations have existed in the shadows of larger, more urbane black communities, whose experiences have been regarded as representative. The story of black Richmondites implies that black political leadership, social activism, cultural instruction, gender equity, and personal achievement, far from being the exclusive domain of a black middle-class and professional elite, also emanated from the ranks of working-class men and women, who frequently stood in the vanguard of change.

In preparing this work I consulted several manuscript collections that were tremendously helpful. The Regional Oral History Office at the University of California, Berkeley, has compiled a number of excellent oral histories of African Americans who resided, worked, or had some dealings in Richmond and the Bay Area. These transcripts provided insight into the lives of a broad cross section of African Americans. In addition, the Records of the National Association for the Advancement of Colored People, West Coast Region; the Kaiser Papers; and the papers of C. L. Dellums in the Bancroft Library proved to be invaluable manuscript sources. The National Archives' Records of the President's Committee on Fair Employment Practice were essential sources of information about the wartime and postwar experiences of black Richmondites. I found working with the actual papers, letters, notes, and ephemera, rather than the microfilmed collection, to be a productive, satisfying, and moving experience. The Richmond Public Library's Richmond Collection was also extremely useful in my research, as were the holdings of the Richmond Museum.

These excellent collections notwithstanding, most histories of Richmond have virtually ignored the presence of black people. Traditional historical sources yield scant information on prewar black Richmondites and generally focus on wartime migration. Therefore, I conducted more than one hundred hours of oral interviews, both in person and by telephone, that have been equally (if not more) important than traditional sources for this study. I was fortunate to meet many of my interviewees through my personal network of friends and acquaintances. This network continued to expand as my contacts introduced me to their friends, relatives, and acquaintances whom they believed might be helpful.

Some of my contacts appeared bemused at my request for an interview, insisting that their experiences in Richmond were "not important," or that there was "nothing special to tell." However, everyone welcomed me warmly and provided detailed and often surprisingly candid responses to my questions. Most of the interviews were conducted informally, within the natural flow of people's lives: I interviewed people as they were preparing meals, seeing children off to school or preparing them for bed, tending their gardens, or planning family outings. Other interviews were conducted in business establishments or workplaces, where the interviewees took ringing telephones and constant interruptions in stride. Sometimes, in the middle of an interview, an informant would insist on calling a friend or relative to clarify a dimly remembered event. Some took me on guided tours of old neighborhoods and shared half-forgotten secrets about what transpired in those neighborhoods.

I am grateful for the generosity of these women and men, who are living repositories of African American history. This book is an attempt to place their deeds on the historical record and illuminate the intricate texture of the African American experience.

CHAPTER I

Richmond before the War

A "Slow, Gradual and Comforting" Change

In those days, when someone referred to a home, a street, or a neighborhood, one had a fairly clear picture of its location, condition and character. There was a sense of identity with Richmond, and a feeling of belonging that comes naturally to a small established city.

Richmond City Planning Commission
report, 1958

In 1940, before the tumultuous events of December 7, 1941, thrust the United States into World War II, Richmond was a sleepy coastal city of approximately twenty-four thousand lying along the east shore of the San Francisco Bay in Contra Costa County. No more than a dot on the map since its incorporation in 1905, Richmond languished in the shadows of cosmopolitan San Francisco, fifteen miles across the bay, and Oakland, the East Bay's most populous city, about twenty miles to the south. However, with its mild climate, deep harbor, and vast tracts of unused land, Richmond was ripe for commercial, industrial, and real estate exploitation. Thus, city founders pursued a dream of making Richmond the industrial giant of the Pacific Coast, the "Pittsburgh of the West." Within a decade of the city's incorporation, politicians and land speculators wooed and won major industries like Standard Oil, the Santa Fe Railroad, and the Pullman Coach Company. This coming of industry, combined with a stable labor force and a political climate hospitable to business, earned Richmond the title "The Wonder City," despite its small population and semirural atmosphere.[1]

African Americans had resided in Richmond since its founding and were part of the city's industrial life as well. African Americans in Richmond numbered just 29 out of a total population of 6,802 in 1910, but by the mid-1940s, with the coming of the Kaiser shipyards, Richmond's black population had increased dramatically. In 1940, the city's 24,000 residents included 270 blacks. By 1943 this number had soared to 5,673 (in a total population of over 100,000). The municipal health department estimated the population to be 106,000 in 1945, with blacks numbering nearly 8,000. (The National Urban League revised these figures in 1952, setting the 1945 total population at 99,976 and the black population at nearly 10,000.) In 1947 a special federal census estimated that 13,780 African Americans lived in Richmond. In seven years Richmond's black population had swelled by more than 5,000 percent.[2] Yet prewar patterns of land settlement, ethnic composition, and industrial development shaped the African American experience in Richmond.

The site that became Richmond was settled about ten thousand years ago by Indians known as Huichin, one subgroup of several hundred culturally and linguistically related native groups who were known collectively as Ohlone Indians. European diseases and exploitation by missionaries and other land-hungry whites decimated their numbers, so that at the end of the nineteenth century all that remained of them was the shell mound burial sites hidden in the marshlands that would later accommodate twentieth-century shipyards.[3]

Mexican, or "Californio," settlement followed in the early 1820s as Spanish and later Mexican military officers and politicians were deeded vast tracts of California land by their governments. The gold rush of 1849 dramatically increased the demand for the ferry services as would-be miners, flushed with gold fever, arrived in San Francisco and ferried across the bay to purchase provisions in Contra Costa County.[4] In 1894 Richmond's city-building period began in earnest as American land developers won legal title to large portions of Mexican land grants and set out to convert the region's small agricultural outposts into blocks of tidy city lots on subdivision maps.[5] Attracted by the availability of free commercial lots, businesses from around the Bay Area and the country relocated to Point Richmond, in particular, and by 1902 it had become the heart of the city.

Alfred Sylvester Macdonald, an Oakland real estate developer, is credited with the discovery of what would become downtown Richmond, and he was largely responsible for the downtown's emergence as the seat of power and commerce after intense competition with Point Richmond for the title. Macdonald and other businessmen realized that the ubiquitous grain and hay fields and the adjacent deep bay could be transformed into lucrative commercial, residential, and maritime developments. Therefore, in 1902 he, in association with Santa Fe Railroad officials and oil well developers, purchased 457 acres of a grain ranch that had been part of a historic Mexican land-grant ranch.

Macdonald and company immediately subdivided the property into business, commercial, and residential lots, locating all business lots along Macdonald Avenue, the principal thoroughfare on the street grid. Residential lots spread in every direction from the commercial center, and hay fields gave way to macadamized roads and street lights.[6] During the formative years, Macdonald Avenue became established as the major east-west corridor to the county line. Santa Fe made changes in its system to support the new town, renaming its East Yard station Richmond and moving it so that the train stopped at the west end of Macdonald, rather than near Point Richmond.[7]

The city incorporated on August 6, 1905. Richmond effectively won its struggle with Point Richmond for governmental power by offering attractive business incentives to potential industries, providing workers with transportation and housing, and then annexing all lands lying west of Twenty-third Street up to the Santa Fe tracks. In October 1915, Richmond voters approved local real estate promoter John Nicholl's offer of free land for a new city hall site to be located in central Richmond. In 1917 the municipal government moved from Point Richmond to a two-story building on Twenty-fifth and Nevin Streets downtown. The move symbolized the end of commercial development in Point Richmond. Macdonald Avenue became the undisputed commercial and civic heart of the city (see map 1).[8]

The city's attempts to accommodate industrial change and retain its existing political, social, and cultural identity became another source of tension, however, as Richmond's distinct prewar neighborhoods began to experience the first unsettling jolts of industrialization.[9] The 1910 census shows that only 48 percent of Richmond's population were native-born whites with native-born parents. Some 24 percent of Richmond's white residents were foreign born, and 27 percent of white Richmondites born in the United States had parents who were foreign born. In 1910 about 2 percent of Richmond's population of 6,802 was "nonwhite," a category that included Asian (Japanese and Chinese) and Native American residents. African Americans made up 0.4 percent of the city's population, numbering 29 total, including 5 children under ten

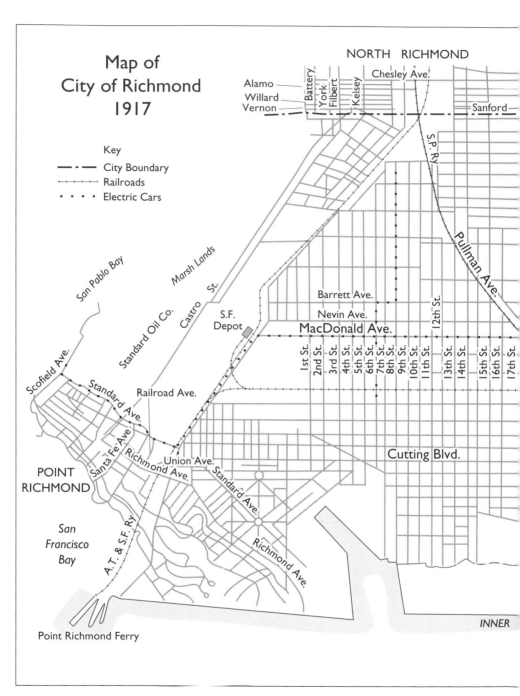

Map 1. The City of Richmond, 1917. Based on a 1917 map by G. H. Miller, Richmond Museum Collection

N

San Pablo Ave.

Barrett Ave.
Nevin Ave.
MacDonald Ave

Silva
Rosalind

19th St.
20th St.
21st St.
22nd St.
23rd St.

Pullman
Palace Car

Wall Ave.

24th St.
25th St.
26th St.
27th St.

Pullman Ave.

San Pablo Ave.

HARBOR

Marsh Lands

Columbia Blvd.

Table 1 *Race, Gender, and Nativity in Richmond, by Decade, 1910–1940*

	1910	1920	1930	1940
Total population	6,802	16,843	20,093	23,642
Male	4,045	9,378	10,666	12,354
Female	2,757	7,465	9,427	11,288
Whites	6,649	16,628	18,800	23,234
Male	—	9,218	9,962	12,138
Female	—	7,410	8,838	11,096
Native whites	5,009	13,026	15,365	19,766
Native whites of native-born parents	3,238	8,215	9,934	—
Native whites of foreign-born/mixed parents	1,771	4,811	5,431	—
Foreign-born whites	1,640	3,602	3,435	3,468
Blacks	29	33	48	270
Male	—	17	28	134
Female	—	16	20	136
Other races*	124	182	1,245	118

SOURCE: U.S. Department of Commerce, Bureau of the Census, *Thirteenth Census of the United States, 1910*, vol. 2 (Washington, D.C.: GPO, 1911), 184, table 4; U.S. Department of Commerce, Bureau of the Census, *Fourteenth Census of the United States, 1920*, vol. 3 (Washington, D.C.: GPO, 1921), 119, table 10; U.S. Department of Commerce, Bureau of the Census, *Fifteenth Census of the United States, 1930*, vol. 3 (Washington, D.C.: GPO, 1931), 261, table 15; and U.S. Department of Commerce, Bureau of the Census, *Sixteenth Census of the United States, 1940*, vol. 3 (Washington, D.C.: GPO, 1943), 610, table 32.

*Includes Indians, Japanese, and Chinese. By 1940 Mexicans were counted as white in the census.

years of age. Black men and women were evenly divided; overall, males comprised the majority of the city's residents (see table 1).[10]

By 1920, the population had more than doubled to 16,843. Native-born whites of native parentage remained a minority (49 percent of the total). The "non-white" percentage increased to 6 percent, with the African American ratio dropping to about 0.2 percent. By 1920 the overall sex ratio had begun to change as the number of female residents increased. Men remained in a slight majority in Richmond through 1940. Families, both native- and foreign-born, also began to increase in the 1920s. By 1930 the population had grown to 20,093. Italians comprised the most numerous of the foreign-born group, followed by immigrants from the British Isles, Germany, and Austria. African Americans accounted for 48 of the total population. In 1940 Richmond's population of nearly 24,000 contained 15 percent who were foreign born, but the census no longer enumerated native whites having native- or foreign-born parents. The African American population had grown to 270 people.[11]

Native-born whites born of native parents, who were in the minority in Richmond, dominated the political and civic life of the city and directed its vision of industrial ascendancy. Most wealthy residents did not live in Richmond. However, below them in status came an influential group of professionals and industrial executives who lived with their families in hillside neighborhoods above the town on the eastern side of San Pablo Avenue. Though religiously, educationally, and socially diverse, the members of this group provided the active leadership in the city's political, economic, and social development. They formed the "informal ruling council of Richmond."[12]

The largest group of Richmond's residents was a "class of high grade workers and specialized mechanics" who sold their services to the city's factories, industries, and waterfront businesses. Employed as craftsmen, foremen, and other wage earners, this group comprised 40 percent of the workforce, and most were white. When clerical workers, sales workers, teachers, and service trades workers earning salaries comparable to factory workers are included, Richmond's high grade workers and specialized mechanics accounted for about 60 percent of the workforce. This group lived in distinct neighborhoods in the flatlands and in Point Richmond.[13] They were marginal participants in public life, deferring to the native-born residents of the managerial and professional classes. For example, local elections (with the exception of the 1912 contest with its antisaloon measure) routinely saw a turnout of less than 15 percent of all eligible voters, with the highest concentration coming from the wealthier hills districts. School board members were often elected by only a few hundred voters, and the turnout for city council elections showed little increase over the years. Professionals, local businessmen, and local government officials sat on Richmond's primary and secondary school boards. The more prestigious high school board usually selected its members from the upper management and professional classes. Neither the city council nor the school boards included representatives from Richmond's labor unions or from members of the working classes.[14]

In 1909 the Richmond Industrial Commission emerged as the city's representative, charged with attracting "good clean money from the outside world" that would be "expended, in the main, right at home in building up the city in a thousand different ways."[15] Their efforts were rewarded as major industries flocked to the city. As early as 1900 the

Santa Fe Railroad shops employed several hundred people, all of whom earned "first-class wages" that were "expended here [in Richmond] in the building of homes and the upbuilding of the community." In 1901 the Standard Oil Refinery arrived and "virtually put [the town] on the map." Originally producing limited quantities of kerosene for export to the Orient, the refinery rapidly expanded to become the second largest in the world. Standard Oil, with its annual payroll of two hundred thousand dollars, became the city's largest and most influential employer.[16]

The Pullman Coach Company relocated from San Francisco in 1910, persuaded by the city's offer of a twenty-acre tract of land along the Southern Pacific line. The one- and three-story Pullman shops lined Cutting Boulevard and eventually grew to a massive complex of sixteen steel, brick, and concrete buildings. The company employed about 525 people who repaired, refurbished, and constructed all Pullman coaches west of the Mississippi River, turning out sixty-five coaches a month.[17] The remainder of the Pullman tract was subdivided and sold as lots to private individuals, most of them Pullman employees, who purchased their property by putting a "small amount down" and paying the rest in "monthly installments—whatever they could spare from their salary." Eventually, fifty houses were built on the townsite, and the Richmond Industrial Commission established an electric trolley line to the townsite.[18]

Smaller industries soon followed the major ones. American Standard Porcelain Works, the Western Pipe and Steel Company, the Southern Pacific Railroad Company, and the California Wine Association Plant (the largest winery and storage plant in the world at that time) all added to the city's industrial vision. City officials predicted that Richmond would become the key to the East Bay and projected a population of 250,000 by the second decade of the century. It appeared that Richmond was well on its way to becoming the "Pittsburgh of the West."[19]

However, some consequences of industrial growth were unwelcome. The city's industrial boom also attracted less desirable businesses like saloons, brothels, and gambling houses. In 1911 the prevalence of prostitution prompted the Women's Improvement Club to denounce the brothels and "love nests" that were "becoming an eyesore" for the town. The *Richmond Daily Independent* of February 26, 1911, reported that many Richmond men fell prey to their "cheap piano drumming out tantalizing tunes . . . [into nights] of debauchery with the fair inmates of the disreputable joints." The newspaper called for the closure of all brothels. Richmond's Women's Christian Temperance Union, pledged to combat the burgeoning saloons.[20] However, judging by the outcome of the 1912 election in which voters overwhelmingly defeated a measure that would have barred saloons, prohibition was one Progressive Era crusade that found few supporters in Richmond.[21]

Residents achieved a coexistence with the teeming vice centers that flourished in the shadows of the city's industries. When the activities of these centers became too blatant, the police would conduct vice raids, usually in the unincorporated areas of North Richmond where African Americans, Mexicans, Italians, and Portuguese lived. Prostitutes would be rounded up and charged with vagrancy, and the most egregious establishments would be shut down. After a decent interval, "the entire matter would be forgotten, the clubs would quietly re-open, and business would go back to normal until another wave of civic virtue would compel more raids."[22]

Life in prewar Richmond followed the contours defined by work and neighborhood identity. For most whites, steady employment and "long-term acquaintances" were proof of success, status, and identity. For the native-born, professional, and managerial classes, success was also determined by the longevity of their reign as arbiters of power.[23] Indeed, the majority of Richmond's public officials were native-born men who had held their positions for many years. By 1940, the city manager had been in office for twenty years; the school superintendent had served since 1901; and the chief of police had been on the force since 1915.[24] Thus, a city planning commission concluded that prewar Richmondites had attempted to reduce change to a "slow, gradual and comforting experience."[25]

Most white Richmondites subscribed, in theory at least, to a philosophy of upward mobility in which "men and women were supposed to rise or fall according to their inherent merit." Friendships were to be based on "personal traits of unpretentiousness, respectability, friendliness, and 'character' rather than family position, race, national origin" or other "artificial" criteria.[26] People of color, however, faced a different reality. A front page editorial in the *Richmond Record* of July 7, 1900, reported: "There are no Japanese at work for the Santa Fe about Point Richmond. The Chinese are limited to cooks at the boarding camps. White men have full sway here."

African Americans, the third largest nonwhite group in Richmond (after the Japanese and the Mexican Americans), lived with that fact, as did other nonwhite residents. During the first two decades of the twentieth century, the majority of Mexican Americans in Richmond worked for the Santa Fe Railroad. They were housed in small company-owned cabins at the foot of Macdonald Avenue.[27] In exchange for right-of-way over tribal lands in New Mexico, Santa Fe hired Native Americans who were brought from New Mexico to work in the rail yards according to treaties made during the nineteenth century. They lived in converted boxcars in the Santa Fe yards.[28]

Japanese, the largest Asian group in Richmond, had resided in the area since the nineteenth century. Compared to the rest of Richmond's adult population, white and nonwhite, they were a highly educated group, having attended school for more than the median nine years attained by the general Richmond population. They tended to be employed in the greenhouse agriculture that flourished on Richmond's outskirts in the prewar years.[29] Chinese migrated to the Richmond area in the late nineteenth century and controlled most of the shrimp fishing business in the area by the early twentieth century.[30]

San Francisco was the focus of black life in the Bay Area, but the end of the Spanish American War, the rise of racist labor unions on San Francisco's waterfront, and the earthquake of 1906 contributed to the emergence of the East Bay as the hub of African American life by the first decade of the twentieth century. Richmond's teeming industries held employment opportunities for dislocated black workers settling in the East Bay. The city's industries made it an appealing workplace for blacks who lived in the more "fashionable" cities of Berkeley, Oakland, and Alameda.[31] However, African Americans lived a tenuous existence on the outer edges of the city's industrial vision, trapped at the bottom of the economic and social hierarchy.[32]

In 1910 Richmond's black population of 29 was far smaller than that of either San Francisco (1,642) or Oakland (3,055). However, African Americans in Richmond had resided in the area many years and had already begun to plant deep roots. Some prewar Richmond blacks had originally come to California from Louisiana, Texas, Mississippi, or Arkansas. In a larger context, the early black settlers in the city were part of the Great Migration that swept almost one million African Americans out of the South between 1890 and the 1920s. Southern political and social realities of disfranchisement, segregation, sharecropping, and lynchings provided the impetus for the exodus. About thirty-five thousand participants in the Great Migration made their way to California and other states of the Far West. The census of 1910 indicates that several black Richmond residents were part of the first Great Migration, coming from Mississippi, Texas, North Carolina, and even Pennsylvania. For black

Richmondites and their counterparts across the country, migration became "a process of self-transformation" symbolizing their quest for economic advancement and educating them to urban industrial discipline.[33]

For example, after a stint as a logger in a Canadian logging camp, Walter Freeman Sr. realize that "living in the South did not suit" him any longer. He returned to Kentucky to marry Jessie Freeman; and after carefully planning their departure, the Freemans "jumped on the train and come right out here to [California]." The newlyweds arrived in San Francisco in 1910 and moved to Richmond in 1915 (see figure 1).[34]

In 1919, Joseph Griffin, a sharecropper in St. Landry Parish, Louisiana, moved his entire family to Richmond, blazing the trail for many others. The move was facilitated by his discovery of a "box full of money" that had been "buried for a long time" in the Louisiana fields he plowed. The Griffins purchased property in Richmond, where their home became a "way station" for other family members and friends. Similarly, Matthew and William Malbrough, two brothers from Louisiana, decided that they "could make more money and provide better" for their families in California than they could working as "muleskinners" in their home state. On the counsel of a cousin in Berkeley, the Malbrough brothers made the long trip out to the Golden State by train, staying with relatives until they found employment in a Richmond factory. Within a year, they were able to send for the rest of the family.[35]

The push of racial violence and poverty and the pull of California's reputation for freedom and economic opportunity were important factors in black migration to Richmond. However, the migrants were not passive victims pushed and pulled in a drama beyond their control. The dynamics of black migration to Richmond were aided and abetted by ties of family and friendship. In almost every case, migrants to Richmond relied on relatives or friends to help them make the decision, to provide them with a place to stay once they arrived, and to otherwise ease the transition while they pursued employment.[36]

As a Pullman porter on the Missouri Pacific Railroad in Louisiana, Louis Bonaparte Sr. first came to Richmond on a vacation pass in the 1920s. Impressed with the "freedom that colored people" seemed to enjoy in California, he decided to make Richmond his permanent home in 1924. He "made up his mind to settle there for good" and "told other people about it" when he returned to Louisiana.[37]

Mildred Hudson Slocum, great-niece of Joseph Griffin, recalled that word of the Griffins' prosperity "got back to other people" through family letters and "the grapevine." This persuaded her brother, Girtha Jr., to come out to Richmond and join "Uncle Joe." Girtha Jr. left Mansfield, Louisiana, first but was later joined by his wife, Lilly, and his father, Girtha Sr. Within a year, fourteen-year-old Mildred and her sister, Mattie, embarked for Richmond on a train "that looked like it took forever." They were greeted by "quite a few people that come to meet the train to welcome [them] to Richmond." The Hudson family crowded into a small apartment above the Griffins' North Richmond store until they could get a place of their own.[38] In lieu of organizations like the National Urban League and the NAACP in Richmond, personal networks assisted black newcomers at every stage of the migration process.

Despite expectations of improved fortunes, employment and housing opportunities for African Americans in Richmond and elsewhere in the state were circumscribed by law and custom. Conditions in Richmond may have been better than in the South, but one longtime resident recalled, "they [whites] still let you know how far you could go." In the workplace blacks performed the hardest and most menial tasks, with little chance of advancement. One resident observed: "You see, if you were just brute strength, they could hire you for lifting pieces of steel, but if you had a little bit of education, [they would not hire you]."[39]

The 1910 census showed that most black men in Richmond did "job work." Albert Bean, a forty-nine-year-old Texan who lived in one of the city's ubiquitous boardinghouses, was listed as a "job worker" in a Richmond barbershop. South Carolina native William Bost boarded at the same house and was employed as a "concrete worker." Walter Freeman Sr. was self-employed but supplemented the income from his drayage business by hauling ice for Richmond's National Ice Company from 1915 until the company closed. He went on to work at North Richmond's Standard Sanitary Company manufacturing porcelain fixtures and breathing "all that dust that was bad for his lungs."[40]

William Malbrough's most memorable job in Richmond consisted of "making concrete pilings for the Golden Gate Bridge" in the 1930s. He worked on the project for about two months before the rigorous labor forced him to quit. However, his first job came in 1927 when after putting in applications with most of the factories in Richmond, he and his brother, Matthew, were hired by the Certainteed Manufacturing Company in North Richmond to make roofing paper and mattress products. Matthew led an all-black, sexually mixed rag-sorting crew, which separated rags for the "heater" that converted the cloth into paper. They were paid less than a dollar an hour, "but that was pretty good." Walter Freeman Jr. recalled that when he worked at Certainteed making house shingles during the Depression, the factory employed "fifty to a hundred" workers, about twenty or thirty of whom were black. The men were required to "hand pull" twelve-hundred-pound bales of rags. "They would take a hook, put it in the bale, pull it down and bring it in." Several foundries located in North Richmond hired black workers and paid "decent wages." Foundry work was particularly hard, however. Irene Malbrough Batchan recalled that men who worked in foundries "could take that iron for about twenty years before breaking down, hernia. I'm talking about what the men did!" Whites and blacks worked side by side doing the same jobs, but for black workers this was "just about all you could get." Nevertheless African Americans from around the Bay Area sought work in Richmond's industries.[41]

The Santa Fe Railroad hired African American workers who manned track crews and equipment maintenance crews, performing general labor for about forty cents an hour (see figure 2). John Maynard and Sammy Graves worked at Santa Fe as boilermakers "back in the old days when they had the steam engine." One of Joseph Malbrough's in-laws walked fifteen miles to his job at Santa Fe from his home in Oakland because there were no buses. The "only thing that run was the street car and it didn't run until after six [A.M.]. The railroad run at standard time. Six o'clock the whistle would blow and he'd walk down along the railroad track."[42]

Richmond's major industries enjoyed a reputation among whites of paying "decent" wages, "anywhere from thirty-five cents to fifty cents an hour," with blacks generally confined to the lower paying, unskilled category. For example, administrators in the Pullman shops (which employed five hundred workers) earned about sixty-eight cents an hour in 1918. Workers classified as semiskilled earned an hourly wage of forty-seven cents, and unskilled laborers were paid forty-two cents an hour for shifts of eight to twelve hours. Its national employment policy reflected prevailing racial stereotypes that assumed African Americans were fit only for menial work. However, Pullman specifically hired black workers to block the inroads unionization had begun to make in the railroad industry and to "undercut labor organizing among white workers." In Richmond the company locked out its white workers in a 1922 strike, established an in-house union, and hired its first black employees that year. From 1922 through 1929 blacks comprised 11.3 percent of new hires at the Richmond shop. As late as 1940 the company union was still using race to keep the union at bay. Pullman officials agreed to a scant two-cents-an-hour wage increase above current railroad rates to mollify its nonunion workforce, asserting that the "mostly colored men, Italians, and a few Portuguese on the laboring gangs" at Pullman were still better off than the "99 per cent Mexican" railroad laborers who "have no standard of living."[43]

Joseph Malbrough worked in the Pullman shops in 1934 and recalled that there were about seventy other African Americans employed there as seasonal laborers: "In the summertime they'd lay us off and in the wintertime they'd call us back to repair the cars." He put wheels on the coaches and installed "batteries and things to make them light up. We'd paint them and they'd look like brand new cars when they came out there. Remodel them wherever they were damaged. You know, rocks would hit them and they'd have dents. Sandblast them and we'd paint them all over."[44]

African American men in Richmond worked within a precarious employment environment in which competition for jobs was so keen that "you'd have to wait for somebody to die" to get hired. The practice of "putting in a good word" to a supervisor was not widespread or effective in securing a factory or industrial job for a relative or friend. William Malbrough remembered: "you'd just get out and get going place to place. Depending on where business was good, that's where you would go."[45]

African American women in Richmond fared no better. Moreover, they labored under a triple yoke of oppression. Racism confined them to the lowest rungs of the employment ladder; they were stigmatized by their Richmond residency; and they were constrained by male notions of female propriety: "If you were married and your husband had a steady job, you might stay at home. You did that. But most had to work and the men seemed to think that only day work, or housework was suited to a black woman."[46]

Indeed, before World War II most black women worked as domestics in the homes of affluent whites in Oakland, San Francisco, and other Bay Area cities, where they earned two to five dollars a week. Irene Malbrough Batchan recalled that before the war black women who "weren't too old . . . were working cleaning up white folks' kitchens, cleaning [and] cooking." The 1910 census shows that Orilla Varlick, a thirty-four-year-old married black woman from Mississippi, worked as a "servant" in a Richmond boarding house that catered to an all-white clientele. In 1915 Jessie Freeman cooked for a white family in San Francisco and came home to Richmond only on weekends. Mattie Hudson, who arrived with her sister, Mildred, in 1939, became the family's biggest breadwinner, "working for the whites mostly in the outer areas, in towns like Orinda and over in the Oakland hills doing housework."[47]

Like their counterparts around the country, black women in Richmond were better able to obtain stable employment than men, who frequently had to settle for seasonal or "occasional" work. Domestic work, though low paying and arduous, was at least steady. It brought women into routine contact with the white world. Jessie Freeman's cooking job in a doctor's household allowed her to acquire "lots of good medical sense," which she took home to "doctor" her family when they were ill. In the 1920s, Ida and George Johnson worked as maid and chauffeur for a wealthy East Bay banker, who taught them about the stock market, warning them of the impending crash. George Johnson noted, however, that "it didn't matter since we didn't have any money to invest anyway."[48]

African American women acted as "employment ambassadors" in the workplace for their men. For example, a black Richmond resident noted that "if [white people] liked the way the women would work in their homes or did ironing, they might throw some work to your husband or son or something from time to time." Thus, female domestic employment provided the foundation upon which a great deal of the community's prewar economy rested.[49] Black women not engaged in domestic work sometimes joined Mexican American, Portuguese, Filipina, and Italian women in the seasonal, predominantly female labor force in Richmond's fish and produce canneries. Longtime residents Charmie Jones Williams and Liddy Freeman worked in a Richmond cannery back in the thirties. Williams's son recalled: "It was my mother and Liddy. . . . There wasn't many [black female workers]. About three or four I guess, back then." Pearl Malbrough, Beryl Gwendolyn Reid, and Irene Malbrough Batchan had to travel to Oakland and Emeryville to sort tomatoes and peaches in the Del Monte canneries each summer.[50]

Before Richmond's wartime shipyards lured women away with higher paying jobs, dozens of black and Filipina women found seasonal employment at the Red Rock fish cannery, where "only the floor ladies were white" and the men brought the fish in. Throughout the 1930s and 1940s cannery workers earned about thirty or forty cents an hour and worked an eight-hour day, five to six days a week.[51]

As late as 1940 the city still retained large tracts of undeveloped pasturage which enabled some African Americans to derive at least a portion of their livelihood from agriculture.[52] Black residents nicknamed North Richmond "Cabbage Patch" because of the numerous Portuguese- and Italian-owned truck farms located there, and they often hired themselves out as workers on the small farms there: "I can remember north of Chesley Street was all open fields. There were practically no houses. Right down on Seventh Street and First Street there was a farm and a man, an Italian man, grew lettuce. . . . There were a lot of truck farms." [53] More typically, black residents in North Richmond raised farm and dairy animals for personal use and to supplement their incomes. The Freeman family raised and sold chickens and rabbits. Walter Freeman Jr. delivered milk from the family cow to customers in Albany and Berkeley (see figure 3). [54]

Before the war Richmond had few black-owned businesses. This fact distinguishes Richmond from larger urban black communities in the Bay Area and around the country, where black-owned businesses did develop. Samuel C. Rogers, an Ohio native who arrived in Richmond in 1909, became the Bay Area's most successful black entrepreneur with a thriving construction firm. [55] However, the Richmond Cafe, owned by E. H. Oliphant, was the earliest black prewar business. It was located on Washington Avenue and in 1905 advertised the "best meal in the city." [56]

The North Richmond store of the Griffin family was more representative of prewar black businesses. After moving from Louisiana, Joseph Griffin and his wife, Betty, opened a small, chronically undercapitalized grocery and sundries store in North Richmond in 1919. It offered a limited number of staple goods to its customers, most of whom were black and shopped at the store only "when they run short." Most black Richmondites preferred to do the "big shopping" in the downtown city markets, or, as one resident recalled, "we'd get in our little car and go shopping at the Housewives [Market] in Oakland." [57]

During the late 1920s the Griffins' daughter Hattie Griffin Vaughn inherited the business and expanded to include hardware as well as groceries. Despite operating "on a shoestring," the Griffins were successful enough to buy "the first Durant car. . . . It was brand new" and the talk of the neighborhood (see figure 4). [58] The Griffins' modest success reflected hard work and determination but highlighted the limited opportunity structure for black entrepreneurship. Larger urban black communities in the East and Midwest, whose populations were more rigidly segregated, developed a network of businesses that were dependent on the ghetto population for patronage. In contrast, the size of the black population in California retarded the widespread development of such enterprises in all but the largest African American communities, such as those in Los Angeles, Oakland, and San Francisco. The absence of a substantial black customer base and the improbability of significant white patronage confined black businesses in Richmond to marginal profitability at best.[59]

In theory, African American residents could live anywhere they could afford. Some blacks resided in the boardinghouses and rooming houses close to the factories and shops where they worked, and others lived in the houses they built themselves. The *Colored Directory of the Leading Cities of Northern California, 1916–1917* listed a total of twenty-two black Richmondites scattered throughout the city.[60] Harry Williams recalled that in the 1920s and 1930s

in the entire Richmond itself there was about fifteen black families. . . . Where I lived on the South Side, there was me and my cousins, named Graves. There was a big family of them. They lived a block from me. Then there was Irene Fraser. That was just in the area where I lived, South Third, between there and a street south of Ohio [Street]. Those were the black families I knew. There were two black families that lived over by there—Lily Petgrave and the Ellisons.

However, segregated housing patterns began to emerge within the first decade of the city's incorporation.[61]

As early as 1909, Richmond developers were inserting restrictive covenants into deeds of sale. A real estate brochure advertising a new housing development in south Richmond alluded to racial exclusiveness, invoking images of "savages running wild in central Africa" and appealing to "white men, civilized men, twentieth century Americans" who could appreciate the "beauty of owning property—real property— a HOME."[62]

Restrictive covenants shut out "undesirable racial and ethnic groups" when property was sold or transferred, thus quietly accomplishing what southern Jim Crow achieved through violence and racial intimidation. By 1918 the California Supreme Court clearly stated that racial restraints, "properly phrased," would be enforced. By the 1920s restrictive covenants were commonplace in Richmond real estate transactions. Thus, racial segregation in Richmond housing, de facto and de jure, predated the wartime influx of black newcomers and lasted well into the 1960s.[63]

By 1940, therefore, most of Richmond's African American population was concentrated in and around North Richmond, one-third of which lay inside city limits, with the rest located in the unincorporated area. It was in close proximity to a garbage dump, it had few street lights, and its unpaved streets became muddy quagmires in the rain. North Richmond lacked adequate fire and police protection, depending on a

single sheriff's car to patrol the entire county section. Before the war
North Richmond had been a rural, ethnically diverse area where blacks
lived alongside Portuguese, Italian, and Mexican Americans. However,
by 1943 North Richmond had become virtually all black. By 1947 nearly
fourteen thousand African Americans lived in the city, one-fifth residing in North Richmond.[64]

Although the seeds of black ghetto formation had been planted in
pre–World War II Richmond, the hard lines of segregation did not fully
emerge until the war. African American residents of Richmond insisted
that the city offered more social freedom, in comparison to "how it was
down South." Blacks could attend downtown theaters without having
to sit in segregated sections and were permitted to shop in the city's retail stores, although they could not try on clothing or hats. In the 1930s
Ivy Reid Lewis remembered that her father could cash his paychecks in
downtown stores, but the white merchants discontinued this practice
during the war, fearing "other coloreds would want to do it too." Sunset Cemetery, located in the county, allowed black interment but re-
voked the "privilege" during the war.[65]

Racial diversity also typified Richmond's prewar public schools.
Many residents insisted that the "schools were integrated in Richmond."
Ivy Reid Lewis recalled that her teachers "did not discriminate against
me because I was black." Indeed, Lewis had no black classmates until
the fourth or fifth grade, "when the war began." Nevertheless, the school
board hired no teachers of African American, Native American, Mexican American, or Portuguese backgrounds. A principal at Peres Elementary School in North Richmond recalled that during the 1930s only
one teacher ever visited the community or attempted to develop a representative classroom curriculum. Her efforts resulted in her dismissal
because "a few of the teachers had an active dislike for these culturally
different children."[66]

Black school children, like their elders, learned to accommodate racial
boundaries that were real, often invisible, and sometimes difficult to negotiate (see figure 5). Stanley Nystrom, a white prewar resident, explained: "In high school there was a handful of colored kids my age, but
we were all one. They lived on their side of town, and we lived on our side.
But that was because they wanted to live there."[67] Walter Freeman Jr.
recalled that the boundaries frequently bristled with tension: "I saw
there's a [white] boy who [lived] between Lincoln and Sixth Street. They
lived right around the corner from us. We was on this side of the track
and he was on the other side. Every time we'd go that way to Peres

school, he'd come out and start something. . . . So him and my brother would go to fighting. . . . He just wanted to whip a white boy."[68]

Black accommodation to the racial status quo may have appeared as acceptance to most whites, but the threat of violence and intimidation lurked just beneath the surface of the city's seemingly placid race relations. For instance, as early as 1917 the Ku Klux Klan openly participated in Richmond's civic celebrations, parading down the main thoroughfares in full regalia and staging rallies and cross burnings in the hills and parks surrounding the city.[69] Walter Freeman Jr. recalled that some of the most well known white residents openly engaged in Klan activities: "They were in the parade. I don't know if it was a special day. I know American Standard had a truck all draped out. That's where they make them bathtubs. And I was in the parade sitting up in one of them tubs. The Klan was in the parade. They gathered at Sixth and Macdonald. My dad knew half of them."[70] The *Richmond Independent* endorsed "freedom of association" for Klan members in a 1922 editorial. The editorial deplored the "invasion of homes" and the infliction of "cruelties" by the Klan, but it asserted that the KKK was like any other fraternal organization. It concluded that "every free-born American citizen" had the right to "join a secret society every day of the year" because Americans as a people are "jiners."[71]

Racist activity in Richmond reflected the Klan's widening geographic and ideological influence in the United States during the 1920s. Racial attitudes formerly associated with the South had by then permeated the entire fabric of American cultural, social, and political life. National Grand Wizard Hiram Evans's claim that the Klan was a "movement of plain people" appears to have found resonance in prewar Richmond. In Richmond blackface minstrel shows became popular entertainments among whites, continuing for almost three decades. The annual all-white Elks club minstrel and variety show, featuring the "Shinola Shines," became a tradition that lasted until the 1940s. Whites who participated in such activities were not just from the "marginal" or lower class, not just "Southern rednecks." They included people from some of the "first families." While prewar Richmond managed to avoid the race riots that plagued other American cities after World War I, Klan parades and minstrel shows reinforced the racial status quo.[72]

The uniformity of the African American experience in prewar Richmond prevented intraracial class stratification. Status in prewar black Richmond appears to have been derived not from socioeconomic condition but from length of residence in the community. This measure

held for white Richmondites as well, but the larger size of their population and the greater number of economic opportunities available to
whites contributed to a greater degree of white differentiation. Mildred
Slocum explained: "There wasn't no middle class or upper class. We all
just did the best we could. We were all of the same cut." There "may have
been some [black] 'gentry' here, but that was just because they lived
here longer."[73]

Faced with such constraints, prewar African Americans turned inward
to those aspects of their lives that were within their control. Like turn-
of-the-century white working-class immigrants who drew on tradition
and cultural resources to facilitate entry into the urban industrial proletariat, black Richmondites turned to their religious institutions, voluntary organizations, and homes to ease the transition and fulfill personal
ambitions. Since slavery, the church has been an important force in African American community life. W.E.B. DuBois asserted that the black
church antedated the black family in the United States. E. Franklin Frazier noted that the church provided the community with a refuge in a
hostile white world and a place where "the Negro could give expression
to his deepest feeling and at the same time achieve status and find a
meaningful existence." In Richmond the black church stood as the primary repository for values of black initiative, self-help, and community
solidarity. It provided an arena for education, social interaction, and
transmission of values.[74]

Because no formally organized churches existed in Richmond before
1921, many residents traveled to Berkeley or Oakland to attend Sunday
services. On Sundays it was common to see a steady stream of well-
dressed black people boarding streetcars, climbing into cars, or walking
to services in neighboring cities. Even after churches were built in Richmond, outside churches continued to attract black Richmondites who
believed those congregations were "quality looking." The Reid family
attended the Episcopal Church in Oakland, where Father Wallace's congregation arranged themselves in a color hierarchy. All the "Louisiana
people who were light-skinned would sit on one side of the church and
all the dark folks sat on the other side."[75]

Harry and Charmie Williams sent their children to the predominantly
white First Christian Church in Richmond. Harry Jr. recalled: "I went
there. My sister went there. . . . My parents never did go to this First
Christian Church. They would go to their Church over there. . . . We
went to that church and took place in the Christmas pageant and everything. There were three black kids, young black kids, and they treated
us fine. An all white church. There wasn't any problems there."[76]

However, many black residents were eager to establish their own churches because "most people wanted to stay in Richmond to go to church. Didn't want to travel all that way." Therefore, in the first two decades of the twentieth century, home church services became the dominant form of religious worship among African Americans in the city. These were interdenominational gatherings in private residences and appealed to a cross section of the community.[77]

North Richmond Missionary Baptist Church (NRMBC) was the first black Baptist church in Contra Costa County, and it became the most prestigious of Richmond's prewar churches (see figure 6). It had its beginnings in the Baptist gatherings in the Alamo Avenue home of Mr. and Mrs. Willie Miles of North Richmond in 1919. Later, a group of Richmond residents prevailed upon the Reverend G. C. Coleman, pastor of North Oakland Baptist Church, to conduct a home worship service in the Miles residence. Sister Rosa Robinson was the first to be baptized in the new church. Because the congregation did not have a building of its own, "the mother church, North Oakland, opened its doors so that she could be baptized in their pool."[78]

By 1921, however, the small Richmond congregation had "worked and saved long for a simple structure" in their city. The church's construction became a community project, cutting across denominational lines: "Everybody chipped in and helped." The sixtieth anniversary program for NRMBC noted that some in the community had been "used to Negro Baptist Churches" as "old established organizations, but here [in Richmond] a few had to do the work of many." Store owner Joe Griffin was instrumental in the church's construction, providing money and material. His efforts made him a "big cheese in the church." Twenty founding members bought simple wooden pews and made their own stained-glass windows. They found an old organ that "with much coaxing could be played." The church dedication ceremony turned out to be a joyous community celebration. Walter Freeman Jr. recalled: "They had a full house. Lot of people. We thought it was a lot of people. It was an all day thing; it was really nice." The Reverend Holmes of Berkeley was "appointed to be the leading shepherd of the flock." Similarly, North Richmond's Colored Methodist Episcopal Church and the Church of God in Christ (COGIC, which later became McGlothen Temple), evolved from other home church gatherings and were established in the 1920s.[79]

Despite obvious community commitment, Richmond's prewar black churches were treated as religious outposts and became objects of skepticism and derision from blacks in neighboring cities.[80] The *Western Ap-*

peal, an African American newspaper, announced the 1921 dedication of NRMBC's permanent building: "A new church was dedicated in Richmond June 11. Let them dedicate a steam laundry next so that the members of the church may have employment. That will enable them to pay for it and take care of a pastor." [81]

Although a few months later another article noted that the church had managed to survive "under the efficient leadership" of the Reverend Holmes, other East Bay churches still considered Richmond churches to be unstable, disorganized, and financially vulnerable. Ministers' salaries came from a "small collection" that was often given back to the church. Despite the lack of funds and its small size, NRMBC "played its part in joining other Baptist organizations" and being a "very active church" in district and state work. The church was represented at state and national religious conventions and received small cash awards from the third session of the Negro Baptist Missionary Associates in October 1922 for its achievements. [82]

Richmond congregations and ministers were attacked by other congregations for being "unsophisticated and too emotional." [83] Richmond's ministers generally received their training from small, southern church–affiliated schools. Some, known as "jack-leg preachers," simply "got the call" and became self-ordained ministers of the gospel. The most successful ones were unpretentious and "close to the people." [84] The congregation had the final say over whether a minister would remain in the pulpit. The Reverend Holmes, imported from Berkeley, did not inspire his NRMBC congregation, which demanded that he "put more life" into his sermons. [85] He was replaced by F. W. Watkins, whose rousing sermons were "very, very loud and they would stomp, you know." Walter Freeman recalled it was "real back home Baptist Church preaching and I never been back home. But I can remember the way they'd preach." [86]

Pentecostal church services at McGlothen Temple in Richmond were even more spirited than those of the Baptists. The contrast was "the difference between night and day." It was not unusual for the singing, shouting, and "joyous noise" emanating from McGlothen Temple to shatter the quiet of a Sunday evening. McGlothen's services were powerful magnets for young people looking for something to do:

At night North Richmond was really kind of quiet so we'd go to . . . MGlothen's Temple and they'd be *sanctifieded* ![*sic*] In other words, the joint be jumping! Whereas, it look like North Richmond [Missionary Baptist Church] be asleep. I mean it's according to who was preaching at North Richmond but like I say, you go to McGlothen's Temple and they'd just be *up* there! Everybody got the Holy Ghost, you know—dancing, playing music loud and all that stuff. There was a great difference. Yes, was a great difference on Sunday night.[87]

Like the storefront churches that sprang up in major northern and midwestern cities during the Great Migration, McGlothen Temple and NRMBC provided their congregations with personalized, intense worship. Unlike their storefront counterparts in other cities, Richmond's prewar churches were not upstarts; they represented black Richmond's religious mainline. Their "down home shouting" services, while anathema to middle-class blacks, were acceptable to most black Richmondites. The class divisions that emerged in larger cities between uninhibited storefront newcomer congregations and the staid middle-class congregations during the Great Migration did not appear in Richmond until thousands of black newcomers arrived in the second Great Migration, sparked by World War II.[88]

Generational rather than class tension surfaced in Richmond's prewar black churches. Children frequently traveled "back home" to visit relatives and friends in the South, but it appears that they were becoming "bicultural." As a child Irene Malbrough Batchan was teased by her Richmond schoolmates because of her Louisiana "French patois." Yet on summer visits back home, her relatives and "the people in the church" teased her for "talking funny" and being "Too California!" One Richmond resident explained: "Here [in California] it was different, almost like the air you'd breathe was different, it changed you. You didn't never want anyone to think you weren't with it." Although church was important in their lives, "that didn't mean that the young people could relate to everything that went on there." Many young people found it difficult to identify with the agrarian roots of the black churches in prewar Richmond. Irene Malbrough Batchan recalled that the "old timey preachers" at NRMBC would "load up their preaching" with "crazy old [country] sayings" that seemed incomprehensible to the young. Moreover, the ministers could seem overbearing in their concern with morals and religious piety. The Reid children became the subjects of pulpit sermons by ministers who "preached against" them for being "those new people from Oakland" who would "[go] swimming on Sunday instead of coming to church."[89]

Despite these conflicts, the church remained an important community focus in prewar Richmond, attending to material as well as spiritual

needs, validating individual milestones, and celebrating community accomplishments. Church bake sales, picnics, raffles, and musicals provided
recreation and generated income for pastors' salaries, community projects, and charitable activities. Choir competitions provided the opportunity for travel and socializing as participants performed in churches
around the Bay Area. NRMBC picnics became interdenominational,
community-wide affairs: "Well, the one that I really remember was that
there were a bunch of trees out there by Lambert's place on the right
hand side. They always had sack races and all kinds of activities. Then
they'd have a big feed." [90]

Occasionally, youthful romances developed under the watchful eyes
of the adults. Sixteen-year-old Mildred Hudson and twenty-four-year-
old Jessie Slocum met and courted at NRMBC in 1940. A year later the
couple eloped and were married in Reno (see figure 7). [91] Walter Freeman Jr. meet his first wife, Regina Hinkle, at NRMBC, where she attended regularly with her foster parents. After a carefully supervised
courtship, Walter and Regina were married at NRMBC in 1934. Thus
the church remained central to the life of the prewar black community.
Mildred Slocum explained: "There wasn't any other place [to go] but
church" (see figure 8). [92]

Black Richmond's secular institutions fulfilled similar needs for the
community. The social clubs, fraternal organizations, recreation groups,
and entertainment spots provided an economic base and promoted interdenominational cooperation. Through these institutions black Richmondites developed leadership skills and cultivated political awareness
that would flower during the war and postwar periods. The activities of
these organizations reflected a tradition of service and self-help that had
been part of African American ideological discourse since slavery. Nowhere was this tradition more evident than in the women's clubs founded
in prewar Richmond. [93]

For example, the Chlora Hayes Sledge Club, established in 1919, was
one of Richmond's first black female voluntary organizations. It pursued an array of health, educational, and political goals. The club was
named in honor of a former Richmond resident and Bay Area activist
who served on the board of directors of Oakland's Fanny Wall Home
for Colored Orphans and who presided over the California Association
of Colored Women in the 1920s. Club members met in private homes,
where they offered programs that included classes in home nursing,
cooking, and arts and crafts. [94] In 1928 the "elderly women [in Rich-
mond]" organized the Women's Progressive Club. Unfortunately, no

records exist of this club's activities. In 1926 black Richmond women, intending to "inspire every woman to take advantage of opportunity for a broader education in the home-making arts," founded the Richmond Self Improvement Club. This organization represented Richmond at the National Association of Colored Women's (NACW) fifteenth biennial convention held in Oakland in 1926. Top priority on the convention's agenda was given to establishing a national educational scholarship for black women and to passing antilynching legislation.[95]

Thus, black working-class women in prewar Richmond were engaged in a sustained program of institution building and community service that connected them to a larger network of black voluntary institutions. Through their efforts these women became part of a national community of African American female progressivism that had begun to mount an assault on racial, gender, and class stereotypes.[96]

The important work of community building and preservation of culture was not exclusively a female domain, however. African American men were instrumental in establishing voluntary associations and mutual aid organizations as well. In 1921 a few "leading [black] citizens" initiated the Ashler Masonic Lodge in North Richmond. After receiving "special dispensation" from the parent lodge in Oakland to allow members "to join at a cheaper price," Ashler Lodge No. 35 opened its doors at 200 Grove Street on June 6, 1922. Lawrence C. Strickland Sr. presided as Ashler's first "Worthy Master"; Walter Freeman Sr. and Samuel C. Rogers became charter members.[97] From the start, Ashler "welcomed everyone; bootblacks, everything," as long as they were "freewill, honest men."[98] Black workers at the Certainteed company devised a unique way to study for their initiation: "Whoever had to come on the shift, he had to tell him [the man who was getting off] something about his [Masonic] Degrees before he could go to work. That's the way we got into the Lodge."[99]

By 1930 about forty men belonged to Ashler lodge, with many others attending occasional meetings and functions from as far away as San Jose and Pittsburg, California. Ashler's chapter, or the women's "auxiliary," was also an active part of black Masonry in Richmond. The auxiliary held "parties and formulas" to raise funds for programs that included children's Christmas parties and academic scholarships. Such auxiliary functions were open to the entire community and attracted black people from all over the Bay Area.[100] In addition to raising funds, Ashler provided its members with life- and burial-insurance policies for a minimal monthly contribution and distributed food, money, and clothing to the widows and orphans of lodge members through their Widow's Mite Fund.[101] In 1930 Ashler lodge relocated to a two-story brick building in downtown Richmond, which the members had purchased from a "white labor union." To raise money for the purchase, Ashler's building fund committee hosted a fund-raising dance and barbecue in East Oakland, offering a "1930 Ford Roadster, Fully Equipped" as a door prize. Over one thousand people paid fifty cents each to attend.[102]

Black Richmondites also established an Elks club in the 1930s and located it in a North Richmond recreation center known as the "little neighborhood house." Irene Malbrough Batchan and her brother Joseph Malbrough helped establish the center because, Joseph explained, there was "no place for the niggers to go unless you have house parties. . . . We said we needed some place for all the niggers to go." The building belonged to the Griffin family and was a "big building with open floors." It had a "little kitchenette," complete with sink, running water, and electricity. The little neighborhood house "got to be like a family. There would [even] be wedding receptions."[103]

The Elks club, like the community's other voluntary organizations, provided a much needed recreational outlet and "made them feel like worthwhile human beings." The Elks' fund-raising dinner dances and boat rides on the bay "help[ed] the kids with going to school." Elks members would "pick out someone who was about to graduate" and "give him so much" money to help meet school expenses. The Elks club, like the Masons, also offered its members life- and burial-insurance policies.[104] Serving as bulwarks against an often hostile society, these black voluntary, fraternal, and mutual aid organizations were the bedrock upon which community rested. They provided the nexus to a tradition of service and activism that spanned generations, class, and geography.

The commercial orientation of North Richmond's prewar taverns and nightspots distinguished them from black voluntary institutions but did not diminish their role in fostering community cohesiveness. These places served food and offered their patrons music and other entertainments. The atmosphere in the clubs provided a supportive context in which to escape some of the "day's troubles." Blacks, unwelcome in the downtown white establishments, found "a place of [their] own where [they] could relax." The clubs were rooted in black cultural traditions, reminiscent of the southern "jooks" described by Zora Neal Hurston: "Jook is the word for a Negro pleasure house. It may mean a bawdy house. It may mean the house set apart on public works where men and women dance, drink and gamble. Often it is a combination of all these."[105]

North Richmond's Pink Kitchen, owned by the Griffin family, resembled Hurston's jooks. It was a pink stucco building where "adult black people went to drink beer, play music and dance." The jukebox would "play something slow" and patrons would do a dance "called belly rubbing. Get up against the wall and let it all [go]." Prostitution and gambling provided patrons with other illicit diversions.[106]

These establishments provided a degree of refuge from racial hostility, but some also embodied California's and Richmond's ethnic and cultural diversity, providing an eclectic musical and cultural experience for black Richmondites. For example, blacks, Mexicans, Italians, Portuguese, and Asians sometimes attended "polka dances" in a popular North Richmond tavern. It was a "shoestring operation" owned "by a Mexican man," where local residents went to dance, drink, and socialize. As a child Ivy Reid Lewis learned to dance the polka by peeking into the tavern and watching the patrons: "Everybody, not just the blacks, went there to dance. I can still do that dance. . . . People laugh at me when I do that dance but that's the dance I saw when I was a kid."[107]

Cross-cultural interaction took place outside the clubs as well. Symbolic of this were the bullfights that attracted a diverse crowd to wager on the Mexican matadors who fought in the makeshift rings in the fruit orchards and fields of North Richmond and Point Richmond during the 1910s. Walter Freeman Jr. remembered: "[It was] just a big oval. . . . Let the bulls get in it but they weren't supposed to wound them or anything like that. They put pads on them. Guys would come from Mexico, would come up there and [fight]."[108]

Ivy Reid Lewis, wanting to fit into the *fiestas, cumpleaños* (birthdays), and other festivities that were part of her Mexican American neighbors' lives, learned Spanish from her Spanish-speaking playmates in North Richmond. Lewis recalled: "if World War Two hadn't come, I would have had to marry a Mexican or something because there were no blacks, not my age."[109] Similarly, Harry Williams recalled: "I grew up with a lot of Mexican kids. A lot of them. . . . There was Mexican and Italian kids." As a youngster Walter Freeman Jr. was "raised up in an Italian neighborhood" in North Richmond where he played "run, sheep, run" and "pig in a corner" with his Italian friends. They taught him to speak Italian and he was "doing pretty good." Young Walter reciprocated by giving English lessons to their parents.[110] Black Richmondites recalled visiting their Portuguese and Italian neighbors in North Richmond, trading family recipes, and sharing meals of "salami and French bread. They would make that 'dago red' wine they called it. People sort of shared."[111]

Despite cross-cultural interaction, prewar African Americans were aware of the realities that circumscribed their lives. Therefore, they also engaged in a variety of activities to fight racism and discrimination. In the 1920s Garveyism found a receptive audience in the Bay Area. In the East Bay, Oakland became the location of the Universal Negro Improvement Association (UNIA). In 1927 the Oakland UNIA held an areawide convention in which issues ranging from community unity to a "Negro Bill of Rights" were debated. There is little evidence that Richmond was a hotbed of Garveyism, but the working-class backgrounds of black Richmondites and their connection to Oakland suggest that some Richmond residents participated in the UNIA activities at least occasionally. Walter Freeman Jr. never joined the movement but noted: "There was a big hall in Oakland that lots of people went to. Maybe some from Richmond too, but I don't know."[112]

In the 1930s blacks established two civil rights organizations in Richmond. The North Richmond Improvement Club (NRIC) and the Negro Protective League drew their membership from the Masons, the Elks, and the clergy. Both organizations took community grievances to city hall meetings. In 1939, after several appeals to the Richmond City Council, the NRIC succeeded in having a streetlight installed in North Richmond. In 1940 the Negro Protective League unsuccessfully petitioned the city for a children's playground in North Richmond. In 1941 the league filed a complaint with the city council protesting discriminatory hiring practices in the local fish canneries but got no response from city officials.[113]

Religious, recreational, and mutual aid institutions provided black Richmondites an opportunity to craft interpersonal, social, and political skills, but Richmondites' homes represented the most fundamental aspect of community building. In 1921 a local black newspaper noted that the "colored population [in Richmond] are purchasing lots and building homes thereon" in those areas open to them.[114] The Freeman family was in the vanguard of this trend. Walter Freeman Sr. "had so much work" from his teamster job for the Panama Pacific International Exposition that he was able to buy property in North Richmond, move from San Francisco, and construct a house in 1915.[115] Walter and Jessie Freeman—with help from Jessie's brother, Oliver Fountain—built their home on Monroe Street by working evenings and weekends. On Friday evenings Walter Jr. would accompany his father to Oakland to pick up Uncle Oliver, who took the ferry from San Francisco: "He came off the boat one night I guess about eleven or twelve o'clock. I can remember Dad had a lantern out in front of the team and another in back. And my uncle he had one too. So we came right out San Pablo Avenue. It took us all night to get from down there [Oakland] and then to get out here [Richmond]. It took us all night. They were big horses, but boy, they had a load."[116]

The Freeman's gray and white frame house became a source of pride and the focal point of family activity. Jessie Freeman, an avid gardener, filled the front yard with roses and planted a vegetable garden in back (see figure 9).[117]

In 1928 the Malbrough brothers bought side-by-side lots on Vernon Street in North Richmond for twenty-five dollars each (the same lots would sell for seven hundred dollars each during the war). Armed with a rudimentary knowledge of building and paying little attention to existing codes, William and Matthew Malbrough, aided by family and friends, set about constructing their houses: "It was a rough town then. If you had lumber you could build anything you wanted to. No permits or licenses were necessary. I had some friends who helped me build it. I didn't know much about building but I learned."[118]

The Freeman lot was fairly large in 1915, and the Malbroughs' narrow lots with frontages measuring twenty-five by one hundred feet, were more typical of North Richmond lots (see figure 10). Most of the dwellings were one- or two-bedroom structures made from materials "scrounged" from everywhere. In an "under the table" deal, the company foreman at Certainteed gave and sold black Richmondites shingles after designating them "off color" or "seconds."[119] In 1938 Girtha Hudson Sr., who "worked on cars . . . electricity" and "just done things," built his family's North Richmond home "out of . . . stuff that he salvaged from the dump . . . [and] stuff he would sell." He constructed another house on the same street as a gift for his newlywed daughter, Mildred.[120]

African Americans in Richmond painstakingly built up many hours of "sweat equity" in their homes, making needed repairs and adding cosmetic touches. Walter Freeman Jr. worked several years to restore the house given to him by his mother and aunt as a wedding present in 1934. He reroofed the house so that it "didn't have no more leaks or nothing like that." A few months later, he applied white terra cotta shingles to the house, shingles which he obtained from Certainteed. Finally, "waiting until [he] got that all paid off," he "put a little fence around it" and "built . . . a big barbecue pit in the back."[121] George and Ida Johnson built their rambling house on the outskirts of southwest Richmond in 1937. The Johnsons endured two years in a one-room shack on the property, making monthly payments to the white landlord until they purchased the land for about two hundred dollars. George "worked the midnight shift" at Mare Island Naval Yard and then came home to work with Ida building the "foundation, mix[ing] the plaster and hammer-[ing] every nail" until the job was completed in late 1939 (see figure 11).[122]

Thus, the homes of black Richmondites, like their religious institutions and voluntary organizations, proclaimed their self-sufficiency and symbolized their hopes for the future. By the 1930s, however, the Depression had tarnished prospects considerably. The economic crisis that gripped the nation hit black Americans, already clinging to the bottom, especially hard. In 1931 a national unemployment census revealed that black urban workers suffered twice as much unemployment as white urban workers. The same correlation held for black people in all regions of the country, including Richmond.[123]

Nevertheless, even as Richmond's industrial growth slowed, the African American population continued to grow while the white population remained stable.[124] Several factors account for the increase. California's reputation as the Golden State continued to attract black migrants. Blacks joined their white counterparts in pouring into the state seeking work. A black newcomer from Chicago, described as a "typical tramp" by state employment officials, explained: "we hear so much about California and as times are so hard with us back there I thought that I would come out here to try my luck. . . . I've been writing my friends to come out here."[125]

Between 1930 and 1940 the Ford assembly plant was the only major industry to locate in Richmond. Although many businesses reduced shifts and cut wages, none of the city's major industries shut down, thanks to New Deal programs like the WPA (Works Progress Administration). Richmond's WPA industries "adopted a share-the-work plan by which employees were kept at work a limited number of days per week so they could maintain themselves."[126] The relative health of Richmond's industries remained a powerful magnet for the black unemployed, even though, as of 1940, 1,298 workers, or 13 percent of the city's total labor force, remained without work or were employed by the WPA, the National Youth Administration (NYA), or other public relief agencies. African Americans, comprising 1 percent of the city's population, accounted for almost 2 percent of the unemployed.

Richmond's economic outlook had begun to improve by 1940 because increased federal defense spending had stimulated industrial output. Yet for the "Negroes, Mexicans, Native Americans and other minorities," there had been little improvement.[127] African American workers found that they were the "first to be let go" when the hard times hit and the "last to be brought back when things picked up." Irene Malbrough Batchan observed, "you didn't have no way to make a nest egg if you didn't have a way of getting a nest egg. Black people they caught it real bad. They weren't able to go back to work."[128]

Being laid off posed particular hardships for black residents because "almost all of them owned their own homes and . . . didn't have any money coming in and they didn't have other [financial] resources." One resident noted that "if you didn't have any social security, you'd have to make it the best way you could. The county would give you a little commodity." Relief trucks would come in "with the food and the people [would] line up." The WPA paid eighteen dollars a month to the unemployed, but most black workers were "at the bottom the list."[129]

Impatient with the pace of industrial recovery, Richmond's unemployed, black and white, joined their national counterparts in taking direct political action to alleviate their plight. During the 1930s the Workers Alliance of America became a strong, militant organizing force for the CIO, which in 1936 initiated the most far-reaching labor organizing campaign in the country's history. From the beginning, CIO policy banned racial discrimination and segregation. The Workers Alliance organized a cross section of unemployed groups across the nation, especially targeting African Americans. CIO leader John L. Lewis deliberately sought out members of the Communist Party to serve as organizers because of their "special interest in the unity of black and white labor and the achievement of such unity" in organizing trade unions.[130]

In Richmond the Workers Alliance was a racially integrated group composed of "unemployed persons and those on work relief projects." Richmond's business community accused the alliance of being a "radical, somewhat disreputable organization," controlled by Communists intent on "instigating a social and economic revolution." Hard times had indeed radicalized a number of black Richmondites. One longtime resident recalled, "lots of them joined the Communist Party for freedom."[131]

Richmond's Workers Alliance "was nearly as conservative as its detractors, however." It focused on morale-boosting social activities, such as holding Christmas parties for children of the unemployed, refurbishing a health center, and participating in a street-widening project. Its most militant action was to demand that the city council declare March 13, 1940, "End to Unemployment Day." Richmond's Workers

Alliance flourished between 1939 and 1940, but when wartime mobilization saw the return of economic prosperity, the organization faded. Many black radicals "had to hush it up after the war," fearful of the repressive postwar political climate.[132]

While some black Richmondites turned to interracial groups such as the Workers Alliance and the Communist Party to ameliorate their condition, most relied on individual initiative and community institutions to see them through. Black residents who owned horses or mules hired themselves out to work the truck farms that dotted North Richmond and were paid "whatever they thought you was worth." Some planted gardens and sold the produce in nearby cities. Others found that hunting provided a source of cash and food.[133] Walter Freeman Jr. had grown up hunting birds with his .22 rifle, but during the Depression his boyhood pastime became a matter of survival: "That's where I started hunting. Well, the Italians liked meadowlarks, robins, blackbirds. They made blackbird pies. I'd hunt them. Take them to them and they'd pay me for them. For sparrows I got one penny a piece. For the meadowlarks [I] would get five cents. For a robin you'd get ten cents. I kept money in this pocket. Yes sir, kept me moving with money in my pocket!"[134] To augment the family food supply, Ivy Reid Lewis shot the mud hens and sparrows that flocked in her North Richmond neighborhood: "Now when I see people kill birds, I think it's terrible because they don't eat them. When I was a kid, people ate birds. They killed them and ate them." Young Harry Williams helped his family make ends meet in the Depression by sneaking into the Chinese shrimp camp on lower Third Street and helping himself to the shrimp that lay drying on the sidewalk: "I pilfered them. . . . I wasn't the only one. Everybody did it." His mother would "fix that shrimp with rice. You had to survive back in the thirties."[135]

As black Richmondites struggled to maintain their homes and families during the Depression, their community institutions provided them with vital services that public agencies, city government, and local employers could not or would not provide. NRMBC held canned food drives and sponsored a "clean clothes closet" for needy residents. Church-related "feeding stations" organized by community women during the 1930s provided food to anyone in need. From the porch of her house in North Richmond, Beryl Gwendolyn Reid, a "soft-hearted woman" who liked to help people, prepared "big pots of beans and fed all the people who were hungry. And there were a lot of hungry people." Ashler Masonic Lodge's Widow's Mite Fund helped sustain needy women and children throughout the Depression with cash donations collected from lodge members and other community residents.[136]

Comprising only 1 percent of the city's total population in 1940 and enduring denigration from the black middle class in other cities who believed Richmond offered no social or cultural amenities, black Richmondites nonetheless held a positive view of themselves and their community.[137] The growth of the African American population in the city attests to more than the lure of its industries.

Black working-class men and women chose to live in Richmond for reasons other than economic ones as well. Charles Reid hoped to escape the social pretensions of blacks who were "try[ing] to have [a] society they didn't have." Therefore he took his family from their "much grander house" in Oakland to Richmond, despite strong disapproval from relatives. His sister informed him that "she thought it was a shame" he moved his family "back there in Richmond with all those backwards, backwoods people." She was "always mad about it." Ivy Reid Lewis recalled that her "grandmother didn't like it either."[138]

Matthew Malbrough quickly tired of life in Berkeley because there "wasn't a lot of work" there and because it was "too much of a city." He moved to North Richmond to work and for the added benefit of having room to "plant a patch" in his backyard. It appears that the semirural quality of life in prewar Richmond was important for many blacks.[139]

Thus by the eve of World War II, African Americans in Richmond had developed a stable, close-knit community with thriving institutions. Though most had been nurtured in a southern agrarian economic and cultural matrix, the war would accelerate their entry into the urban industrial workforce and transform the community they had created.

CHAPTER 2

Shipyards and Shipbuilders

*It looked like just about everybody was going into the army or
doing war work [so] I sold my tools and mules and come out
to Richmond.*

Unemployed black shipyard worker, 1947

World War II had a profound impact on every aspect of
life in Richmond, drastically altering black and white assumptions about
the future. The coming of the Kaiser shipyards was the most visible symbol of the war in Richmond. Shipyard work offered African Americans an
economic shift upward, placing them in the midst and at times the vanguard of Richmond's (and the nation's) economic, industrial, and social
transformation.

By 1940, as Congress turned its attention to California, where mild
climate, vast open spaces, and abundant natural resources made it an
ideal site for defense production, the government began to invest almost
half of its seventy-billion-dollar national defense budget in the Golden
State. This influx of money rejuvenated Southern California's languish-
ing aircraft industry and converted Northern California cities like Richmond into bustling shipbuilding centers. Therefore, war mobilization
sparked a western migration rivaling the gold and silver rushes of the
nineteenth and twentieth centuries. Of the 8,000,000 people who
moved west of the Mississippi in the 1940s, nearly one-half came to the
Pacific Coast. California received 3,500,000 new residents. From 1942
to 1945, after the passage of Executive Order 8802 and the creation of
the President's Committee on Fair Employment Practice (also known as

the Fair Employment Practices Commission, FEPC), nearly 500,000 African Americans poured into the state. This represented the largest voluntary black westward migration in the nation's history. Almost 125,000 black newcomers settled in the Bay Area, and nearly 15,000 came to Richmond. The city's total population soared to over 100,000.[1]

The coming of the Kaiser shipyards was the catalyst that transformed the city and seemed to realize the founders' dreams of industrial preeminence. The president of the Parr-Richmond Terminal Corporation persuaded Henry J. Kaiser to bring his newly won federal contract to build thirty British merchant ships to Richmond Harbor, California's second largest port.[2] The city gave Henry Kaiser carte blanche to transform the "boggy tideland" and Ohlone shell mounds into an efficient shipbuilding enterprise. By January 1941 crews had begun construction of thirty buildings, and they quickly completed four shipyards, twenty-seven shipways, twenty-three outfitting berths, and a prefabrication plant.[3] Ship specialists, construction engineers, and local workers removed over six million cubic yards of sludge and sank twenty-four thousand piles into the soggy earth around the harbor. In all, the yards covered almost nine hundred acres and became omnipresent and pervasive in the life of the city (see map 2).[4]

Yet from the beginning, the Kaiser yards proved to be a mixed blessing, exacerbating the long-standing conflict between small-townism and industrialism, increasing racial tension, and thrusting African Americans into the spotlight. On one hand, the shipyards provided the industrial economic base the city had sought since 1905. For example, just four months after the "announcement of the first shipyard," the *Richmond Independent* reported that local merchants were happily overwhelmed by the booming sales generated by the army of Kaiser construction workers who spent freely in downtown establishments. The paper noted that if the trend continued many of the merchants would be "hard put . . . to handle the business offered them." On the other hand, residents and city officials resented the presence of the shipyards and workers, who severely strained city resources and disrupted established patterns of life. Congressional hearings, municipal government reports, and personal experiences all confirmed that Richmond underwent a greater number of acute and long lasting changes than did any other city in the nation.[5] This upheaval caused the city attorney to declare, "Richmond is one town in America that has been deluged by the Federal Government to such an extent that the civil government is about to break down unless we get some help."[6]

African Americans at Kaiser joined their white counterparts seeking

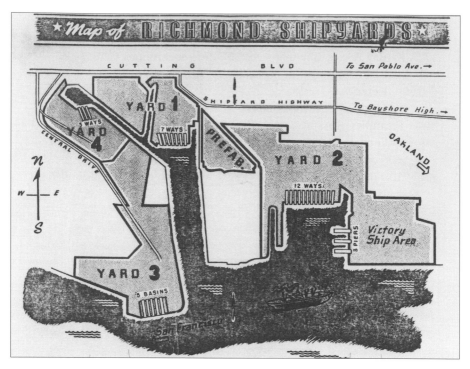

Map 2. Richmond Shipyards, 1944. Kaiser Permanente Metals Corporation, Henry J. Kaiser Papers, Bancroft Library, University of California, Berkeley.

work in Richmond's shipyards.[7] So overwhelming was the rush of African Americans to the shipyards that *California Voice* columnist Louis Campbell cautioned blacks to "look before they leaped" into "temporary posts in the defense program," fearing when "all the shooting and shouting [was] over," black men would be "cast adrift in the army of the unemployed" as white employers turned to "women and Chinese boys" to fill the nondomestic positions remaining after the shipyards shut down.[8] This warning did not slow the influx of African American workers to the Kaiser yards, however. At the peak of shipyard production, blacks comprised 20 percent of the labor force in the Richmond yards.

Black and white workers, 45 percent of whom came from California, flocked there because the work required no special industrial skills or technical expertise. Kaiser's innovative assembly techniques broke down skilled industrial procedures into the most basic components, resulting in faster ship production twenty-four hours a day, seven days a week.

For example, Kaiser scrapped the piece-by-piece craft of welding in favor of prefabrication, doing some work on site and parceling out other tasks to Bay Area companies. Fast welding techniques virtually eliminated the laborious but highly skilled task of riveting. The yards themselves reflected simplicity and efficiency. Laid out like assembly lines, the shipyards kept steel beams and ship parts moving smoothly from flat cars to completed vessels. Thus, shipyard workers became experts not in shipbuilding but in "performing one small job out of the total."[9]

Most workers who came to the yards with "no experience whatever," regardless of race, could start out as either a helper or a laborer. Applicants for laborer positions could "just show up" and be hired, since they could "always be put to work." All workers who aspired to be welders or burners needed additional training and received it through a variety of sources. Even the ferry that brought workers across the bay from San Francisco maintained a floating welding school, which the shipyard workers called "Ferryboat College." Many workers attended the training schools that Kaiser established right in the yards. Yard schools paid would-be welders $.95 an hour for a seven- to ten-day basic course. By 1943 Kaiser, in cooperation with the Federal Public Housing Administration and the Maritime Commission, began offering a complete training program that not only paid single men to come out to Richmond but also provided dormitory housing for a monthly rental fee ranging from $35 to $40 per month, utilities included. The four-week training program included four hours of welding, two hours of lecture, and two hours of "camp duties." The trainees, arriving from all parts of the country, received $33.50 a month minus $22.50, which the company retained for clothing and board expenses. Upon completion of the training, the average worker received $61 a week and had enough left over for modest savings (see table 2).[10]

An unskilled laborer could earn $45.76 per week, and helpers in most classifications received $.95 an hour, or $49.40 a week. A shipyard recruiting pamphlet noted that these workers were observed by supervisors, and "as soon as they show[ed] any aptitude and willingness to learn . . . you are made a trainee, third class in the craft you choose." Third-class trainees remained in that category for up to sixty days and then became trainees, first class, earning $1.05 an hour ($54.60 per week) with the possibility of advancement "to the grade of journeyman." Journeymen received $1.20 an hour ($62.40 per week, or $270 per month).[11]

Even though the shipyards had their greatest impact by being the largest employers — of both white and black workers — in the city, their pres-

Table 2 *Employee Weekly Budget, Kaiser Shipyards,*
         Richmond, 1944

Average weekly salary	$61.80
Expenses	
Food	$18.30
Rent	$ 8.50
Recreation, household expenses	$ 6.75
War bonds	$ 6.10
Taxes	$ 6.70
Clothes	$ 5.50
Transportation	$ 2.45
Miscellaneous and savings	$ 6.70
Subtotal	$ 61.00
Additional expenses	
Hospital plan	$ .50
Incidentals	$ 6.20
Total	$67.70

SOURCE: "Richmond Took a Beating," *Fortune,* February 1945, 264; *A Health Plan for Employees of the Richmond Shipyards* (Richmond: Kaiser Permanente, Inc., 1942), 22–23, series 15, carton 288, Kaiser Papers; William Sokol, "From Workingman's Town to All American City: The Socio-Political Economy of Richmond, California, during World War II," June 1971, 93, insert 5, Richmond Collection, Richmond Public Library.

ence affected other areas of black employment as well. Blacks found that the shipyard boom afforded them new leverage with other employers. For instance, the Pullman Company, which had had no problems recruiting black workers before the arrival of the shipyards, was forced to advertise for workers in black newspapers. In an effort to retain its dwindling black female workforce, the Red Rock fish cannery initiated virtual door-to-door bus service for its workers living in North Richmond. The cannery undertook this extraordinary measure at a time when wartime transportation problems plagued Richmond and other Bay Area cities.[12]

The Santa Fe Railroad, employer of 150 nonwhite workers, experienced shortages and high turnover rates in 1944. The company offered Mildred Slocum, a Richmond resident since the 1930s, a substantial pay raise to entice her to reconsider her decision to quit her job as cook, but she declined the raise and quit anyway. Marguerite Williams rejected shipyard work (even though she was "tempted because of the money") because the "women had to work like men," and she took a job at Santa Fe cleaning troop cars. Black domestic workers also enjoyed increased power as many abandoned the kitchens and laundry rooms of white families for the shipyards. They did not hesitate to let their employers know that they "didn't have to take just whatever [white families] wanted to give you, when you could get work in the [ship]yards."[13]

The prospects for black employment in the city's other wartime industries were not as promising. Other businesses refused to hire blacks workers or hired one or two to comply with government contracts. Standard Oil, citing the discriminatory policy of its "company union," employed "about 9 Negroes" total. By 1944, under pressure from the government, the company had increased the number of nonwhite employees to 114 out of a total workforce of 3,291. After reviewing Richmond's employment situation in 1944, the FEPC examiner concluded that "a considerable number of firms still do not employ any non-whites and . . . only a few firms employ the majority of the non-whites." This situation would be highlighted as critical labor shortages made discrimination in defense industries a volatile issue both in the city and across the country.[14]

In 1942 the War Manpower Commission estimated that California would require at least 123,000 additional shipyard workers. Neither local nor state labor pools could meet the growing shipyard labor demand. Therefore, desperate federal officials and defense contractors devised a number of innovative recruitment and retention strategies, including imposing stringent regulations on worker movement from war-essential jobs and negotiating with Mexico the *bracero* treaty, which opened up to three hundred thousand Mexican nationals short-term employment in Pacific Coast shipbuilding and other industries. More importantly the government, in conjunction with defense contractors, embarked on a vigorous recruitment campaign.[15]

Less than a year after launching its first ship, the Kaiser Shipbuilding Corporation initiated an out-of-state recruitment drive to secure a daily quota of 150 new workers for the Richmond yards. In November 1942 Kaiser dispatched a five-man team to Minneapolis and began a massive midwestern effort. The operation was subsequently expanded to eastern and southern locations, particularly Oklahoma, Arkansas, Texas, Louisiana, and Mississippi. Kaiser also stationed special shipyard "spotters" along the California border to direct newcomers to the Richmond yards. They faced fierce competition from other recruiters, who tried to steer the new arrivals to aircraft plants and other shipyards in Southern California. However, Richmond recruiters held a "tremendous psychological advantage over most concerns bidding for shipyard help" because of Henry Kaiser's popularity with the public.[16]

In another recruitment venture, Kaiser joined forces with the Richmond Chamber of Commerce to distribute over thirty thousand "job fact sheets" to hundreds of United States Employment Service (USES) offices nationwide. The fact sheets informed potential recruits, "with or without experience, there's a job of vital importance to your country waiting for you in the Richmond shipyards." The recruitment sheets, promising a trade, high pay, and a piece of the California dream, were strong inducements for millions of Americans who had endured years of deprivation during the Depression.[17] During 1942 and 1943 Kaiser recruiters paid the fares for 37,852 workers destined for the Richmond shipyards, but hopeful workers also traveled "by car bus, train, even hitchhiking" to get to Richmond.[18]

Despite these efforts, Richmond shipyards experienced chronic worker turnover and substantial financial losses when their "contract men" failed to honor their contracts. In an effort to reduce some of the bureaucratic runaround that characterized shipyard routine and led to recruitment loss, Kaiser management provided transportation and housing counseling services for new arrivals. The company even arranged to install shower facilities in the train depot at Ninth and Nevin Streets in downtown Richmond.[19] Nonetheless, Kaiser's high productivity prompted the regional director of the War Manpower Commission to proclaim the Richmond recruiting program the "hottest in the nation."[20]

Most of Richmond's other defense employers remained cool to mobilizing efforts that would tap the national pool of African American labor, however. Virtually all able-bodied nonwhite city residents (the majority of whom were African Americans) were employed in the shipyards. These statistics alarmed federal officials, who feared that persistent workforce deficits would erode defense production. Concluding that black migration was crucial to the war effort, the War Manpower Commission of the USES in Richmond began a campaign to persuade industries to intensify and broaden their recruitment efforts among blacks, women, "Latins, aliens, minors and handicapped persons." Arthur A. Hall, local manager of the War Manpower Commission, informed a government panel, "we have to get other people in and get them to work. We have to break down the employment standards." The USES campaign called for the abolition of restrictive union policies that shut out African Americans and women from employment in Richmond's defense industries.[21]

Therefore, in 1942 Kaiser labor recruiters began to scour the southern United States specifically for black workers, the last remaining untapped labor resource available. Recruiters distributed brightly colored circulars throughout southern cities. The circulars extolled California's mild climate, its recreational facilities, and shipyard pay benefits and appealed to patriotism. Kaiser also placed advertisements in local newspapers. One "caught [the] eye" of Margaret Starks in Pine Bluff, Arkansas. She urged her husband, "go to California and get a job [then] send for me later." Her husband came to Richmond in 1943 and began work in the shipyards as a laborer. Margaret Starks joined him later that year and also worked as a laborer in Yard 2. In Memphis, William McKinney "looked in the paper" and saw an advertisement for welders: "They'd learn you in three months and guarantee you a job." After McKinney completed a welding course in Memphis, the recruiter told him about opportunities in the Bay Area, "so we chose Richmond." Five other men completed the training course with him: "we drove out. . . . We didn't stop for nothing but the gas and to eat. It took us three days to come here." Upon arrival, McKinney and his colleagues discovered that "every black guy that worked in a shipyard in the United States worked in a Jim Crow union. You was not in the regular union. So we worked there all through the war."[22]

Only a fraction of African American shipyard workers were recruited by these methods, however. Blacks relied on personal and social networks to facilitate their migration to Richmond and other California cities. Unlike black southern migrants to the North during the first Great Migration, World War II migrants received little encouragement from California's black newspapers. African American newspaper editors in the Golden State, fearing a "backlash" from whites if large numbers of job-seeking blacks concentrated in California's cities, had long advised black newcomers to bypass cities and settle in agricultural areas, where they would be more dispersed and would pose less economic competition to whites. Informal networks created by religious affiliations, employment associations, and familial ties helped black newcomers make their way to Richmond during World War II.[23]

Charles Henry Thurston, a school teacher and principal from Jackson, Mississippi, utilized his Baptist church connections to aid his migration to Richmond in 1943. Thurston's travels to Baptist choir conventions as a "singer of some prominence" afforded him the opportunity to exchange views with other blacks about the "state of the race." Thurston "knew people from all over the state; he had been all over the state singing." Bill Thurston, Charles Henry's son, recalled that someone told his father and uncle "that there was work [in Richmond]." Charles Henry's discussions regarding the "future of black people" led him to conclude that Richmond offered more promise for him and his family than Mississippi did.[24]

In 1943, the Thurston brothers boarded the train in Jackson, Mississippi, and arrived in Oakland, California, "about a week later." They lived with friends in Berkeley until they could find a place of their own. Although his brother returned to Mississippi after a few months, Charles Henry took a job at Richmond's Ford Motor Company making steel plates for armored vehicles. He quickly saved enough money to send for his wife and son, who joined him in 1944.[25]

The Southern Pacific and Santa Fe lines that terminated in the East Bay also contributed to the "migration grapevine" that brought African Americans to Richmond. Railroad porters, cooks, and maids based in Oakland spread the word of job opportunities up and down the line in the 1940s, just as their counterparts on the Illinois Central line had done for the millions of black southerners who streamed into Chicago during the first Great Migration. Now, however, the destination of choice for millions of African Americans had become California. Louis Bonaparte, a retired Pullman porter who had lived in Richmond since the 1920s, told his sister and brother-in-law, Vesper and Wilbur Wheat in Port Arthur, Texas, about opportunities in the Bay Area. Wilbur Wheat worked as a barber in Port Arthur and valued Louis's opinions because "people looked up to railroad workers everywhere," and their views about "what to do" and "where to go" carried considerable weight.[26]

Louis Bonaparte's favorable reports about Richmond contributed to Wilbur and Vesper's decision to migrate, but when a prosperous-looking friend from California visited the Wheats in Texas, the friend's "new clothes, new car and lots of money" tipped the scales. In 1942, they set out for Richmond, where Wilbur hoped to get into war work, amass some money, and avoid being drafted into the military: "The main reason I came here, I didn't want to go in the service. . . . I could get me a defense job and make good money." When the Wheats arrived in Richmond, they lived with Louis and Georgie Bonaparte. Wilbur was hired to "pick . . . up scraps" in Kaiser Yard 2. The couple eventually moved into Harbor Gate, one of Richmond's numerous housing projects for shipyard workers.[27]

Personal correspondence networks were vital to African American migration. Like the turn-of-the-century immigrants who settled in eastern cities, black migrants to the Bay Area in the 1940s "would write back home" to loved ones. Their glowing letters said that "there were certainly more opportunities here than in the South" and proclaimed that "there were jobs here, plenty of jobs." For example, one black Richmond shipyard worker recalled: "my brother came out here in 1942. He sent letters and said that wages was good and that we could get some good paying jobs. He wrote a lot of letters and we decided we would come out here and work in the shipyard." Letters from a former co-worker persuaded another to leave his home state: "I had a friend out here who used to work at the lumber mill with me. . . . He wrote me to come out here and get one of these defense jobs." [28]

Yet for many, other factors also contributed to the exodus. The political and social climate of the South in the 1940s was a powerful inducement to black migration. The introduction of the mechanical cotton picker in 1944 pushed thousands of black sharecroppers and tenant farmers off southern plantations and into the urban industrial marketplace. A mechanical picker could do the work of fifty people, reducing costs from $39.41 to $5.26 per bale. Mechanization had political as well as economic implications for black southerners. In those places where blacks outnumbered whites, mechanization could equalize the population ratio or put whites in the majority as blacks left to find other employment. The new technology dispersed entire black agrarian communities and in doing so diluted the potential for black political organization. White growers quickly came to realize that mechanized farming would "require a fraction of the amount of labor . . . required by the sharecrop system" and would "automatically make our racial problems easier to handle." Racial violence also pushed many African Americans out of the South and onto the road west. An outbreak of antiblack violence in the Mobile shipyards, for example, convinced a number of black workers to depart for Richmond. Their reasons for leaving had little to do with the higher wages offered by Kaiser: "They had this riot there [in Mobile] and a lot of the colored workers got beat up and I was afraid to go back in the yard." Having endured a terrifying night in which "white men rode around . . . [and] threw rocks at our houses," one worker and his wife left for Richmond with a group of other blacks: "I didn't even wait for my check. . . . [We] just decided to leave." Despite the good pay and better economic opportunity in the Richmond yards, he said, "I don't guess I would have ever come out here unless they had that riot." [29]

For other black migrants, the spirit of adventure, of doing something different and breaking free of old patterns, proved irresistible. One black newcomer summed up the atmosphere: "It looked like just about everybody was going into the army or doing war work [so] I sold my tools and mules and come out to Richmond."[30] Migration opened up the possibility of change on multiple levels for African Americans. Believing it would lead not only to an economic shift upward but also to the expansion of other opportunities like education and decent housing, black migrants anchored their decision to depart the South in the realities of the present and hope for the future. In Richmond, they would be able to make decent wages, sit in any available seat on the bus, and provide better opportunities for the next generation. A Kaiser shipyard worker explained: "[I] had been working for thirty-five cents an hour [in the South] and we couldn't get a raise. . . . I came right here to Richmond [where] I [make more money]. My wife likes it here, says they have good schools for our kids."[31]

The predominance of women among black newcomers to Richmond and other Bay Area cities suggests that gender played a role in migration as well. In contrast to the first Great Migration and to black migration to other parts of the country during the 1940s, the migration to the San Francisco Bay Area involved more women than men (by a ratio of 53 percent to 47 percent). Twice as many black females as males between the ages of fifteen and twenty-four settled in the Bay Area. Personal and workplace experiences, inextricably linked to race and gender, helped shape women's economic and social expectations of migration.

Kaiser worker Lyn Childs explained why she came to Richmond and worked as a shipburner (welder), "number one, I needed work; number two, I'd had a bad experience in jobs before where I hadn't felt any pride in the kind of work I was doing; number three, there was a war on and the people were all enthused about helping out in every way they could." Margaret Starks followed her husband to Richmond from Arkansas in 1943 and worked in the shipyards until learning that she was pregnant and that her husband was "playing around" on her. Starks resolved to break completely with her past: "I knew I couldn't go back to Pine Bluff. . . . [I] had an abortion, divorced him and with the money I earned from the shipyards I started a life of my own." Still holding down her shipyard job, she began publishing Richmond's first black newspaper, the *Richmond Guide,* in 1944 and became secretary of the newly established Richmond branch of the NAACP. In addition to these duties, Margaret Starks served as a "talent booking agent" for several of North Richmond's blues clubs that flourished during the war years.[32]

Thus, migration and industrial employment could have a liberating effect on the lives of black women. Wartime work afforded them an escape from low paying, dead-end domestic employment to which the double yoke of racism and sexism had consigned them. For some women migration became a quest for personal as well as economic autonomy. Margaret Starks noted that Richmond was a "long way from [her] cooking job in Pine Bluff."[33] A Marshall, Texas, woman articulated the race, gender, and economic nexus that placed African American women in the forefront of migration to Richmond:

I'll tell you. You see, I am a colored woman and I am forty-two years old. Now you know that colored women don't have a chance for any kind of job back there except in somebody's kitchen working for two or three dollars a week. I have an old mother and a crippled aunt to take care of, and I have to make as much as I can to take care of them. . . . I got my neighbors to look after my mother and aunt and came out here on the bus. I went to work for Kaiser and saved enough money to bring my aunt and mother out here.[34]

Almost 90 percent of the black women and men employed in the Richmond shipyards were southerners.[35] They brought with them varying levels of employment skills and education. Most had completed eight years of formal education, which equaled or exceeded that of their white counterparts. Though youth characterized migrants regardless of race, African American migrants who settled in the San Francisco Bay Area were even younger than their counterparts (black and white) in other parts of the country, averaging a little over twenty-three years, and most were married.[36]

They came from the middle stratum of their southern communities. In general, their ranks did not include W.E.B. DuBois's "talented tenth" or Carter Woodson's leaders or professionals, who made up a good portion of the first Great Migration. Rather, the experiences of World War II black newcomers to Richmond resembled the pattern described by historian Clyde Kiser. They gradually expanded their employment parameters in ever widening circles of secondary migration, moving from the rural South, to southern urban areas, to northern and midwestern cities. Black migrants to Richmond extended this pattern to include the urban West during World War II. A 1947 University of California study of fifty black former shipyard workers in Richmond suggests that many Richmond migrants entered urban industrial labor via secondary migration routes. This pattern frequently included a sojourn in transitional southern cities like Dallas, Jackson, New Orleans, and Mobile, where they garnered industrial experience and urban savvy. Only 10 percent of the black shipyard workers studied had worked in agriculture immediately before entering the Richmond shipyards.

At least one former shipyard worker in the study had been a welder in a Mobile, Alabama, shipyard. Similarly, William H. McKinney, a welder at Kaiser Yard 4, had been employed as a carpenter in a Memphis furniture plant, where he worked as a case fitter: "I was running that machine. The first black guy running that machine." McKinney discovered that a white trainee under his supervision was earning a higher wage: "He said, fifty cents an hour. I said, oh, no it ain't. So he showed me his stubs. . . . I was making forty-five. . . . So I hauled it to the office. I told them, I can't work for this. I got to have more money! That was where I made my mistake." McKinney quit and decided to move to Richmond.[37]

Thus, African American networks, deeply rooted in the social and cultural fabric of the South, propelled the movement of black men and women to Richmond. These black newcomers hoped to escape racial and gender stereotypes and looked forward to greater economic and social opportunities in the West. The Kaiser shipyards seemed to offer most of them the best means to achieve these goals. These aspirations contributed to black shipyard employment and to the growth of the city's black population. In 1943 Kaiser's black workforce, most of whom resided in Richmond, totaled nearly 8,000 men and women, or about 9 percent of the entire shipyard labor force. The black shipyard employment figure peaked at almost 25 percent of the total shipyard workforce of over 100,000. By 1943 blacks numbered 5,673 in an overall city population of more than 90,000.[38]

The migration of African Americans to Richmond was an ongoing and complicated process, a process that began in the nineteenth century and accelerated with the massive movement to California during the 1940s. Prewar black migrants like Matthew Malbrough and Girtha Hudson, who left Louisiana to work in Richmond's early industries, represented the first wave. The World War II influx of blacks to Richmond's shipyards merely extended and intensified it.[39] For longtime residents of Richmond, black and white, and for the vast majority of newcomers of all races, shipyard work resulted in a distinct "shift upward" in economic position, skills, and occupational status. However, African Americans encountered obstacles to shipyard employment not experienced by their white counterparts. Regardless of their skills, blacks were severely limited in the workplace because of racist union policies that were abetted by Kaiser management's acquiescence. Shipyard unions assumed an ambivalent and often hostile position toward all new recruits, fearing the massive influx of new workers would jeopardize their control over hiring and wage policies in the yards.

A Boilermakers Union publication characterized the new recruits as an odd assortment of "shoe clerks, soda jerks, professors, pimps and old maids." White newcomers, called "Okies" and "Arkies" by residents, flooded into the city and faced resentment from union members, Kaiser officials, and local residents.[40] A white character in Joseph Fabry's shipyard novel *Swingshift* remarked: "Those Okies just swamp us. You can't get a room to live in and you can't get a seat in an eat joint because they're all over the place. American history is wrong. General Grant didn't take Richmond, the Okies did."[41]

The harshest criticism, however, was reserved for African Americans, who were considered the "dregs of the recruitment barrel." Native-born white residents worried that blacks brought with them the "cultural mores of the south." Richmond's director of recreation testified before a government committee that the arrival of "several thousand colored workers and their families . . . from the southern lower economic groups" complicated working and living conditions in the city. Even the Arkie protagonist of William Martin Camp's novel about wartime Richmond complained that when the shipyards "gits t' a-hirin' lazy negroes, they shore must be hard up fer h'ard hands." W. Miller Barbour, western field director of the National Urban League, noted that the "hostility toward the white southerner" in Richmond had "modified considerably," but the "big problem that remains is the Negro."[42]

Shipyard employment promised economic advancement and independence, but racism restricted the ability of black workers to achieve equity. Union membership was required of all shipyard employees, but shipyard unions prohibited black membership. Thus African American workers were caught in a vicious cycle that kept them from being hired, paid, and promoted like their white counterparts.

In 1941 the Tolan Committee report on the state of American labor found "a dozen great trade unions with constitutional provisions barring Negroes from membership." A similar report by *Fortune* magazine concluded that out of nineteen international unions, ten with AFL affiliations discriminated against African Americans, sometimes violating the nondiscrimination pledges in their own charters and flouting Executive Order 8802. Malcolm Ross, national chairman of the FEPC acknowledged that racist practices "clearly indicated that there would be difficulty in achieving the full use of the labor" of black men and women. William McKinney attempted to "get in the shipyard working anywhere in the United States" but was informed by union officials, "we don't have no openings no where in the United States for Negro carpenters." He was told to look in "Honolulu or South America, that's the only thing we have carpenters for a Negro." Despite an acute labor short-age, African Americans, regardless of skill level, ability, or training, were last hired, first fired, and least promoted in defense industries across the country.[43]

Because the Kaiser shipyards in Richmond employed more black workers than any other industry in the city, Kaiser's union practices put black workers at an even greater disadvantage. The steamfitters, ma-chinists, and painters unions all followed exclusionary and discrimina-tory practices in the Kaiser yards. Initially, Kaiser attempted to use only whites in its skilled shipyard trades but abandoned this strategy when a firestorm of protest from African Americans prompted the War Man-power Commission to pull "Kaiser, Richmond out of inter-regional re-cruitment because of the attitude toward negroes [sic]."[44]

The Boilermakers Union was the most powerful shipyard union on the West Coast. Richmond's Boilermakers Local 513 controlled almost 70 percent of all shipyard labor and proved to be the biggest impedi-ment for African American workers in Richmond, since it controlled the shipyard jobs most frequently held by black workers (chippers, welders, burners, riggers, flangers, and laborers). In 1940 Kaiser signed closed-shop contracts with the Boilermakers locals, and in two years the union controlled virtually every aspect of shipyard hiring. Under the terms of the agreement, the union was given the power to hire, promote, and set work rules. Kaiser management was allowed to recruit and hire only when the union was "unable to furnish needed workers." The director of the local office of the USES bluntly admitted that "the hiring prac-tices of the Boilermakers' Union have prevented Negro men and women from being employed in shipyards at Richmond solely because they are Negroes."[45]

Even skilled black workers found their paths to employment thwarted by Richmond's unions. For example, Samuel D. Hudson, a plumber from Mississippi with over ten years experience, and Marcellus Knox, a plumber from Texas with more than twenty years experience, com-plained that Steamfitters' Local 590 turned down their applications for membership. Informed by the business agent that there were "no open-ings" and that "there weren't any colored in the union" despite a stand-ing "blanket order" by the USES for pipefitters in three of the Rich-mond shipyards, Hudson and Knox turned to the FEPC. Under federal pressure, the union eventually extended a "relaxation" of its exclusionary policy for Hudson and Knox only. This temporary solution prompted one USES administrator to admit that "if any cases come to our attention in the future it will again be necessary to work out a clearance of the individual worker with the unio[n] representative as no commitments have been made by Local 590 as to future cases." In 1943 two black journeymen welders with "substantial experience in their trade" appealed to the Bay Area Council against Discrimination for help in securing shipyard employment. Because of the "discrimination in treatment at the hands of the union, they were nearly ready to throw over their jobs here and return to their homes in Illinois. They'd take their chances there."[46]

The 1947 University of California study of black shipyard workers in Richmond also indicated that many black newcomers brought with them industrial skills and experience. Only 10 percent of that group had been employed on farms immediately prior to their migration to Richmond. Forty percent came from small urban areas of the South, where they had worked in nonagricultural jobs. Four workers in the study had been employed in construction; twelve were listed as laborers; and four had worked in the service industry as washroom attendants and domestic servants. About twenty-five of the fifty surveyed had worked in nonfarming jobs, earning their living as, for example, carpenters, compress machine operators, stonecutters, welders, truck drivers, clerks, sheet metal workers, cement handlers, and stationary firemen. They were also able to attain more education than newcomers from rural areas of the same states. The picture painted by the 1947 study contrasts with the popular image of black migrants as unlettered, rural peasants.[47]

Thus, many black newcomers with industrial trades or skills and educational levels comparable or superior to those of white workers experienced a "downward thrust into unskilled labor" and a decline in occupational status as a result of entry into shipyard work. Like the midwestern black workers of an earlier era described by historian Joe William Trotter Jr., a number of black workers in Richmond during World War II were compelled to "learn over again what they had mastered" or, locked out of skilled trades, were forced to enter the unskilled labor force.[48] For some, entry into Richmond's wartime industrial labor force meant an increase in income but a decrease in professional status. Charles Henry Thurston found that his pay of fifty to sixty dollars a week as an assembly-line worker in Richmond's Ford Motor plant represented a "vast amount more" than his salary as a school teacher and principal in Jackson, Mississippi, but it represented a "step down" socially. Realizing that "credentialing was very loose in the South" and that Richmond schools "did not hire black teachers," he did not seek a teaching position but pragmatically decided to "forget the prestige and make the money." Similarly, Wilbur Wheat's barber training gave him a professional occupation that became only a "sideline" once he started working as a laborer in Richmond Yard 2. Only after quitting over a racial dispute did he return to his previous occupation, working out of his housing project apartment.[49]

Training dormitories and unions, like other aspects of shipyard work, were generally segregated or inhospitable to blacks. Most who aspired to become welders, for example, received training at the unofficial "ten-day schools" that sprang up in home garages all over the area and were taught by workers who had only recently learned the task themselves.[50] The shipyard unions classified nearly 80 percent of Kaiser's black work-force as unskilled or semiskilled trainees and concentrated them in the "hull trades," where they were employed principally as chippers, welders, flangers, and burners (see figure 12).[51] African American workers also experienced wage discrimination. Because they most often started out and remained in the unskilled categories, they earned about $.88 to $.95 per hour on an eight-hour shift in contrast to whites, who came in at higher levels and were promoted more quickly, earning between $1.00 and $1.25 an hour for an eight-hour shift.[52]

In November 1943 the FEPC conducted hearings in Portland and Los Angeles on racial discrimination in West Coast shipyards and heard testimony from African Americans who were refused admittance by the Boilermakers Union. The Richmond yards figured prominently in the complaints and charges of discrimination heard by the committee. Many complaints dated back to the latter part of 1942, before a separate "auxiliary" union had been established for black workers in the Richmond yards.

In an affidavit submitted to the FEPC, Sylvester White complained that Welders Union Local 681 had refused his application for membership with the "flimsy excuse" that "they aren't clearing any more Negroes until they decide on how to handle their union membership." War Manpower Commission investigators reported that White's actions had "caused considerable feeling in Local 681 against Negro workers." After a meeting between the Boilermakers "International Representative" (Thomas Crowe) and the president of the International Boilermakers Union in Kansas City, the Boilermakers affiliates were advised that "Negro workers accepted by them should be transferred to the nearest auxiliary." Thus, White's membership was sent to Local 26 at Moore Dry Dock Company in Oakland. White reported that a union representative warned "that if he didn't like the Jim-Crow local he would see to it that he didn't get a welder's job." Moreover, Crowe "indicated he felt it unwise of the management of the shipyards to place Negroes in certain types of positions particularly those in which they would have supervision over other workers." He noted that the "Richmond shipyard had attempted this resulting in the southern White workers rebelling against it." [53]

Isaiah Brooks, who had been a shipyard worker in 1918 and 1919, submitted an affidavit to the FEPC after he was denied membership in the union and blocked from working in the Richmond shipyards in September 1941. The assistant business agent told Brooks that "he was instructed by the Business Agent not to take any applications from Negroes, Filipinoes [sic], Japanese and Chinese." When Brooks showed the agent his "Riggers union card, which [he] carried while working in the shipyards in 1918 and 1919," the agent said that "he did not want to see it as it did not mean anything to him." The union representative added, "a lot of your Colored fellows have been here to join the union and we have told them all the same thing." [54]

African American women faced dual discrimination in their pursuit of shipyard employment in Richmond. The Kaiser yards hired its first ten female welders, heralded as the "vanguard of American women gone to work," in July 1942 for the prefabrication plant. The overwhelming majority of women employed in the Kaiser shipyards worked as welders; the second largest group of female workers was classified as "laborers." By mid-1944, women made up 27.5 percent of all Richmond shipyard employees and 24.2 percent of all production personnel. Female shipyard employment peaked at 24,500 (see figure 13). A recruiting pamphlet announced that female shipyard workers earned "precisely the same wages as men, doing comparable work." Black women were refused union membership, were concentrated in the lower paying hull trades, and were refused promotions at higher rates than were their black male coworkers and their white coworkers of both sexes. The manpower utilization division of California's War Manpower Commission concluded that "there is considerably more discrimination against Negro women than men." [55] In 1942 Flora M. Hilliard enlisted the aid of the War Manpower Commission to help her obtain union clearance through Oakland's Shipfitters and Helpers Local 9 for employment as a shipfitter's helper in Richmond Yard 3. Local 9 refused Hilliard's application with the explanation that they "did not have an order from this company [Kaiser Yard 3] for women Shipfitter Helpers." Moreover, when she applied for membership, the union "had not received instructions from [the] International President . . . on how to handle this type of membership." With the intervention of federal authorities, Hilliard was cleared for work at the Kaiser Richmond yards on October 3, 1942. Her letter of thanks to the commission hinted at the struggle black women faced in trying to penetrate the white, male domain of the shipyard unions: "[I] am sure that with out [*sic*] your consideration, I would not have been cleared through this particular Local #9."[56]

That same year Oakland resident Elmira Ake, a self-described "true American" wife of a draft-age husband and mother of a son who "in a few days will Join the arm[ed] force[s]," complained in a letter to President Roosevelt that "the colored womens are being refuse [t]he chance to Join the Boiler maker unions as Helpers or Trainee Burners or welders." Ake was employed as a laborer in Richmond's Yard 3 but attempted to join the AFL, which informed her that "they Did not take negro woman in the Boiler makers union." Demanding to know "why I can't have a [decent] Job as other american Citison," she implored the president to "rite me [immediately] and tell me why cant [I] Become a member." The White House referred her letter to the FEPC, which informed her, "If . . . your membership in the union does not affect in any way, your employment, wages, opportunities for promotion, or other conditions of work, the Committee would have no jurisdiction to intervene in the matter of your failure to secure union membership." Ake, like thousands of other African American workers, was certain that union membership represented the surest path to the higher paying, skilled, "decent jobs" in the urban industrial labor force.[57]

As late as 1944 the shipyard unions still balked at accepting African American women. William R. Brown—shipyard worker, Richmond resident, and "grand president" of the Richmond branch of the United Negroes of America, a militant civil rights organization concerned with workplace discrimination—noted: "for the last two years to my knowledge the Richmond Yards have accepted Negro women reluctantly; at present, supposedly because Boilermaker's Local 513 will not accept them into membership they are not accepting them at all."[58]

Local 513 was able to maintain an all-white, predominantly male union until 1943, when longtime Bay Area resident and community activist Frances Mary Albrier challenged the union's color and gender bars in the Richmond shipyards. Albrier went to work in Yard 2 in 1943 after completing a training course at Oakland's Central Trade School. She put in twice the sixty hours of training required: "I felt I had to be better because I *was* a black woman." After passing the welder's test "with flying colors," Albrier had her application for union membership rejected because Kaiser "had not yet set up an auxiliary [union] to take in Negroes."[59]

Yielding to her threat of a lawsuit and to pressure from the black and progressive communities in the East Bay, the shipyard union devised a temporary solution to the dilemma. Local 513 would accept Albrier's union dues in Richmond but immediately transfer them to the auxiliary at Moore shipyards in Oakland until Richmond could establish its own auxiliary. Despite this less-than-satisfactory arrangement, her accomplishment was greeted with amazement by other black shipyard employees when she reported to work outfitted in full welder's regalia: "The black shipwrights stopped and said, 'how did *you* get in here? . . . Because they are not hiring any black welders out here.' I said, 'well, I just happened to *bust* my way in here.'"[60]

From 1941 to 1942 the Boilermakers locals in the Bay Area managed to avoid a direct challenge to their discriminatory policies "simply by issuing clearances to black shipyard workers without requiring them to join the union or pay dues." In February 1943, when its rigid stance against black workers threatened to disrupt shipyard production and exacerbate labor shortages, Boilermakers Local 513 established an auxiliary union, Local A-36, for black shipyard workers. African American employees now would be required to pay dues to the auxiliary in order to receive work clearance but were "not privileged to attend the meetings of any local, even in order to be informed." Furthermore, auxiliary members had "no voice or vote in the selection of collective bargaining representatives, in formulating the demands nor in approving the collective bargaining agreement" but would nevertheless be bound by election results. With the tacit consent of Kaiser officials, who were concerned more with production schedules than workplace equity, Local 513 managed to retain "control [of] the jobs in the Richmond yards."[61]

Local A-36 could not "refer workers directly . . . to jobs" and was "unable, in the main, to help a colored worker who wants to work in the Richmond yard." Yet from its inception Local A-36 stood as a paradox. Legally subordinated to Local 513, the auxiliary operated within the context of segregation but became an institution through which African American workers began to challenge workplace segregation. Although allegations of fiscal mismanagement and corruption plagued Local A-36, it represented an important step in the processes of black urbanization and proletarianization and enabled black Richmondites to expand their power beyond their numbers.[62]

For thousands of black newcomers streaming into Richmond, Local

A-36 stood as the primary and most accessible industrial institution they had encountered in their search for employment. It provided them with their first orientation to the workplace and to their new community. Under the direction of the Reverend William B. Smith, himself a recent arrival from Texas, Local A-36 was able to place more than ten thousand black workers in shipyards and other positions during its first year of operation. In addition to locating shipyard employment, Local A-36 found jobs for fifteen black women in the city's newly expanded recreation department. Because many members lived in North Richmond, the auxiliary devoted a portion of its time and finances to improving conditions in that district, which lacked, among a great many other things, "decent recreational facilities." The auxiliary won the approval of most black longtime residents for its "meritorious work accomplished in so short a time among the Negro workers of the Richmond Shipyards."[63]

The auxiliary served as a transitional vehicle to "union consciousness" for black workers, 60 percent of whom had come from areas that legally banned organized labor, and for whom the union concept was a "completely new and different thing." Their struggles in the workplace fostered a realization that "discrimination [could be] expected for years to come" and that they would need some protection from low wages and exploitation. Their experiences in Local A-36 helped black men and women develop organizational skills, political discernment, and public-speaking expertise. Bill Thurston, an employee in Yard 2 explained: "For the first time you had poor black people from the South working with the union and all kinds of people who knew the ropes. It made them feel like they could do something too. It wouldn't be the same old story."[64]

By 1943 union consciousness had spilled over into a general racial awareness, and African American shipyard workers organized to fight workplace inequities and discrimination in the community. The creation of Shipyard Workers against Discrimination (the forerunner of Richmond's NAACP) by black newcomers and longtime residents was visible proof that a new spirit was flowering in Richmond. The organization targeted the auxiliary system. William McKinney recalled: "every black person [who] worked in the shipyard was in the auxiliary. . . . They had formed an organization in this whole Bay Area to break down discrimination in the union because we wasn't in the union. And I joined that organization, Shipyard Workers Against Discrimination. We worked all through the war trying to break that thing [the auxiliaries] down."[65]

Shipyard Workers against Discrimination tackled the unions' anti-black policies by picketing and sitting in at the headquarters of Local 513 in downtown Richmond. Yard 2 leaderman Cleophas Brown joined a delegation of United Negro Labor Council (UNLC) members at a national conference of the Boilermakers Union and successfully persuaded the union to allow auxiliary members to vote in the national convention, though there was no change in union policy on auxiliaries.[66] These tactics were responsible for a few more black shipyard hires and for focusing public attention on the problem, but as late as 1944, the United Negroes of America complained that Local 513 had "only accepted Negro members into their auxiliaries a total of four months in the last year" and that those months were "divided into two periods about May 15 and November 17 when we threatened to call a strike."[67]

In July 1943, under the sponsorship of the UNLC and Shipyard Workers against Discrimination, African Americans in Richmond, led by Cleophas Brown, joined with other black workers in a national boycott of the auxiliaries, refusing to pay dues. Brown, who had been active in the NAACP in Los Angeles before moving to Richmond in 1942, worked with C. L. Dellums and Marinship welder Joseph James to bring a class-action suit against the Boilermakers Union. In Marin County, in the North Bay, almost half of the nearly eleven hundred black workers at the Marinship yards, who were governed by the Boilermakers Union's closed-shop contract provisions, refused to pay union dues and went on strike. In shipyards around the Bay Area, African American workers protested in solidarity.

In Richmond, most black shipyard workers supported the Marinship strike but did not walk out. Instead they withheld dues. Cleophas Brown recalled that many Richmond shipyard workers "dropped out of that second-class union" and "never paid a nickel dues into this auxiliary. . . . That was the campaign: we won't pay dues into a second-class thing." In retaliation against the protesters, the "Boilermakers tried to get you fired. They had quite a bit of influence and they would draft guys in the army, blacks who wouldn't join the union." However labor was at a premium, and the shipyards "needed us so bad." Brown used this to his advantage as he continued to fight the auxiliaries: "I could read blue prints and . . . they exempted me from going into the war because they needed me in the shipyard, because so many people in the shipyard could hardly read and write."[68]

In 1945 Joseph James's class-action suit resulted in a landmark Supreme Court decision (*James v. Marinship*) that called for the dismantling of the auxiliaries. Thus, as the war against fascism overseas wound down, African Americans won an important victory in their "Double V" campaign against Jim Crow on the home front. Their victory represented "quite a blow" to segregation on all fronts and "kind of kicked off things," since "out of that, here in Richmond we built the NAACP branch and this fight went on quite a bit in the courts, you know." The activism of black Richmondites attracted national attention. Walter White, executive secretary of the NAACP, frequently visited Cleophas Brown: "I was living in public housing. . . . and Dr. DuBois was a visitor in our house because they appreciated the fact that I was organizing this [NAACP] branch here." It appeared that "real change was happening and it took us working folks to make it happen. Wasn't like in the old days, no! We learned too much."[69]

The activities of black Richmondites in Local A-36 and their stand against auxiliaries accelerated their entry into the urban industrial labor force, legitimized their presence in the workplace, and shattered antiunionism among African Americans. The interests of black newcomers and black longtime residents in Richmond converged most notably in the workplace, where racism and discrimination prohibited all blacks from advancement. Both groups understood that the abolition of segregation was the prerequisite to economic and social mobility. Despite its segregated context, Local A-36 eroded intraracial divisions and brought the African American community together in the common cause of breaking down workplace barriers. Even though Cleophas Brown admitted that initially leaders "had a hell of a time organizing them," African American newcomers gave energy and direction to labor and civil rights organizations like the UNLC, Shipyard Workers against Discrimination, and the NAACP. Many black newcomers, who "weren't used to too much fighting in the South" and who were "so accustomed to separate things," nevertheless became the voice and conscience of the new organizations.[70]

Newcomers became the majority of Richmond's black population. They quickly adapted to their new circumstances, shed the racial deference born in the Jim Crow South, and took their places in the community, eventually supplanting black longtime residents as community, political, and cultural leaders. Cleophas Brown recalled: "they just kind of forgot the people who were already here" and became the vanguard of change in Richmond. These experiences provided thousands of African Americans with practical experience and a deeper understanding of the complexities of workplace and governmental bureaucracies. This confidence spilled over into all aspects of black life and set the stage for more assaults on Jim Crow in and beyond the workplace.[71]

In addition to fighting against official discrimination in the Richmond shipyards, black workers had to contend with a constant undercurrent of racial conflict in the yards. Sociologist Katherine Archibald's study of Oakland's Moore shipyards noted that "Negroes and whites cooperated in countless tasks, white shoulders straining beside black. . . . The slightest touch, however, revealed the impermanence of the surface calm and the depth of the hatred beneath." Although Kaiser officials tried to minimize it, this atmosphere also prevailed in Richmond. For example, a proposed *Life* magazine photo project documenting the "FEPC's work in the Kaiser shipyards" caused considerable anxiety among shipyard administrators, who worried that the project might "create additional tension in the East Bay" and contribute "to the already existing tension" in the Richmond yards by portraying the "Kaiser interests" as "violators of a national order." Furthermore, Kaiser officials worried that the story's emphasis on harmony and production might cause some black workers to construe it as antiunion. Harry Kingman, regional director of the War Manpower Commission, reluctantly gave his approval for the project, "since the assignment was to be carried out regardless of whether FEPC desired it," and thought it better to "show a cooperative attitude . . . to influence the project as constructively as possible."[72]

However, not even the most optimistic public relations spin could mask the reality of race relations in Richmond's shipyards and the frustration of most African American workers. Most officials attributed rising racial friction to an influx of Okies and Arkies, whom they considered "dirty and dumb [but] smart enough to cheat." Kaiser management conceded that the "men from the South complain more about the fact that the shipyards employ, and they must mingle with, all races, creeds, and colors." In the shipyard novel *Swingshift* a white shipyard worker complained: "How can [my supervisor] do this to me? It's bad enough to have a stupid nigger in my gang, but on the same machine! I'd rather quit!"[73]

Undoubtedly, the presence of thousands of white southerners, steeped in the racial customs of the South, contributed to Richmond's native white community, or "core community," becoming "somewhat southern in its ideas" and the "southern community" becoming "a little more northern in its ideas." Many white newcomers bristled at having to deal equitably with blacks in the workplace. Wilbur Wheat, a worker in Yard 2, recalled that "some whites were nice, [but] like all peckerwoods [they] couldn't stand being around colored people. They would do anything to mess you up!"[74] However, racism, segregation, and discrimination did not suddenly descend on Richmond with the influx of white and black southerners during the war. Migration only magnified racial tensions that had been present since Richmond's founding. White newcomers, as vexing as they might be to Richmond natives, enjoyed more access to the city's economic mainstream than their black counterparts. Native-born whites tended to accept white newcomers, grudgingly acknowledging that they were "little different from those already there, only requiring that the rough edges be worn off through the pressure of conformity to prevailing social standards." Thus, white newcomers encountered comparatively few compulsory obstacles to employment or promotion in the shipyards or in Richmond's other industries. They experienced greater economic and social mobility than their black counterparts even as they clung to their cultural heritage, distinctive speech patterns, and music and religious preferences. Whites accomplished the transition from sojourner to resident with relative ease. African American newcomers, plagued by racial discrimination inside and outside the workplace, did not enjoy such a smooth transition.[75]

Despite these obstacles the Kaiser shipyards continued to be powerful magnets for thousands of African American workers. Black men and women preferred employment in the Richmond yards, attracted by modern technology, an array of incomparable benefits, and of course, the higher wages offered by Kaiser. Black shipyard workers considered the Richmond yards to be safer and better maintained than other Bay Area yards and industries. Frances Mary Albrier recalled that the Kaiser yards "were not cluttered up with a lot of beams and things in the walkways which you had to walk over and drag your welding hose over like Moore's Shipyards." In addition, the Kaiser yards operated as a complex city within a city, providing workers with unequaled pay and personnel, medical, and recreational services.[76]

In an effort to reduce absenteeism Kaiser provided an array of innovative services. Busy workers could purchase food, clothing, and sundries in the numerous cafeterias and shops that operated around the clock in the yards. Kaiser even offered a carryout meal service for workers who had no time for shopping or food preparation. Company theaters provided inexpensive, nonsegregated leisure activity for those who had spare time. Kaiser initiated several intramural sports teams, but Vesper Wheat recalled that "not too many Negroes" participated in them. Several housing project–sponsored softball teams were more popular among black Richmondites than the intramural teams.[77]

In 1943 Kaiser's child care center, operated by the Richmond school district, became the first "multiple unit" nursery school opened in a Maritime Commission–sponsored building, caring daily for fourteen hundred children ages two to five and one-half. In addition to employing a faculty of thirty certified teachers, the center was staffed with a nurse, a nutritionist, and a psychiatrist. Eventually Kaiser operated a total of "thirty-five additional nursery units . . . in housing centers and schools." However, many black women recalled that company child care services were "available to the whites" only.[78]

The Kaiser health plan proved to be the most attractive benefit for blacks and whites. For most workers, whose health "had been found to be below average," the medical plan provided the first professional health care they had ever received. Kaiser introduced the plan in 1942, after epidemics of influenza and pneumonia devastated the shipyard workforce. Initially, coverage was restricted to shipyard employees, but dependents were permitted to enroll in the plan after the war. Although no separate figures for black workers are available, records show that nearly 87 percent of all workers contributed to the health plan. For a weekly membership fee of fifty cents, they received "preventive protection, complete hospital, medical and surgical care; ambulance service and emergency treatment." In 1942 the health plan employed 6 doctors and 6 nurses and cared for industrial cases in Yards 1 and 3, which employed twenty thousand workers at that time. By 1944 the two hospitals had 90 doctors, 526 nurses, and 350 beds and "would add 100 more beds in the Oakland hospital."[79]

All of these experiences generated and reinforced a culture of expectation among African Americans in Richmond. Every challenge to racism they mounted and each concession to equality wrested from shipyard authorities represented a blow to Jim Crow, no matter how symbolic. For example, the pageantry surrounding a ship launching in the Richmond yards assumed greater significance for blacks when the vessels bore the names of famous African Americans. Three ships launched from the Richmond yards were named for prominent African Americans (Robert S. Abbott, publisher of the *Chicago Defender;* educator John Hope; and renowned scientist George Washington Carver.) In April 1945 Yard 2 launched the S.S. *Fisk Victory,* in honor of Fisk University, the African American institution founded in Nashville in 1866.

On May 7, 1943, the *George Washington Carver,* under the sponsorship of the UNLC and Local A-36, slipped into the water from Yard 1 while African American commoners and dignitaries—including representatives from Tuskegee and other luminaries such as Walter A. Gordon, distinguished attorney and secretary of the Alameda County NAACP, and C. L. Dellums, West Coast representative of the International Brotherhood of Sleeping Car Porters—cheered its maiden voyage. Thousands of black people, far more than could "simply be accounted for by black shipyard workers and their families," crowded into the yard. As the ship "shivered and slid into the water," a black woman "threw up her arms and raised her voice above the crowd. 'Freedom' she cried." These events may have been token gestures of wartime unity, but to black Richmondites and African Americans around the Bay Area, they symbolized the determination and achievement of all African Americans (see figure 14).[80]

For the majority of African American workers the simple act of receiving a weekly paycheck became the most tangible evidence of black achievement, even though some required an initial period of orientation to the industrial wage system. Some black workers found it difficult to equate the "official looking slips of paper" (paychecks) given to them at the end of each work week with real money. One black newcomer, facing eviction for nonpayment of rent, quickly learned the protocol with the help of the Richmond Housing Authority: "He said he was willing to pay his rent . . . but the boss had not paid him. . . . they had given him a piece of paper, whereupon he opened his wallet and showed checks for the entire period he had been working. The Housing Director told him this was money. . . . The Housing Director then had to take him to the bank, vouch for him and get the checks cashed." Wilbur Wheat observed that black newcomers "took a while to catch on about money, but after a while they did fine."[81]

The relentless pace and the tedious, exacting nature of shipyard work also required a period of adjustment for many shipyard employees. Workers, regardless of race, devised ways to protest the extreme regimentation that left many feeling like interchangeable parts in the vast shipyard machinery.[82] On at least one occasion, a worker frustrated with the music constantly piped into the yards by loudspeaker resorted to sabotage, cutting the loudspeaker wires "every other day for two months" before being apprehended by the FBI. The employee confessed that he could no longer tolerate the repetitious music, which had become "just so much noise."[83]

Black men and women were part of a general shipyard "work culture" that placed a premium on harmony, productivity, and discipline, but they also created a work culture of their own to counter racial hostility and affirm values that often conflicted with those of the industrial workplace. Within the black shipyard work culture, seasoned workers took newcomers in hand, instructing them in strategies to make life in the yards more bearable. Black shipyard work culture was also influenced by the desire to affirm cultural and social values nurtured in a southern agrarian matrix and was nuanced by issues of gender as well. It included but was not limited to protest against shipyard regimentation and discipline.[84]

Challenges to shipyard regimentation came in the form of high absenteeism and frequent requests for transfers to other yards. Workers of all races applied for interyard transfers, hoping to gain a change of scene if not condition. Wilbur Wheat recalled that workers would "apply for a transfer real quick" following a "run in" with a supervisor or if they "just got fed up" working in the same place. People were "always coming and going." Statistics compiled for the shipyards during the peak employment period of 1943 show that the yards experienced an "extremely high" turnover of twenty-four thousand people a month. These figures represented workers who moved on to other yards or to new jobs outside the shipyards.[85]

To combat the trend, the Federal Labor Stabilization Program required that workers present a "justifiable" reason for changing jobs. The "inclination of a large number of laboring people to jump from job to job without sufficient reason" prompted the government to impose the threat of military draft for any worker found guilty of "loafing" on the job. Kaiser management broadly defined loafing to include those workers who requested job transfers without "sufficient reason."[86]

For African Americans, transfers also represented attempts to ameliorate racial discrimination. Wilbur Wheat collided with the new federal regulations when he refused to work as leaderman of a segregated "all colored crew" in Yard 2 and demanded a transfer, which was denied. His white supervisor tried to use the draft to intimidate him into returning to work: "He said, 'Okay, Wheat, pack up your tools. . . . We're going to put you on the boat. . . . Let's go down to the Marine Department and we'll put you in the Army.'" Telling his boss to "stick that and shove it too," Wheat quit the shipyards altogether.[87]

Short of quitting, all shipyard workers at one time or another registered their discontent with regimentation by "just not showing up." The USES calculated that "avoidable absenteeism" in the yards ran at about 10 percent a day, or approximately ten thousand people during the peak employment period. On Sundays the figure could easily reach

as high as eighteen thousand. The manager for the local War Manpower
Commission in Richmond told the committee investigating conditions
in congested areas that the turnover rate reached about fifteen thousand
people a month.[88]

Although workers of all races routinely took unauthorized time off
work, in the racially charged environment of the shipyards, many blacks
were ambivalent about embracing work patterns that rewarded attendance and punctuality over interpersonal obligations. Black newcomers
were reluctant to relinquish the work patterns that had characterized
their lives in the South. These patterns were reinforced by cultural sanc-
tions that placed equal or higher value on kinship, friendship, and religious ties. Margaret Starks noted that "lots of the people from the South
resented having to work on Sundays no matter how much money they
made. They didn't think it was right so, honey, they didn't do it. Sunday was kept for church, family and kinfolks." Even the less devout had
reservations about Sunday work. Some considered it a "family day,"
made for renewing kinship and friendship ties.[89]

Black shipyard workers in Richmond refused to give up their social
obligations and preferences, which in many cases provided them with
the only opportunity for relaxation in a hospitable environment. Although Kaiser sponsored activities for its employees within or near the
work site, the majority of black workers preferred recreational pursuits
in their communities, even when transportation and housing problems
made commuting to those communities difficult. Therefore, in many
cases taking unauthorized absences and arriving late represented attempts to retain culturally sanctioned traditions, even when doing so
meant a breach of industrial discipline.[90]

Kaiser officials noted that women employees had higher absentee rates
than their male coworkers because of the "nursery problems." The on-
site day-care facilities could not keep pace with the demand and were
not available to African American women. Thus, black women in the
Richmond shipyards were compelled to rely on relatives, friends, and female coworkers to care for their children more often than whites were.
Some black women improvised an "absence exchange," which was an
informal but common arrangement whereby they took turns caring for
each other's children using deliberately designated but unofficial time
off work. This informal support network not only filled a pressing need
but also fostered a sense of extended family that wartime dislocation
had disrupted, and it established a camaraderie among black women
that lasted long after the shipyards faded away. Vesper Wheat, recalling

her harried existence as a wife, mother, and shipyard worker said, "thank God for those girls. You were so busy and tired from children and work. I really needed their help."[91]

Child care was not the only issue that gave black shipyard work culture a gender dynamic. African American female workers tended to measure their performance in the yards against the standards of their male counterparts, knowing that their qualifications would have to meet and usually surpass those of men in order for them to get and keep their jobs. Therefore African American women often expressed pride in their ability to climb, lift, and handle equipment as well as or better than their male coworkers. Moreover, they tended to minimize the social conventions of femininity in the workplace. One worker recalled that women would gather to discuss workplace hairstyles: "Not how to keep it pretty, but how *not* to have to mess with it. You couldn't be primping in the hull of a ship, carrying a hot welder's torch."[92]

Black women often sought advice from the more senior female workers regarding the best way to contend with white female coworkers, deal with menstrual problems on the job, handle unwanted advances from male coworkers, and cope with the double burdens of family and work. Richmond resident Marguerite Williams disdained shipyard work, believing it was inappropriate for women to be compelled to work "like men." However, the workplace culture shaped by black women "created a real bond between the colored women. We had to stick together." In this respect the work culture created by black shipyard workers in Richmond was less an expression of protest than an attempt to retain dignity and community in an environment that devalued both.[93]

African American shipyard work culture included other, more surreptitious aspects as well. Bob Geddins, songwriter and founder of the Bay Area's only black record company in the 1940s (Big Town Records), worked in Yard 2 in 1943. Always scouting for new talent to record and promote for his company, Geddins sometimes auditioned prospective blues and gospel singers "right there in the [hull of the] ships." He noted that "you could do a lot of other things in the yards, too."[94] Joseph Malbrough, a shipyard rigger foreman in the Richmond yards, recalled that prostitution was a fact of life in the yards. Prostitutes did a brisk business with workers who had money "burning a hole in their pockets:" To "the fellows in the shipyards a hundred dollars was [more] like a one dollar bill. They'd go right down there in the bottom of the boat. . . . Shit, you had to have more than a hundred dollars 'cause that wasn't shit! You was just standing up there looking and wasting your time thinking here was your three or four dollars! Before [the war] it was $2.50 for fifteen minutes."[95]

The work environment was both frustrating and encouraging for the black men and women who streamed through the shipyard gates. Shipyard employment meant an upgrading of skills and status for the majority (though not all) of African American workers. The work culture and strategies they developed within the yards helped mitigate some of the harshest aspects of their new work environment. Moreover, the shipyard experience helped black Richmondites develop political and social proficiencies that gave them a new perspective on their place in Richmond, the state, and the nation. This culture of expectation would be severely tested during the boom years and when postwar demobilization pulled the shipyards out of the city.

Figure 1. The Freeman family, North Richmond, ca. 1919 (*left to right:* Walter Freeman Jr., Walter Freeman Sr., Jessie Freeman). Courtesy of the Freeman family.

Figure 2. Santa Fe Railroad workers, ca. 1920.

Figure 3. Walter and Jessie Freeman with the family dairy cows in North Richmond, ca. 1920. Courtesy of the Freeman family.

Figure 4. The Joseph Griffin family and their new Durant car, ca. 1930. Courtesy of the Freeman family.

Figure 5. Richmond High School shop class, ca. 1928 (*far left*, Walter Freeman Jr.). Courtesy of the Freeman family.

Figure 6. North Richmond Missionary Baptist Church, ca. 1940. Courtesy of the Slocum family.

Figure 7. The Slocum family, North Richmond, ca. 1939. (*left to right:* Jessie Slocum Sr., Mildred Hudson Slocum, Jessie Slocum Jr.). Courtesy of the Slocum family.

Figure 8. Sunday morning, North Richmond, ca. 1940. Courtesy of the Slocum family.

Figure 9. Jessie Freeman displaying one of her quilts in front of her North Richmond home, ca. 1925. Courtesy of the Freeman family.

Figure 10. Mr. and Mrs. Joseph Malbrough, North Richmond, in front of the house built in 1928 by his father, Matthew Malbrough. Photograph by Joe Louis Moore, 1985.

Figure 11. Ida and George Johnson and the Richmond shack they built into their "dream home," ca. 1937. Courtesy of George Johnson.

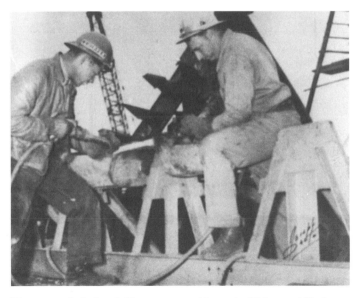

Figure 12. *Left,* Louis Bonaparte, a chipper in Richmond Yard 2, ca. 1943. Photograph by E. F. Joseph. Courtesy of Mrs. E. F. Joseph.

Figure 13. Black women workers in the Richmond shipyards, ca. 1943. Photograph by E. F. Joseph. Courtesy of Mrs. E. F. Joseph.

Figure 14. Lena Horne officiates at the launching of the S.S. *George Washington Carver,* Richmond Yard 1, 1943. Photograph by E. F. Joseph. Courtesy of Mrs. E. F. Joseph.

Figure 15. Shipyard workers in downtown Richmond, 1942. Copyright the Dorothea Lange Collection, The Oakland Museum of California, City of Oakland, Gift of Paul S. Taylor.

Figure 16. Richmond shipyard workers end shift, 1942. Copyright the Dorothea Lange Collection, The Oakland Museum of California, City of Oakland, Gift of Paul S. Taylor.

Figure 17. Former Arkansas sharecropper at her North Richmond trailer home, 1942. Copyright the Dorothea Lange Collection, The Oakland Museum of California, City of Oakland, Gift of Paul S. Taylor.

Figure 18. Shipyard worker on her day off in front of Richmond Cafe, ca. 1943. Copyright the Dorothea Lange Collection, The Oakland Museum of California, City of Oakland, Gift of Paul S. Taylor.

Figure 19. Richmond wartime housing project, ca. 1944.
Courtesy of the Freeman family.

Parchester Village Improvement Association. Board of direc-
ɔrs, left to right, seated: Mrs. Pearl Hutchinson, Mrs. Shirley,
Ɩrs. John D. Jordan, Mrs. Ersie Howard, Mrs. Campbell, Stand-
ɳg, left to right: J. Johnson, William Beal, Clarence Newby,
ʾhomas M. Dent, and Mr. Langston. (Joseph Landisman, Atty.)

Figure 20. Parchester Village Improvement Association, ca.
1950. Courtesy of the Jordan family.

Figure 21. Well-baby clinic staff in the North Richmond home of Mrs. Emma Jarret (*seated, left*), ca. 1943. Courtesy of Margaret Starks.

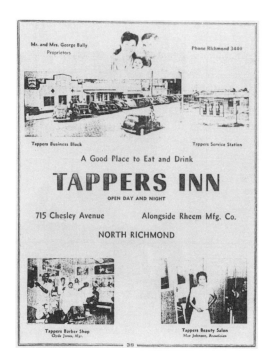

Figure 22. Advertisement for Tappers Inn, the most popular club in North Richmond, ca. 1945. Photograph by E. F. Joseph. Courtesy of Mrs. E. F. Joseph.

Figure 23. Opening night at Minnie Lue's, North Richmond, ca. 1950 (*left behind counter*, Minnie Lue Nichols). Courtesy of Minnie Lue Nichols.

Figure 24. Minnie Lue Nichols (*right*) and assistant serving "home cooking," as they did every night in her North Richmond club, ca. 1950. Courtesy of Minnie Lue Nichols.

Figure 25. The Spiderettes softball team, ca. 1945 (*2d row, 1st on left,* Ivy Reid Lewis). Courtesy of Ivy Reid Lewis.

CHAPTER 3

Boomtown

---

*I don't think there is any comparison between your problem in
Richmond and any other city even though the other cities are bad.*
Congressman George Bates, 1943

*[Even] the Saturday nite poker games have changed from penny
ante to nickel ante. . . . But along with all good things come the
bad also. . . . The present boom is bringing in lots of the undesirable element, namely "Okies" and "Arkies" who are trying to
make it hard for the sepia-hued laborers in California.*
California Voice, 1941

The war boom hit Richmond like no other town in the
United States. Virtually overnight Richmond went from a small bay town
to the quintessential war boomtown as federal defense contracts and
thousands of newcomers poured in. For African Americans the war boom
held out the promise of advancement but also highlighted their tenuous position in the city's economic, political, and social structures as
Richmond, like municipalities across the state, erected more-stringent
restrictions on black people. Therefore, black Richmondites, with newcomers leading the way, established new institutions like the United
Negroes of America (UNA) and the NAACP to fight Jim Crow in housing and the workplace. These organizations nurtured and sharpened
black activism and political leadership and challenged the city's racial
status quo. However, even as black newcomers and old-timers attempted
to subordinate their differences in order to present a unified front against

racism, the most influential black organization (the NAACP) was racked by intense intraracial class and ideological conflict.

Although Kaiser was the city's largest employer, fifty-five other industries helped fuel Richmond's wartime boom. However, city planners and developers hoped to retain prewar economic, political, and social boundaries by carefully orchestrating municipal and industrial growth. In 1944 city officials optimistically projected that "only one of the four shipyards will continue in production" after the war and that the housing authority would "tear down the temporary buildings now in use." Richmond officials planned to use the remaining shipyard as the centerpiece in an industrial complex where local residents would be given hiring priority.[1]

This scheme would ensure the prewar integrity of city neighborhoods and help retain small nuclear families (3.1 people per family) in those neighborhoods. These plans left no room for the upward mobility of blacks and other "unemployed laborers on the social fringe of the community." However, city officials miscalculated their ability to regulate the rush of federal monies and the onslaught of newcomers who permanently swelled the population, outstripped city resources, and eclipsed hopes for a sustainable mixed economy.[2]

The testimony of Arthur A. Hall of the United States Employment Services (USES) at a House of Representatives hearing on congested areas showed that plans for regulated, orderly growth and a mixed economy were wishful thinking on the part of city planners, since virtually the entire city was now involved in some aspect of war production. The Standard Oil Refinery, the largest prewar employer in Richmond, was "engaged almost 100 percent in the production of war materials critical and vital to the prosecution of war effort." Ford Motors assembled jeeps and tanks; the Pullman shops manufactured cars for troop transports, and the Santa Fe Railroad was engaged in conveying war material. In addition, there were "innumerable chemical companies" that provided war materials. The Berkeley Powder Plant and the Hercules Powder Plant produced munitions. Rheems Manufacturing Company made bomb casings, and the California Camergic Corporation manufactured detonators for large shells.[3]

Congressman George Bates of Massachusetts, member of the House committee investigating congested areas, noted all of California "is profiting more as a result of the activities of the Federal Government than any other [state]. . . . It is a tremendous source of revenue." Richmond business owners were "pleased with the booming business brought to town by the newcomers" and welcomed the industrial revitalization.[4]

However, the war boom strained city resources to the breaking point. Prewar whites resented the thousands of newcomers of all races who crowded downtown streets and stores. Longtime residents accused this "avalanche" of newcomers of destroying their neighborhoods and altering established customs. The sidewalks were now "blocked by gaping strangers in cowboy boots, blue jeans, and sombreros." Women "in slacks and leather jackets and shiny scalers' helmets wait in long lines to buy food. Pale-haired children and mangy hound-dogs wander the treeless streets. Nobody knows anybody" (see figure 15).[5]

Moreover, the abundance of federally controlled defense industries, which were exempted from local taxation, led to a precipitous decline in property tax revenues. Therefore, Richmond officials turned to the federal government for relief under the Lanham Act of 1940, which authorized "payments in lieu of taxes" to municipalities requesting aid for specific wartime programs. The city also sought special consideration for the U.S. Maritime Commission housing units that were constructed for Kaiser shipyard workers. This was a particularly pressing problem, since shipyard housing projects utilized city resources but were excluded from taxation and did not come under Lanham Act jurisdiction.[6]

Of course, other communities across the country suffered acute problems of overburdened housing facilities, inadequate public transportation, and understaffed schools and police forces. Communities from New York to Mississippi experienced skyrocketing populations and dwindling resources as war production industries located there. For example, the Ford Motor Company's massive B-24 aircraft plant in the Detroit suburb of Willow Run employed over forty-two thousand people, who more than doubled the population and virtually exhausted housing supplies. Seneca, Illinois, experienced a fivefold increase in population when the Chicago Bridge and Iron Corporation constructed a shipyard there. In the Los Angeles area, the enlarged wartime population virtually depleted available housing, tied up transportation, and aggravated crime.[7]

The problems that beset other cities, however, paled in comparison to those of Richmond. Congressman Bates declared: "Here is a community . . . which, I think is undoubtedly the worst that we have run across in the entire country in these congested areas." Richmond's city manager went before a federal committee to plead for federal aid because, he said, "even normal social controls could not be maintained." The result was "congestion and utter confusion. Richmond was literally bursting at the seams."[8]

Nowhere was the population explosion more evident than in the public school system. A special census taken in 1943 showed that the 23,805 children under age fourteen in Richmond equaled the city's entire population only three years earlier. Richmond's small neighborhood schools, with classrooms designed to accommodate twenty or thirty students before the war, now bulged with sixty or more children. In the 1944–45 school year the city's total school enrollment stood at 28,851 students. School days were extended to include double or triple sessions.[9]

Compounding the crowded conditions were the varying levels of educational skills brought by the students, who came from all regions; the schools became more like holding tanks. Most newcomer children were concentrated in a few schools on the periphery of the defense housing projects. Harbor Gate School was built in the housing projects. Okie and Arkie students vied with southern black newcomer children for school services and the attention of overworked teachers. In addition, many of the public school faculty were themselves newcomers to Richmond. They were wives of workers from the northern midwestern states and were drawn from the "only major pool of teachers still available in the area." Armed with out-of-state credentials, they were hired to fill the "many vacant spots in the schools near the shipyards." By the war's end about 25 percent of Richmond teachers were teaching on "emergency certification." While teachers saw that most newcomer parents "didn't have much education themselves," most conceded that the newcomers "wanted their kids to have what they didn't have so that their lives would be easier." However, the teachers had little experience and less patience with the children of diverse educational and cultural backgrounds who now crowded their classrooms. Richmond educators characterized the newcomers as "floaters [and] drifters" who viewed education as "only a necessary evil, or just an evil." In addition many public school officials believed newcomers "had no feeling of belonging or community, or they wouldn't have left their own community to come here." School authorities, like city planners, mistakenly believed that the situation was temporary and would be resolved when the newcomers returned to their home states.[10]

The wartime boom also encroached on Richmond's once quiet neighborhoods as bars with names like the Nut Club (Richmond's Nuttiest Joynt), the Fern Leaf, the Denver Club, and the Red Robin sprang up all over the city. These round-the-clock enterprises eclipsed Richmond's prewar saloons. Wartime drinking establishments raked in monthly profits totaling eight thousand dollars as defense workers, flush with money, flocked to them for liquor, gambling, and other illicit activities. A city judge noted that "plenty of girls proposition in [those] bars and take their clients to [the] rooming houses" that proliferated. Even Richmond's two ornate prewar downtown movie theaters did not escape the squeeze: twelve additional movie houses opened for business, operating twenty-four hours daily, seven days a week. Moreover, they often doubled as flophouses for workers who were unable to find other accommodations.[11]

Wartime housing shortages frustrated city officials' attempts to regulate growth and change in their city. The population explosion forced thousands of newcomers into haphazard living quarters which were usually cramped, dirty, dangerous, and unhealthy and always expensive. Former sheriff John Miller testified before a House committee that newcomers paid premium prices for meager living spaces in "trailers, tents, in houses, cardboard shacks, greenhouses, barns, garages, in automobiles, in theaters, or just fenced-off corners with the stars for a roof." For fifty cents each, desperate shipyard and other defense workers could rent a "hot bed" in which they took turns sleeping after completing their shifts. Usually three or four different people used the same bed, and the rental price did not include a change of sheets. Marguerite Williams recalled that her husband's aunt who lived in North Richmond "really took advantage of the people because she used to raise chickens . . . [and] they would whitewash the chicken houses and they were renting that out. They weren't the only ones."[12]

Because living space was so scarce in Richmond, thousands of defense workers were compelled to live in other cities and commute to their jobs in Richmond. Richmond city planners experimented with a variety of transportation alternatives to accommodate the crush of commuters coming into the city. The U.S. Maritime Commission resurrected old ferry boats, pressing them into service between San Francisco and the Kaiser shipyards. The commission imported several discarded elevated railway cars from New York City's Third Avenue line, refurbishing and running them as the Richmond Shipyard Railway. The revitalized streetcars traveled a twelve-mile route from Fortieth and San Pablo in Oakland to the Richmond shipyards and transported twelve thousand workers daily.[13]

In an effort to combat the rising crime rate that accompanied the war boom and to restore Richmond's tidy neighborhoods, city officials petitioned the federal government for increased funding to augment the police force. In April 1943 the chief of police testified before a federal

Table 3 *Yearly Incidence of Selected Crimes and Total Arrests in Richmond, 1940–1943*

	1940	1941	1942	1943
Total arrests	415	5,421	10,910	16,854
Accidents	375	442	659	961
Auto theft	18	27	125	396
Burglary	85	94	131	255
Drunkenness	56	501	908	3,761
Larceny	5	63	71	136
Murder*	1	5	10	4
Rape	—	6	4	5
Assault**	—	33	60	84

SOURCE: Subcommittee of the House Committee on Naval Affairs Investigating Congested Areas, *Hearings before the United States House Committee on Naval Affairs,* 78th Cong., 1st sess., April 12–17, 1943, 871–79.

*Murder includes negligent and non-negligent homicide.

**Assault includes aggravated and other assaults.

committee that the entire police department "consisted of 35 men, and an additional 19 men have been employed in the department in the past year to help maintain law and order in the community." In that same year an "increasing number of robberies, burglaries, hold-ups, thefts, juvenile delinquencis [*sic*], and drunks, overwhelmingly indicates the inefficiency of our present force of 54 men." Arrest figures and crime statistics seemed to confirm these fears. Wartime arrests increased dramatically in Richmond. From 1931 to 1940 the number of arrests averaged 2,149 per year, but by June 30, 1941, the annual arrest figure had grown to 5,421. By March 1943 the total number of arrests had climbed to 16,854 (see table 3).[14]

    In the summer of 1943 Richmond received federal funding to hire seventy-five more police officers, but initially "the city could find only eight men who wanted the jobs." Eventually an infusion of federal monies tripled the city's police force. By June 30, 1944, the yearly arrest figure had jumped to 43,754, although "serious crime" declined that year in the city due to "a much larger force." The police department, with the approval of civic leaders and elected officials, undertook a stringent law enforcement campaign. Those arrested faced fines ranging from $25 for public drunkenness to $250 for drunken driving. City Manager James McVittie explained: "We hit them heavy. . . . They can behave or pay." Police were charged with the dual responsibilities of combating crime and upholding "custom and matters of taste." In practical terms this meant that dustpan- and broom-wielding police officers routinely cleaned up broken glass from the sidewalks of Macdonald Avenue and swept "drunks and other undesirables" from the downtown area. The strategy resulted in some four thousand arrests a month.[15]

Ironically, the rising crime rate, like the wartime boom that produced it, proved to be an economic bonanza for the city. In November of 1944, Richmond police court collected $34,000 in fines, in contrast to the $800 collected for the same month in 1937. During the fiscal year of 1944 police court fines accounted for $235,000, or 10 percent of Richmond's gross revenue. This money helped offset the revenue lost to the city because of the tax exempt status of the shipyards, federal housing projects, and other defense industries.[16]

Newcomers bore the brunt of Richmond's wartime crackdown. Law enforcement officials generally characterized them as "drunks, knifers, rapers, attackers, hop-heads, harlots, wife beaters, murderers—anything you like." They were "persecuted and stigmatized as hardened lawbreakers" and as a result comprised a disproportionate number of those arrested. One newcomer bitterly complained: "If you wait for your wife on the station platform you're picked up as a vagrant." Even though the more-serious crimes of assault, robbery, and homicide rose in Richmond during the war years (with the exception of 1943), the majority of newcomers who were arrested were rounded up on the catchall pretexts of drunkenness and traffic and parking violations. Like white migrants to Richmond, African American newcomers had to cope with all the problems of a war boomtown, but racial hostility and intraracial class and ideological conflicts further complicated their entry into the community. White Richmond natives derided the Okies and Arkies, but they abhorred black newcomers, characterizing them as "Chicago Negroes, a different breed from the quiet, decent, and docile Blacks" who had resided in Richmond before the war. Black newcomers increasingly became identified as uncouth troublemakers by police, city officials, and the local press, and by some longtime black residents as well.[17]

Although no racial breakdown of arrests exits, African Americans complained that they were disproportionately harassed and arrested by Richmond police. The *Richmond Independent,* aligning itself with the forces of "law and order," identified criminal suspects by race only if they were black, thereby presenting a misleading picture of lawlessness in the city. The local press pursued an editorial policy that linked criminality with African Americans. Chick Roberts, editor of the *Indepen-*

dent, framed the city's crime reduction efforts in racial terms: "We haven't had a white murder for eight months . . . and only four Negroes in that time."[18]

Many black longtime residents believed that black newcomers were prone to violence as well. Ivy Reid Lewis claimed that "when the black people came they'd start cutting up each other. You'd see more people get killed." When African Americans became involved in confrontations, they were labeled the instigators. Local media routinely attributed racial conflicts to black aggressiveness and blacks' inability to assimilate.[19]

On August 10, 1943, the *Independent* reported that a race riot between black shipyard workers and sailors in Oakland was caused by "500 negro [*sic*] swing fans." In May 1944, after a Richmond policeman was beaten by a gang of "youthful zoot suiters," the police department vowed a crackdown on "zoot suit gangs." In January 1945 a black worker "jostled" some white sailors on a crowded bus. When the black man departed the bus, six whites chased and cornered him. Striking out in self-defense the man slashed two of the white sailors with the knife he carried. The *Independent* concluded "that the Negro was to blame for stepping on the sailors' toes."[20]

In 1944 the *Independent* reported on "a raging club and knife battle" between three white men and three sanitation workers described as "Negroes from Richmond." One of the black workers, identified as Turner, was murdered. The garbage truck on which he and "two other negroes [*sic*] were working" bumped a car carrying three white men. "Turner [took] a swing at one of the white men. The battle started and knives flashed. . . . one witness . . . saw a negro stab a white man." William Martin Camp's novel about wartime Richmond, *Skip to My Lou,* pitted white and black newcomers against each other: "A few poor-white trash [were] trying to scare up a riot to get the colored folks run out of Richmond," on the pretext that black housing-project residents were holding secret "voodoo meetings" directed against whites. Indeed, the county probation officer estimated that "two-thirds of the crime in Richmond originated in the war-housing areas," where the majority of the city's black residents lived.[21]

Before the war, black Richmondites who attended Richmond High or the ethnically diverse Peres Elementary School in North Richmond sat in integrated classrooms and perceived no difference in treatment from their peers or teachers. However, this changed as the war boom brought thousands of black and white newcomers to the city. One black Richmond High graduate recalled that during the war black students would always get into fights because white school kids would call them names. Moreover, as more children crowded into overflowing classrooms, teachers and school administrators increasingly labeled black students as educational "problems" and troublemakers, assigning them, regardless of origin, to separate, lower level classes in Richmond's public schools.[22]

Hoping to defuse the explosive racial situation, Mayor Mattie Chandler in 1943 appointed a "tolerance committee" composed of businessmen, shipyard representatives, the YMCA director, and African American community leaders. After deliberating for several weeks, the committee recommended that Richmond develop "a more friendly understanding" between minority groups, merchants, and other residents. A subsequent editorial in the *Independent* entitled "Tolerance" urged citizens to avoid a Detroit-type race riot by "beating down" their racial prejudice, but it gave little comfort to African Americans with its suggestion that the presence of blacks and other minorities added to a "feeling of inadequacy" among whites that spilled over into violence and discrimination: "People in Richmond . . . are forced to stand in overcrowded busses; wait for service in packed restaurants, cafes and overcrowded business establishments, while a member of a minority race may be sitting down or getting the service others are waiting for."[23]

Therefore, race rather than behavior, appearance, speech, or place of origin, was the most formidable obstacle to acceptance for black Richmondites. White newcomers could enter the city's mainstream in a year or so after their "rough edges" had been softened, but African Americans, no matter what strides they might make in the workplace or elsewhere, would remain outsiders.[24] The predominantly black North Richmond community was despised during the war years "because [its residents] were Negroes *and* because they were newcomers." By 1947 the black population, almost invisible as late as 1940, had increased by 5,000 percent and became for whites, the cause of the unwanted transformation of the city.[25]

Testifying before a House committee in 1943, Richmond's recreation director, Ivan H. Hill, asserted that the city's problems were "complicated by the addition of several thousand colored workers and their families who stem from the southern lower economic groups." Their "unaccustomed high wages" earned in the shipyards resulted in "expenditures and activities which may have serious effects upon the stability and peace of the community." For most white Richmondites, the rough edges on black newcomers could never be smoothed away. As the war boom gripped the city, all blacks, regardless of length of residency, became troublesome presences to most white Richmondites.[26]

Renowned photojournalist Dorothea Lange did a photo essay on wartime Richmond for a special West Coast edition of *Fortune* magazine in 1945. These pictures were intended to illustrate the rhetoric of wartime patriotism and depict harmonious cooperation in the battle against a common enemy. For example, one full-page photograph caught hundreds of black and white shipyard workers during a shift change. The picture suggested a unified, race-blind civilian army (see figure 16). In all photographs dealing with the war effort, black and white workers, faces tired but determined, interacted with unity, dignity, and equality—all necessary conditions for victory against the Axis powers.[27]

However, Lange's photographs had some unintended consequences and in some cases managed to "summarize every major [negative] impression" whites had of black migrants. White newcomers were depicted as ordinary people who might easily fit into community life when the war ended. A photograph of a white trailer park couple from Iowa who lived "on the edge of Richmond for two years" conveyed industriousness. The accompanying caption explained that even on his Sunday off the man found time to paint the couple's tidy trailer.[28] These images of whites are contrasted with images of black newcomers, who seemed more alien. A picture of a black Arkansas mother of eleven seated in front of her makeshift trailer in the North Richmond mud and a photo of a bejeweled, fur-draped black shipyard worker enjoying her day off in downtown Richmond could, on the one hand, reinforce white fears of black profligacy (see figures 17 and 18). On the other hand, such pictures could also convey images of black autonomy, perseverance, and determination—qualities that many white Richmondites may have recognized in African Americans but refused to acknowledge because they were equally as unsettling as the perceived negative qualities.[29]

While racism and discrimination were the major external factors shaping the process of proletarianization for African Americans during World War II, a growing body of recent scholarship on African American migration has begun to examine the impact of intraracial class and ideological conflict on the process as well. In addition to white hostility, black newcomers to urban centers like New York, Pittsburgh, Chicago, and Cleveland encountered opposition from longtime resident blacks as well. Perceiving the newcomers to be lower class and ill prepared for urban life, the old-timers feared that their growing numbers would upset the fragile racial equilibrium that existed in most northern cities. Afri-

can Americans who streamed into Richmond during World War II encountered similar hostility from prewar black Richmondites.

Black newcomers to Richmond initially received a chilly reception
from longtime black residents who feared that massive numbers of unsophisticated, ill-educated, southern black migrants would destroy the
gains and privileges they already enjoyed. The former director of the
North Richmond Neighborhood House recalled that prewar black Richmondites "resented very much the blacks coming from the South. Because prior to the blacks coming from the South, they had far more freedom and felt more accepted." Black newcomers were accused of a variety
of social transgressions from poor personal hygiene to destruction of
private property. Some black newcomers were chided for being unduly
subservient, while others were condemned for being "overly belliger-
ent." Most often, prewar black residents complained of the newcomers'
"foreignness." Their outsider status was betrayed by their "dress, speech,
and public behavior." One prewar black resident claimed: "they talked
differently; you couldn't understand them and I wasn't used to that."
Beryl Gwendolyn Reid regarded "all these black people . . . from the
shipyards" as "lower class blackguard people who didn't have any man-
ners." They appeared to be a "completely different sort of people." [30] A
black San Franciscan remarked: "You could pick them out from among
all the others. Just like that [snaps his fingers]." It would take years "before they seemed to get Americanized." Walter Freeman Jr. recalled that
his encounters with some black newcomers left him with the feeling that
they spoke a different language: "I didn't understand them. They'd say
something and I wouldn't know what they were talking about. It was
flat, the accent. I just got out of high school and I didn't know anything
about that. I didn't understand any of it. . . . I never understood them." [31]

Although earlier black newcomers to other U.S. cities experienced a
similar reception from black old-timers, internal and external factors
unique to Richmond in the era of World War II made their entry into
that city's urban industrial arena somewhat different from that of black
migrants to the larger, older black urban communities of the East and
Midwest. In those areas racism had confined the black population to
ghettoes decades before such concentration occurred in Richmond.
Black newcomers to eastern and midwestern cities during the first three
decades of the twentieth century entered black communities that were
older, larger, more spatially defined, and more economically and socially
diverse than those of Richmond. Black migrants to other cities lived
with and interacted daily with a cross section of the black population,

including laborers, physicians, teachers, lawyers, and shopkeepers as well as the chronically unemployed and criminal elements.

The African American population in Richmond was smaller, had no middle or professional classes until the 1950s, and had a more tenuous economic base. Indeed, black professionals, like working-class blacks, came to the Bay Area during the war years seeking new opportunities, but they chose to live in Oakland, Berkeley, and San Francisco, not Richmond. In addition, the crucial transitional institutions like the National Urban League and the NAACP that helped orient black newcomers to eastern urban centers during the Great Migration and thereafter were absent in Richmond. In fact, black newcomers to Richmond took the lead in founding such organizations during World War II.[32]

Moreover, black newcomers to Richmond were similar in background to those blacks already there. Many compared favorably in education and employment experience to white newcomers and black residents. Some arrived with no schooling or "spotty education" but eagerly sought a better opportunity for their children. Todd Iverson, deputy probation officer for Alameda County in the 1940s, suggested that black newcomers' "aggressive" reputation stemmed from the fact that their newly acquired status as vital war workers made them "independent of natives to find jobs." Determined never to go back to the deference and discrimination that had marked their lives under Jim Crow, black newcomers defended any infringement on their newfound freedom by acting "rough, very ready to fight and to use any method to win."[33]

Thus, intraracial conflict in Richmond had at its core contrasting assumptions about the possibility, nature, and scope of black progress. Before the war white Richmondites had been relatively tolerant if not "unconscious of the few Negroes that existed in its environs," and the small black population had pursued a course of accommodation that afforded them a degree of freedom and certain privileges but kept them economically and socially marginalized. When the war boom hit, even those small gains vanished. For example, Sunset Cemetery, located in the county, had permitted black burials but initiated a whites-only interment policy during the war. Charles Reid routinely had cashed his paycheck at the Subway Bar in downtown Richmond before the war but was told now not to come back "because [the owners] didn't want the rest of the black people coming in there." Some downtown merchants placed signs in their shop windows that said "Negro Patrons Not Wanted." William McKinney found that the situation in Richmond was "as bad as in Mississippi. You couldn't eat a bite nowhere. . . . We had one place that we ate at down at Fifth and Macdonald, a restaurant there run by whites. . . . That's the onliest place we could go in and eat all through the war." The wartime influx of blacks doomed the integrated school life Ivy Reid Lewis had known. She recalled that school administrators "even told us they were thinking about having segregation since the [black] kids fought so much." [34]

As black migration swelled Richmond's population, the walls of segregation and discrimination hardened in the city and affected the entire black community. African American newcomers took the lead in the struggle against racial barriers in the workplace and other areas of their lives. In doing so they energized all black Richmondites, providing the momentum for change. Newcomer activism ended black racial deference and swept away the romanticized notions of prewar race relations, revealing the fragile foundation on which those notions rested. Such bold changes, initiated by presumably uneducated peasants, highlighted the comparative complacency of prewar blacks. Texas migrant Wilbur Wheat explained: "They who was here wasn't doing much of anything when they that come started doing [some]thing, making a little progress. The [black old-timers] didn't like it very much." [35]

Longtime black residents might have had misgivings about the capabilities of black newcomers, but both groups saw their interests converge as proscriptive racial boundaries grew increasingly more rigid in the workplace, in the classroom, and in city neighborhoods. This convergence of interests redirected and transformed black activism in Richmond. Black residents believed that their goals could be realized most successfully by closing ranks and deemphasizing intraracial, class, residency, or ideological differences. Their success lay partially in the manipulation of white stereotypes that "lumped us all together anyway." Of course black Richmondites did not unanimously agree on this course of action, nor was it explicitly stated as an official policy of black civil rights organizations and institutions. The strategy evolved from the workplace and life experiences of black Richmondites during the war boom. William McKinney explained: "we needed to stand together, walk together, and not be divided." [36]

Black activism and racial solidarity coalesced most dramatically around the issues of employment and housing. For most African Americans, these issues were inextricably linked. In contrast to their white counterparts, black Richmondites found only two housing choices open to them: they could be put on the long waiting lists for public housing projects and hope to be placed before the war ended, or they could seek private housing. Both options presented considerable drawbacks. Thus, black Richmondites, regardless of length of residence, place of origin, or economic status, encountered barriers that not only limited their economic mobility but shut them out of decent dwellings as well.[37]

As early as 1941, Richmond's chamber of commerce, in an attempt to regulate growth and prevent federal intervention into traditional housing patterns, began to develop plans for public housing. After considering the options, the *Richmond Independent* threw its support behind the creation of a local housing authority.[38]

Fearing that federal or "directly-managed" housing projects would follow the racially integrated pattern of Berkeley's Cordonices Village, Richmond's chamber of commerce attempted to block such a development. Most city officials concurred with the mayor of nearby Vallejo, who declared that "there is much objection to the Negroes and Filipinos being indiscriminately placed in these housing projects alongside of white workers."[39]

Thus, the Richmond Housing Authority was established in January 1941 to "represent the community in carrying out the Federal Public Housing Administration program for low-income families." The Richmond Housing Authority immediately contracted with private builders to construct almost 2,400 dwellings to house the increasing defense-worker population (see figure 19). Although this construction represented a 30 percent increase in housing units, it made only a small dent in the housing crisis. By 1943 the Federal Public Housing Administration and the U.S. Maritime Commission had erected 21,000 housing units. These federally managed units took in seventy thousand people and had overflowing waiting lists. Private housing contractors had been issued construction permits to build 4,557 more units, but this did not begin to meet the demand. A little over 60 percent of the city's total population now lived in war housing projects. Whites comprised about 79 percent of project residents, and African Americans made up 19 percent. These racial percentages remained constant from 1943 through 1951, despite fluctuating turnover rates.[40]

Whether locally or federally regulated, the projects were "completely segregated, certain units having been set aside for Negro tenants, others for Orientals, and others for whites." The Richmond Housing Authority managed its projects in such a way that "the racial stigma toward the Negro was carried out in so subtle a manner that the violation of the Federal and State laws regarding non-discrimination in public housing was hard for the average person to detect." As late as the fall of 1952 "no Negro had lived in any of Richmond's permanent low-rent housing," namely, Triangle Court and Nystrom Village. Atchison Village, the "third project built for permanent low-rent occupancy but used for temporary occupancy, never had Negro tenants until 1953." The law might require that the housing projects admit black tenants, but achieving that equal treatment was a different story.[41]

The housing authority devised a racial formula that required admission of one black person for every four whites admitted. Moreover, African American families were segregated by building, block, or division. For example, blacks were generally housed in the projects located south of Cutting Boulevard, a major east-west corridor leading to the shipyards. In an effort to keep the neighborhoods of "private dwellings scattered around" the area near the housing projects all white, housing authority officials barred blacks from units in the "adjacent area north of Cutting Boulevard and east of South First Street." Wilbur and Vesper Wheat resided in the Harbor Gate housing project, located in south central Richmond. They recalled that black people "lived in that area, and towards the back was where the white people lived. . . . Where the blacks lived was nothing but blacks and where the whites lived was nothing but whites. The only place in the Bay Area that was integrated was Berkeley." The Wheats paid thirty dollars a month for their single-frame, one-bedroom unit. Housing authority officials cited "pressures from the southern whites" who objected to living with blacks as justification for their policy of segregation. They believed this "racial pattern was necessary . . . in view of the necessity . . . of keeping social harmony or balance in the whole community."[42] Project authorities even discouraged blacks and whites from interacting socially by maintaining separate activities for each race. Boy Scout and Girl Scout troops, church services, and movie screenings were racially segregated in the projects. Although the housing authority considered the 403 plywood duplexes of Harbor Gate to be of the "permanent off-site sale category," and more fire resistant than the Canal or Terrace project, the thin walls of the units afforded residents little privacy and minimal protection. Flimsy construction caused a great deal of concern among all project tenants. Harbor Gate resident Bill Thurston recalled that his apartment was so poorly constructed that "you know, you could punch your hand through the wall. [It was] plasterboard or something. One way in, no back doors." More importantly, the crowded frame buildings presented a significant fire hazard. During a one-month period in 1944, fires swept through federal housing facilities five times, killing and injuring several people and intensifying residents' concerns with safety.[43]

Therefore black newcomers and longtime residents banded together to agitate for equity in the wartime housing projects. For example, in 1943 project residents joined black longtime residents to form the United Negroes of America (UNA). This black grassroots organization (one of a very few for which there is any record during this period) appears to have fought housing segregation and employment discrimination primarily. In September 1944, William R. Brown, project resident and spokesman for the UNA, presented the Richmond City Council with a petition protesting "Discrimination and segregation and denying negroes [sic] occupancy of available housing in the Federally operated housing units in the city." The group demanded that the council order the housing commission to discharge Harry Barbour, director of the housing authority, and several other employees who were responsible for the deplorable conditions in the projects. Brown debated the matter with a representative of the housing authority and agreed to meet again at a later date, though nothing substantial came of that effort. The UNA protested to the housing authority again the following year.[44]

In November of 1944, the West Coast Regional Office of the NAACP opened its doors in San Francisco under the direction of Noah Griffin Sr. That same year newcomers William McKinney and Margaret Starks joined prewar residents Cleophas Brown, Juanita Wheeler, and others to form the Richmond branch of the NAACP in the Harbor Gate housing project. Cleophas Brown was elected as the organization's first chairman. Through the NAACP, black Richmondites hoped to present their grievances with one voice so their "efforts were taken more seriously."[45]

In addition to challenging segregated shipyard unions, the Richmond NAACP immediately turned its attention to the issue of housing discrimination. The NAACP drafted a resolution condemning the Richmond Housing Authority for "violating the spirit and letter of the regulations set forth by the Federal Public Housing Agency covering racial discrimination and segregation." The resolution accused the housing authority of violating its own discriminatory four-to-one quota system. Margaret Starks and Cleophas Brown, representing the NAACP, presented the resolution at a special council meeting that included representatives from the city and federal housing authorities and the Kaiser shipyards. They also distributed copies to the press and an array of local and federal officials including the regional director of the Federal Public Housing Administration and Representative George P. Miller. The NAACP threatened to call a rent strike in the projects if its complaints were not addressed.[46]

Starks and Brown strongly objected to housing authority tactics. In response, authority officials accused Brown of "sabotaging" the housing grievance committee on which he sat and subsequently padlocked him out of his project apartment, claiming he "had no legal right to live [there]," even though he was employed by the shipyards. At that same meeting, W. R. Brown, president of the UNA, stormed out after assailing city officials for not taking black grievances seriously. In January 1945 the housing authority attempted to serve eviction notices on thousands of project tenants, accusing them of illegal occupancy. Black residents responded by bombarding officials with petitions, staging demonstrations in front of the housing authority and city hall, and initiating a "no-rent" strike. The strike was supported by a cross section of the black community including the UNA, the black Interdenominational Ministerial Alliance, and the NAACP.[47]

To thwart the spreading strike, the authority moved to lock out all tenants who withheld rent. In an attempt to "teach a lesson" to the strikers, the authority immediately evicted many blacks whom they labeled "troublemakers" and "illegal residents." Accusing the authority of having an "un-American, undemocratic" attitude toward the tenants they were supposed to serve, Margaret Starks and Cleophas Brown demanded that the city council intervene to end the "eviction and lockout of people living in the local Housing Authority units." The council demurred, claiming it had no jurisdiction over their complaints, but promised to call another meeting with the housing authority to "discuss the matter."[48]

The actions of the housing authority intensified African American determination. Cleophas Brown recalled: "They thought they could scare the people, but there were so many of us who were tired of being put last. We were learning fast about how to get some of the things we needed. Lots of people couldn't read or write too well, but they knew what was right. They weren't ashamed of being ordinary working folks." Though the authority eventually broke the strike, the strength of black resistance to the eviction attempts caused the resignation of some housing authority officials and brought a halt to their heavy-handed tactics.[49]

African Americans encountered equally dire conditions in the private housing market. A special government census showed that 5,673 African Americans made their homes in Richmond in September 1943. As thousands more poured into the city, formerly racially mixed neighborhoods reached a "tipping point" where "the portion of non-whites exceed[ed] the limits of the neighborhood's tolerance for interracial living." The number of blacks necessary to trigger this reaction is difficult to determine, but as racially diverse neighborhoods like North Richmond began to receive more black newcomers, white families who had lived there for generations now fled. Ivy Reid Lewis recalled that her Portuguese neighbors, alarmed by the numbers of "black shipyard people" moving into North Richmond, sold their home and moved away. The departing family urged the Reids to do the same before it was "too late . . . just as if we weren't black."[50]

Restrictive covenants, avaricious landlords, and real estate agents who refused to show blacks all listings resulted in the concentration of African Americans in North Richmond. In a desperate search for housing, one black newcomer "went to a real estate office located near 14th and Macdonald Avenue" seeking "help in finding a place to live" for herself and her mother. After making "many trips on [sic] his car to North Richmond," the white real estate agent finally "frankly stated that he was told to take me out there and that's where all of my people are shown places to live."[51]

North Richmond, adjacent to a garbage dump and lying partially in the unincorporated county area, had become a less-than-desirable place to live. Throughout the war years, North Richmond lacked adequate utilities, garbage collection, lighting, and medical facilities. No municipal or federal agency would take responsibility for upgrading sewage disposal facilities, so drainage and overflow problems plagued the community, endangering health and property. North Richmond residents remarked that in rainy weather "you had to swim to get out there." Unusually stormy weather in 1944 and 1945 flooded the area, destroying many of the newcomers' makeshift living quarters. Water and mud rushed into trailers and shacks, transforming the unpaved streets into a "quagmire of mud two feet thick." Seeking relief from that catastrophe, various community organizations went before the city council to "plead for some minimal services," but their efforts were "without any effect whatever." Adding insult to injury, the city housing inspector came out and condemned over 75 percent of the dwellings for being below code standards.[52]

Despite North Richmond's substantial shortcomings, it was for many African Americans the only thing available, and blacks continued to stream in. Their influx represented a financial windfall for many long-time black residents, who rented out extra rooms, garages, and even chicken coops at inflated prices. Black newcomers were charged exorbitant prices for their meager accommodations there, and "the colored shipyard workers could like it or not." Even the most modest of rooms rented for $1.50 a night, and "decent three-room apartments in private houses" rented for $120 a month. Auto and trailer parks, offering little in the way of sanitation or social amenities, did turn-away business, charging $3 a night. The Reid family was among those who took in boarders during the war, including several children who had been abandoned by their parents, but like many other black longtime residents, the family was ambivalent about the newcomers: "Those people needed some place to live, but they brought roaches with them and didn't have any manners." Beryl Gwendolyn Reid regretted that she had ignored her Portuguese neighbors' advice and "wished they had've moved" from North Richmond before the onslaught of the newcomers.[53]

White Richmondites may have considered the situation in North Richmond and the housing projects "temporary" and hoped that the newcomers would "go back where they came from" once the war emergency ended, but African American newcomers intended to stay. With wages earned in the shipyards and other industries, they made down payments on North Richmond lots and lived in trailers, tents, or shacks until they could construct their houses. Finding it difficult to secure home loans or building permits, they "eventually built their own homes, using whatever scrap lumber they could secure from the shipyards in which they worked." Black newcomers did "a lot of scrounging. . . . They went to the dump, and they got what they could" to construct their houses. Wartime restrictions allowed them to purchase only twenty dollars worth of lumber, but "many families bought that $20.00 worth every pay-day, and went on with their building." The structures "violated the county building code and sanitary regulations, but they were homes, and the owners took great pride in their accomplishments." The rickety dwellings erected on the marshy North Richmond lots represented to most black newcomers the first property they had ever owned.[54]

In his study of black migration to the San Francisco Bay Area in the 1940s, Edward France suggested that black migrants tended to accept segregated and substandard conditions because they were "recent arrivals from the south where segregation was the rule" and because they lacked leadership and cohesion. One black newcomer offered a similar explanation: "We know it isn't right to be treated as we are, but we are from the south, and we are used to living all huddled together." While their explanations may contain a measure of truth, the characterizations dismiss and minimize the pivotal role southern black migrants played in mounting some of the earliest and strongest attacks on Jim Crow in

Richmond. Their founding of and activism in the Richmond NAACP challenges the notion of ineptitude and acquiescence among southern black newcomers.[55]

The Richmond NAACP quickly emerged as the most influential black organization in the city, boasting a membership of over five hundred. It became the fastest growing NAACP branch on the West Coast, but from its inception it had the reputation of being a radical organization, infiltrated by Communists. Although black Richmondites hoped to present a united front in their attacks on California Jim Crow, the organization was racked by a hotly contested struggle for power between "conservative" and "radical" factions of the black community and their white supporters.[56]

Fragmentary sources and the reluctance on the part of participants to name names make it difficult to assess who the radicals and the conservatives were. The radical faction appears to have espoused direct actions, such as strikes, boycotts, and demonstrations. They came from the ranks of black and white labor activists, most of whom were or had been employed in the shipyards. Some of the white radicals lived in Richmond, Oakland, and the university community of Berkeley. The radical group was often linked to the Communist Party. Noah Griffin insisted that they were a "small Communist group who practically run the branch." Compared to the entire membership their numbers were small, but they seemed to be tireless participants in labor affairs, electoral politics, and postwar advisory committees. Cleophas Brown, Ray Thompson, AFL activist Louis Richardson, John Hughes, and Mildred Bowen were frequently named as leaders of this faction.[57]

The conservatives came from the ranks of small business owners, clergy, and representatives from "Civic, Fraternal and Social organizations of Richmond, Calif[ornia]." Baptist ministers such as Lofton L. Fowler and Isaac (I. C.) Mickens stood with Margaret Starks and Dr. Paul T. Robinson in opposing the radicals. Starks noted that "the mood of the whole country was [such] that we needed to be in the mainstream, militant but mainstream." Cleophas Brown recalled that Dr. Paul T. Robinson—a Republican and graduate of Meharry Medical College who had settled in Richmond with his wife, Virginia Robinson, in 1953—frequently commented: "We'll get respect when we show we can clean our own house." It seems the battle for power within the organization was also a struggle to legitimize the African American presence in the community.[58]

The ideological divisions appear to have cut across old-timer/newcomer lines. From 1945 through about 1950 Cleophas Brown and a slate a radicals managed to get elected to leadership positions but were opposed by conservatives in the organization. Cleophas Brown was elected president in 1945, when the branch was located at 615 South Thirty-third Street. LeRoy Wheeler, the Reverend W. Dixon, Paul L. Brown, and the Reverend S. E. Diggens were elected as vice presidents. Of this group only Brown and Wheeler could be characterized as radicals. V. E. Butler held the office of treasurer, Margaret H. Starks was listed as secretary, and Juanita Wheeler and Myrtle Fenell were identified as assistant secretaries. Butler and Starks were part of the conservative faction.

Brown was reelected to the presidency in January 1946, with the Reverend Diggens elected as first vice president, Ebb Everett as second vice president, and Louis Richardson, a shipyard worker and part of the radical faction, as third vice president. The Reverend I. C. Mickens was elected as chair of the membership committee. Thus, prewar residents and newcomers, radicals and conservatives were elected to leadership positions in the organization. Margaret Starks was a black newcomer from Arkansas, a staunch Republican, an outspoken opponent of the "radicals," the editor of the *Richmond Guide,* and an entrepreneur. Cleophas Brown was an outspoken labor activist and was also "now in charge of circulation for [the] County of DAILY WORKER [emphasis in original text]."[59]

Despite the range of political affiliations of the executive board and the general membership, the activism and increasing size of the organization made it highly visible during the anti-Communist hysteria of the McCarthy era. The local press and executives from the regional and national NAACP boards voiced growing concerns that the Richmond branch had fallen under the "control and domination" of a small Communist group "who practically run the branch in such a way that every move and action of the branch has been the avowed intention of the party." Noah Griffin feared for the independence of the Richmond NAACP because of its "communist infiltration" and worried that radical influence would cause membership to "[fall] off considerably." Griffin identified Ray Thompson as one of the "chief [Communist] Party members" who participated in Richmond activities. Thompson was an East Bay labor activist, a founding member of the East Bay Shipyard Workers against Discrimination, and the head of the National Negro Congress in Oakland. The regional director also described John Hughes, a white activist and member of the NAACP's executive committee, as "an acknowledged Communist." The *Richmond Independent* reported that Mildred Bowen, a white Richmondite and "Secretary and head of the Communist party in Contra Costa County," was in charge of "publicity for the National Association for the Advancement of Colored People, according to an announcement by the organization." Bowen was elected to the post "after her name had been submitted by one of the members."[60]

The Reverend I. C. Mickens, pastor of an interdenominational church in the Harbor Gate housing project and member of the NAACP, complained to the regional director of the NAACP that a faction of Communists dominated the Richmond NAACP. The regional director reported that "efforts on the part of those not connected with the party to gain any offices in the branch have been fought viciously by the ones in control." Mickens told the regional director that after having been "prevailed upon by many friends and those interested in the NAACP," he finally consented to "have his name placed in nomination for president." However, Mickens informed the regional director that the sitting administration "was very hostile to the nominating committee for even bringing in two nominees." He believed they had intended that only one nominee, "the party member, be brought in." Mickens claimed that acting president Cleophas Brown "is going around to all his group urging them to come and support their candidates." Mickens complained that the opposing conservative candidates were unable to mount their own "canvass of the membership" because they did not hold any of the "top offices" in the organization.[61]

Bernard Evans, another member of the conservative faction, also protested the 1947 election, complaining that the ballot had been prepared in secret by the hand-picked group from the executive committee, who placed the words "majority candidate" behind some of the names and "minority candidate" with others. Regional director Griffin agreed with Evans that the Richmond branch "has a great potential of becoming even larger and more powerful provided we can get the right sort of leadership." National director of branches Gloster B. Current expressed no "doubt that the Nominating Committee was controlled by the Communist Party" but had to concede that the committee acted entirely in accordance with *Roberts' Rules of Order* in nominating the candidates for office.[62]

The factional tug-of-war culminated in a purge of the radicals in the 1950s. Undoubtedly the energy of the Richmond NAACP was influenced by the militancy of its Communist members, but the majority of Richmond's NAACP came from the ranks of ordinary working black people, who had little previous political experience. One resident recalled that the Richmond branch toed no "party line." It was "established . . . as an interracial deal. That's how it was able to survive." Its founders "made it plain" that the NAACP "was first and last for black people." There was "no party line, no difference between this colored person or that one. That's *really* how we could not only survive but make any progress." Otherwise, "they tried divide and conquer." Despite the ideological and intraracial conflicts, the NAACP was, as Margaret Starks observed, "the *only* game in town, honey." Most black Richmondites were willing to let its leaders serve as "spokesmen and advocates for the entire colored minority group." It was the first institution to which most African Americans turned for help during and long after the boom years of World War II.[63]

African Americans, newcomers and longtime residents alike, became integral players in the wartime industrial economy that transformed Richmond virtually overnight. Black newcomers who had never owned property before, who had little experience in political or civic matters, and who were preoccupied with the day-to-day concerns of adjusting to life in a new environment nevertheless began to coalesce as a political and social force in the city. Their participation in and confrontations with labor and municipal bureaucracies taught firsthand political lessons from which they gained confidence and expertise.

The emergence of the NAACP symbolized a convergence of newcomer and old-timer interests as external pressures of racism compelled blacks to publicly emphasize racial congregation and downplay internal divisions, even as those divisions were contested ardently within the community. Race would remain the most salient factor in the existence of black Richmondites long after demobilization closed the shipyards and the war boom ended.

CHAPTER 4

Demobilization, Rising Expectations, and Postwar Realities

Obviously, many people now living in Richmond are going to have to move.

Director George P. Tobin, Richmond
Redevelopment Agency, 1953

Our people will be driven away, that's what. Sometimes I am sure that's what the people running this town really want.

The Reverend W. Lee La Beaux, 1953

The reduction in number and eventual closure of the Kaiser shipyards represented the most profound sign of demobilization in Richmond. As early as mid-1944 Richmond's wartime boom was showing signs of slowing as Kaiser instituted its first round of cutbacks. In the peak production year of 1943, the shipyards employed over one hundred thousand people. By late 1944 that number had dropped to forty-seven thousand. In 1945 Kaiser was laying off workers "at the rate of 1,000 a month," so that by the spring of 1946 only nine thousand remained on shipyard payrolls. African Americans, who comprised an estimated 10 to 20 percent of the shipyard workforce, were first to be discharged and last to be recalled. African Americans found that demobilization translated into economic destabilization, family crisis, and an intensified drive for equal treatment in and beyond the workplace in the postwar period.[1]

In July 1945 Walter White, executive secretary of the NAACP, wrote to Noah W. Griffin, NAACP regional director in San Francisco, about a conversation he [White] had with the "political boss of Richmond whose name I do not remember," from whom he learned about the massive layoffs. White urged Griffin to "drop over to Richmond occasionally to check on" how the shutdown was affecting black workers. Some Richmond officials, "among whom I understand the Mayor is most active," had begun "advocating sending newcomers 'back where they came from,' especially Negroes." The situation was serious since there was "even some talk of vigilantic methods."[2]

The *San Francisco Chronicle* reported that nearly 12,000 people a week were lining up at the unemployment office to collect twenty dollars in weekly unemployment benefits. The newly established Richmond Council on Civic Unity reported that by mid-May 1946, unemployment stood at 13,800. African Americans made up 2,760, or 20 percent, of the unemployed. In the spring of 1947, overall unemployment had dropped to 8,000, but black unemployment as a percentage of the total had risen by 40 percent, to 2,250 (or 28 percent of the total). Seventy-five percent of unemployed black men and 40 percent of unemployed black women had been shipyard workers. In 1947 a University of California study of unemployed black shipyard workers concluded that more African Americans than whites were unemployed or only marginally employed. In 1949 the situation had not improved: an estimated 32 to 36 percent of the labor force in predominantly black North Richmond was unemployed. This was four times the unemployment rate for the entire city.[3]

The unemployment picture was even bleaker in 1950. Of the 37,579 Richmond residents remaining in the civilian labor force, 13.4 percent (5,024) were without jobs. African Americans, who accounted for about 94 percent of the nonwhite civilian labor force, comprised about 28 percent (1,388, in a total black population of 13,374) of the unemployed (see table 4).Many state and local officials considered "the Negro a poor work risk" and tended to blame high postwar black unemployment on shipyard work's not having prepared "the Negro for the type of work found in competitive industry." Nearly all former Kaiser workers found it difficult to duplicate the wages they had earned in the shipyards. One white worker remarked: "I used to make $1.25 an hour in the shipyards. . . . now the best I can get outside is 85 cents an hour." However, skilled and unskilled whites were better able to transfer to private sector jobs after the war than their African American counterparts.[4]

Some black former shipyard employees found work in other governmental facilities (the Benicia Arsenal, Port Chicago, Mare Island Naval Yard, and Hunters Point), and others were hired in the building trades or on San Francisco's waterfront. In contrast to their white counter-

Table 4 *Unemployment Rates in Richmond, by Color and Sex, 1950*

	Male	Female	Total
In civilian labor force	27,040	10,539	37,579
No. unemployed	3,217	1,807	5,024
% Unemployed	11.9	17.1	13.4
Whites			
In civilian labor force	23,507	9,022	32,529
No. unemployed	2,338	1,209	3,547
% Unemployed	9.9	13.4	10.9
Nonwhites			
In civilian labor force	3,533	1,517	5,050
No. unemployed	879	598	1,477
% Unemployed	24.9	39.4	29.2
Blacks*			
In civilian labor force	3,321	1,426	4,747
No. unemployed	826	562	1,388
% Unemployed	23.4	39.4	29.2

SOURCE: U.S. Department of Commerce, Bureau of the Census, *A Report of the Seventeenth Decennial Census of the United States: Census of the Population, 1950,* vol. 2 (Washington, D.C.: GPO, 1952), 102; Robert Wenkert, John Magney, and Fred Templeton, *An Historical Digest of Negro-White Relations in Richmond, California* (Berkeley: Survey Research Center, University of California, Berkeley, February 1967, rev. September 1967), 75–78.

*Figures for blacks were calculated on the basis of data estimating that blacks represented 94 percent of the nonwhite population in Richmond.

parts, African American workers, regardless of skill level, were essentially blocked from most civilian sector jobs. With the relaxation of "governmental pressures for employment of minority groups," Richmond employers reverted to discriminatory hiring policies "with fewer restraints." Standard Oil employed no black workers. The Filice and Perrelli Cannery hired its first black worker in 1952. The Ford Motor Company employed some black workers but in 1955 relocated to Milpitas, fifty miles away, lured by lower operating costs and frustrated by Richmond's poor meeting of the housing needs of its employees, "especially Negro workers."[5]

The most immediate consequences of demobilization for black Richmondites, therefore, were a sharp decline in economic stability and severely strained marriages and families. For example, a newcomer couple from Arkansas had supported three children and an in-law on their two-paycheck shipyard income of more than one hundred dollars. When pregnancy prevented the wife from working and the husband was laid off permanently from Kaiser in 1946, they were forced to exhaust their savings. The man was "now responsible for the support of six persons"

and had "no immediate prospects of employment" and no transportation, since the family car had been sold to meet household expenses.
Margaret Starks recalled: "when shipyard pay ended, it damaged lots of
marriages. People just sort of split up if there was no money coming in."
Black Richmondite Austin Cuba, a former shipyard driller, was reduced
to working as a bootblack on Macdonald Avenue while he "wait[ed] for
a good job." Others attempted to enroll in vocational classes or complete college degrees as they searched for "a job right now." William
McKinney observed, "colored people had to hustle to get those same
jobs we used to have before the war, no one was hiring, and when you
did get a little something the money was bad."[6]

Many black Richmondites attributed racially based ulterior motives
to the precipitous demobilization that threw so many of them out of
work. They were particularly suspicious of the numerous urban renewal
programs that accompanied demobilization. An infusion of federal monies under the Housing Acts of 1949 and 1950 allowed Richmond planners
to undertake large-scale urban planning programs. However, many of
Richmond's redevelopment plans had been drawn up during the war and
called for postwar reduction of the shipyards and often proposed the demolition of housing and neighborhoods where black people resided.[7]

Thus African Americans' intentions to "make Richmond home" collided with the ambitions of developers, city planners, and public officials, who launched postwar programs for "blight" abatement and slum
clearance. Richmond's postwar redevelopment policies had several pur-
poses. By removing the stigma of temporary dwellings and their "at-
tendant economic and social conditions," city planners hoped to attract
"many of the industries which are locating or relocating in the Bay
Area." Moreover, postwar redevelopment and urban renewal projects
had as their goal reducing the percentage of Richmond's population still
living in temporary war housing projects (50.6 percent). In 1950 Richmond city officials and Contra Costa County administrators proposed to
tear down all wartime housing projects in south Richmond to make way
for private commercial and residential developments. Almost 78 percent
of the 13,374 blacks living in the city resided in the projects. The 1950 redevelopment plan also called for most of the dwellings in North Richmond to be razed. This move would have displaced virtually all of the
three thousand residents living there, 94 percent of whom were black.[8]

The director of the Richmond Redevelopment Agency, George P.
Tobin, explained the city's postwar vision: "The density of population
in Richmond is already too great for the size of the city. . . . We need

more jobs, we need more industry. Obviously, many people now living in Richmond are going to have to move." Tobin hoped to accomplish this phase of redevelopment through programs of "population attrition" and "orderly rebuilding," with highest priority being given to industrial development. Some white residents attempted to encourage this impulse, suggesting racial separation as a solution to postwar problems. For example, the city council received a petition from seventy Richmond citizens demanding restrictions on the sale of property at 749 Sixth Street to "those other than the white race." The communication urged the city to implement a policy of segregation in order to promote "closer harmony in the community."[9]

Black Richmondites believed that the urban renewal aspects of demobilization would be accomplished at their expense. The Reverend W. Lee La Beaux, a Baptist minister who pastored a church in the predominantly black Canal housing project, alluded to a hidden agenda behind redevelopment proposals: "There's a strange undercurrent; you can hardly put your hand on it. . . . You think you understand the game. Then suddenly . . . [you're] losing the game." William McKinney was more direct: "They wanted all the Negroes to leave Richmond after the war. With no shipyards and no place to live, that's what they hoped would happen." Most redevelopment proposals met with strong resistance from blacks, who banded together to halt the reversal of their wartime gains. Black real estate agent Neitha Williams reported that "people at Canal and Terrace [housing projects] were so afraid they were talking about getting clubs and sticks into their homes and hitting anyone who tried to evict them." La Beaux declared: "All of our people are being moved. . . . We're opposed to segregation. Segregation is dangerous business."[10]

Hoping to avoid a repeat of the rent strikes and protests of 1945, city officials took a softer approach to postwar plans. For example, in 1952 City Manager Wayne Thompson organized the short-lived Committee on Housing and Municipal Problems, consisting of himself, two redevelopment agency administrators, "four Negro ministers, and one Negro real estate woman." The committee published a pamphlet entitled "Facts You Should Know about the Solution to Your Housing Problem" and tried to reassure the evictees that they would be relocated to permanent housing, as the law required. However, black Richmondites remained skeptical of the assurances, since most neighborhoods with vacant private housing barred blacks, and the remaining temporary housing was segregated. Within weeks the committee "ceased to exist," having been disbanded by the city council, which informed the committee members that "they were no longer needed." [11]

While the Richmond Housing Authority had little trouble finding permanent homes for most of the 207 white families in the Canal and Terrace projects, it concentrated the majority of the 911 black families in temporary housing located along State Street and Fall Avenue, a "generally undesirable area slated for early demolition." Canal and Terrace were finally cleared in October 1952. Of the 704 African American families who were evicted from the two projects, 84 percent were placed in other temporary housing. Only 56 percent of the white families were relocated to temporary housing. [12]

In 1953 Harbor Gate, the predominately white model wartime housing project that had been reserved as housing for the surplus population, also was slated for destruction. The city made a deal with the Safeway supermarket chain to relocate its regional warehouse complex to the Harbor Gate site. Harbor Gate residents fought the demolition, presenting their concerns not only to the city council but to the Federal Public Housing Administration and to Congress. Their struggles garnered support throughout the Bay Area. The high percentage of skilled white workers residing in Harbor Gate and the desire of local merchants to retain these "quality" residents in Richmond forced officials to relocate the evicted Harbor Gate residents to new homes in recently completed Atchison Village, the largest permanent housing project in the city. In a move that further reduced the supply of low-cost public housing in Richmond, the city sold Atchison Village to a private concern in 1957. [13]

Black resentment increased as housing projects fell to the redevelopment wrecking ball. Neitha Williams explained the housing crisis facing black Richmondites: "There was nothing, absolutely nothing in private rentals or sales available to the minority groups. They had to take what the Housing Authority offered." Speaking for black residents who found themselves on the verge of homelessness, the Reverend La Beaux stated: "Our people will be driven away, that's what. Sometimes I am sure that's what the people running this town really want." [14]

The housing situation was no better in North Richmond, where rehabilitation plans seem to have germinated even before the war ended. City Manager James McVittie's 1944 report on housing in the city-governed portion of North Richmond identified some three hundred predominantly black-owned houses "in violation of city standards" and proposed to abolish them. Moreover, a chamber of commerce map drawn up in 1945 projected future development by superimposing large factories and residential subdivisions on property where black homes already stood.[15]

In 1948, the chamber of commerce presented the city council with an improvement plan that called for the condemnation of all substandard housing in North Richmond to make way for the annexation and resale of the land to "private interests" who would build houses "for rent or sale." The plan gave no indication that the proposed new housing would deviate from the prevailing practice of racial segregation. Although the proposal, which required joint city-county action, did not pass, it confirmed the residents' fears that the city wanted to annex North Richmond to "destroy our homes and sell our property to strangers." Thus, North Richmond residents voted against all annexation proposals. In 1949 a zoning ordinance reaffirmed that most of the area would remain residential, multiple-family dwellings.[16]

In 1950, because the black population in North Richmond showed no signs of diminishing, residents began pressing for affordable public housing. However, the Richmond City Planning Commission appears to have had second thoughts about its earlier decision to let North Richmond remain a residential area. A new commission report stated: "No effort should be made to establish public housing until it becomes clearly evident that no demand will appear for industrial sites in this section that may be of paramount importance to the industrial life of the City of Richmond." Within five years of the issuance of the report, a North Richmond master plan had earmarked the area for eventual industrial use, in effect rejecting the call for more housing in one of the few neighborhoods in which blacks were permitted to live. Father John Garcia, a minister to Contra Costa County's black and Spanish-speaking Catholics, declared: "There is great apprehension among my people. They say they are gradually being forced out of the City of Richmond." Margaret Starks, called the "Mayor of North Richmond" by many black residents, recalled that "the squeeze was on."[17]

Black Richmondites were squeezed on two fronts: they were confined to menial employment in the workplace and shut out of decent, permanent housing in the private sector. In spite of the economic and social setbacks that attended demobilization, most black Richmondites planned to remain in the city. Discharged servicemen returned to civilian life in the Bay Area to start "baby boom" families. Former shipyard workers, flush with wartime earnings, wanted to purchase homes in Richmond and encouraged loved ones to join them. Although some

Table 5 *Race and Sex Distribution in Richmond, 1950 and 1960*

	1950	%	1960	%
Race				
White	85,329	85.7	51,016	71.0
Black	13,374	13.4	14,388	20.0
Spanish speaking*	—	—	5,050	7.0
Other	842	.8	1,400	1.9
Sex				
Male	49,732	50.0	35,309	49.1
Female	49,813	50.0	36,545	50.9
Total	99,545		71,854	

SOURCE: U.S. Department of Commerce, Bureau of the Census, *A Report of the Seventeenth Decennial Census of the United States: Census of the Population, 1950*, vol. 2 (Washington, D.C.: GPO, 1952), 102, table 34; U.S. Department of Commerce, Bureau of the Census, *A Report of the Eighteenth Decennial Census of the United States: Census of the Population, 1960*, vol. 6 (Washington, D.C.: GPO, 1961), 140, table 21; Richmond Model Cities Program and City of Richmond Planning Department, Research and Evaluation Unit, "Richmond Facts" (Richmond: December 1, 1974), 2, table 1, Richmond Collection, Richmond Public Library.

*Spanish-speaking population included in white category.

considered returning to their home states, most decided against it because "things are just as bad there. . . . and it's mighty hard to start moving around a family especially when there are a lot of little kids." Therefore, as whites retreated to newly built suburban housing developments, Richmond's black population increased. At the end of 1945 Richmond's total population was 99,976, which included nearly 10,000 blacks. In the fifteen-year period following the war, the overall population declined, slipping from 99,545 in 1950 (with 85,329 whites) to 71,854 in 1960 (with slightly over 51,000 white residents). In contrast, Richmond's black population rose from 13,374 (20,400 counting blacks residing in the unincorporated area) in 1950 to 14,388 in 1960 (excluding the unincorporated area), or 20 percent of the total, and that population grew steadily as the decade continued (see table 5).[18]

In the postwar era the line between old-timers and newcomers virtually became extinct as all African Americans were lumped together in marginal jobs and substandard housing. Demobilization eroded the veneer of wartime harmony. Pent-up white resentment against black gains erupted in a backlash of prejudice and violence, making all blacks vulnerable. The American Council on Race Relations noted that in Richmond some "white people think that now that the war is over, that it is time 'to get the Negroes in line,' or make them stay 'in their place.'"

California's attorney general, Robert W. Kenny, reported that a Richmond police officer "came upon a Negro and a white boy fighting."
The white boy admitted, "sure, I started it. He's got no business walking on this street. It's just for white people." As a result of such incidents,
black Richmondites were tense, "afraid they are going to be discriminated against in postwar jobs and housing. They will do everything they
can to hold on to their wartime gains." [19]

Cleophas Brown recalled, "after the war many a white man thought
they could get nasty with us again. I saw one man just take off and ha-
rass this one colored hod carrier on a job, didn't think he should be
working with white men, until that boy just hauled off and hit him
square in the face with a two-by-four." Margaret Starks noted: "People
were just about desperate, honey. Those who had some money couldn't
get a decent place to live, and those who needed work couldn't find anything that paid what they made in the war. It was about survival. They
weren't leaving and didn't want to be pushed around by white folks anymore. So they had to get together and fight back." [20] In fighting back,
black Richmondites drew on a variety of civil, legal, and political strategies and met with varying degrees of success.

Like employment and housing, education was a potent symbol of
progress and became a hotly contested battleground after World War II.
African American parents set a high priority on education and were determined that their "kids [would] . . . go to school and get ahead." This
goal clashed with the schools' policy of separating students into "large
categories of academic competence," generally assigning African American students to the remedial or "lower reaches" of the educational system. This policy effectively "place[ed] black students in a position anal-
ogous to their parents' condition in the community—segregated at the
bottom and in some cases despised." [21]

Until the mid-1960s the larger Richmond region was divided into
five school districts: four elementary districts and one for junior-senior
high school. Nearly all elementary-level black children attended school
in either the Richmond or the San Pablo district. All four elementary districts fed into the Richmond Union High School district, which served
grades seven to twelve. [22]

The most serious overcrowding occurred in schools serving the
south side housing projects and in the predominantly black North Richmond area. Even as a flurry of postwar new school construction eased
some of the crowding, "there was a distinct tendency for schools, especially at the elementary level, to be segregated by race." For example

Verde Elementary School, which was constructed in 1947 by the San Pablo Elementary School District served children from North Richmond and the surrounding regions and was predominately black. As early as 1944 the city manager had proposed a new elementary school for North Richmond. In 1955 the proposal was revived, but at a community meeting organized by the West Contra Costa Community Welfare Council, the attendees "voted overwhelmingly against such a school." Residents believed the new school would "have been essentially segregated like Verde."[23]

In 1958 Harry Ells Junior High School became a senior high school. Its boundaries were constructed to "follow the boundaries of its feeder schools" and tended to concentrate "higher socioeconomic groups at Ells and lower socioeconomic groups at Richmond High School." Many black parents feared that "this would affect the curricula at the two schools, making the former a college preparatory school and the latter a vocational trade school, instead of both being comprehensive high schools." In addition, the new boundaries did not correspond to the actual location of the schools. Many students who lived close to one school were required to attend the other. Thus black parents were frustrated in their efforts to obtain quality education for their children, who were being treated as "problems" by backward-looking school administrators.[24]

In April 1945 a teacher at Nystrom Elementary School reportedly was "injured" by a black student. Later that year a fifteen-year-old black Richmond High student "cut two white students" who attacked him because they mistakenly believed he had hit a white girl. This touched off a furor in the school that spilled over to the entire city. The school board held a tempestuous meeting attended by "90 to 199 people," of whom "only five were Negroes." Most white parents in attendance, including City Attorney John Pierce, demanded immediate segregation of the black students, who made up about 10 percent of Richmond High School's student body. Monitoring the situation, the NAACP worked out a settlement with the legal authorities for the black student's probation and supervision, with the goal of "keeping black students in school."[25]

Regional NAACP secretary Noah W. Griffin explained that "this outburst of feeling seems to be the breaking loose of much pent-up feeling that doubtless has been in the minds of many of these persons possibly for a few years. Now that the war is over they feel they have an opportunity to 'put the Negroes in their place.'" Black newcomers and old-timers vowed "not to give an inch." Joseph Griffin III recalled: "We used to walk from North Richmond to [Richmond] High School. And we might have to fight every other day to get back to North Richmond 'cause the white boys, they would like to call you nigger." One might be "the preacher's son, a brain, or a rowdy, they didn't care. All of us were here to stay."[26] The issues of school boundaries, class segregation, and access to equal education continued to be bitterly fought in the city for three decades. Racial polarization around the issue of public schools led to confrontations between whites and blacks that flared up periodically in the postwar years and finally erupted in the mid-1960s.[27]

Workplace equity was another heated issue in the postwar period. The concerted efforts of black Richmondites, in alliance with white supporters, were responsible for dismantling some of the most egregious obstacles to fair employment. The NAACP took the lead in this fight, but rifts that had surfaced earlier in the history of the organization flared into full-fledged red-baiting in the postwar period. The United States' obsession with Communism was a product of the Cold War, which chilled social and political expression in virtually every public and private organization in the country. The national directors of the NAACP, responding to this political climate, initiated a campaign to weed out suspected Communists from the ranks of its branches, including the Richmond branch, the fastest growing and most active branch in the region. The Richmond NAACP's postwar battles were waged within this highly charged atmosphere. The struggle between radicals and conservatives in the Richmond NAACP mirrored the nation's preoccupation with political conformity and ideological purity.[28]

Black activists, however, often attempted to turn this preoccupation to their advantage. Jim Crow stood as an embarrassing contradiction to the rhetoric of freedom and self-determination emanating from the United States as it engaged in the Cold War struggle with the Soviet Union to win the hearts and minds of newly independent African, Asian, and Latin American nations. Ollie Freeman, a Richmond resident since 1933 and a decorated war veteran who had served with the segregated 761st "Black Panther" Tank Battalion of the Third Army, explained: "Everybody agitating for better homes and jobs knew it wouldn't look too good for Uncle Sam if he didn't allow people to live right. People would say, 'might as well be in Russia, no difference.'" While the Cold War "made the hue of one's ideology rather than that of one's skin the overriding test of a worthy American," it also called into question the loyalty of black Richmondites and their white allies who worked to eliminate racism from the system. Therefore, the Richmond NAACP's aggressive assaults on Jim Crow in the city, its tendency to collaborate with activists from all points on the political spectrum, and black Richmondites' increasing willingness to work in interracial coalitions to accomplish their goals made the group's activities suspect in the prevailing political climate.[29]

For example, in December 1946 the NAACP allied itself with a predominantly white and "leftist" organization, Progressive Citizens of America (PCA), to gain jobs for blacks. The coalition picketed and boycotted the Lucky supermarket chain because it did not "pledge to hire Negroes in proportion to the Negro trade which is considerable at the Cutting Boulevard store." The NAACP and PCA received widespread community support, and the boycott's effectiveness was apparent in the reaction of store officials, who enlisted help from the housing authority attorney to "counteract public support of the anti-discrimination campaign." Housing authority employees attended NAACP and PCA meetings attempting to disrupt them by relentless red-baiting. After several months of demonstrations and litigation that reached the state supreme court, black Richmondites prevailed in getting five black clerks hired by Lucky.[30]

In 1947, the NAACP also led campaigns against "Negro Patrons Not Wanted" signs, which merchants displayed in their shop windows along Macdonald, San Pablo, and Cutting Avenues. These campaigns captured the imagination of the entire African American community. Margaret Starks recalled that "a bunch of black folks stormed the City Council," demanding that the *Richmond Independent* exert pressure on the businesses. As a result of their actions, downtown merchants were forced to remove the offensive signs. African Americans also led sit-ins and demonstrations at segregated restaurants and lunch counters in Richmond. Their efforts met with mixed success: they were served for the first time in some and rebuffed in others. Most often, however, "the response was complete shock on the part of the owners." The shock stemmed from the boldness of the demonstrators and from the fact that members of prewar black families were now "out there hollering and screaming side by side" with those whom most white Richmondites had viewed as "trashy wartime people." A white resident remarked, "something happened to the good ones. They changed."[31]

Despite the NAACP's initial victories, a black delegation calling itself "The People of Richmond, California" and claiming to represent the "Ministers of the Churches of Richmond . . . Civic, Fraternal and Social

Organizations . . . , and the Business Establishments of Richmond . . . "
petitioned the NAACP national board. The delegation accused the
Richmond executive board of practicing "usury . . . upon the people of
Richmond at large" and "grossly misrepresenting the National Organization for their own Communistic gains." The petitioners demanded
the revocation of the Richmond branch's charter and asked that a new
charter be "issued under the supervision of the Regional Office." The
ministers announced that they would "refuse to cooperate" with the
present NAACP officers in Richmond because of their "definite Communistic affiliations and inclinations." They pledged to ban executive board
members of the Richmond branch from speaking "in our Churches on
matters N.A.A.C.P." A similar petition from the "Business Establishments of Richmond, Calif. strongly protest[ed] the way in which the
Negro People of our City are being misrepresented by the present
Branch." The group claimed to be the "real clear thinkers" who objected to the Richmond NAACP's "pinkish trend." They vowed "to do
something about the situation" and requested that the branch officers
be "deposed" and "do not again hold Office."[32]

This climate of suspicion and recrimination also affected the postwar
interracial coalitions in which many black Richmondites worked. After
the war the Bay Area became the "center of interracial leadership in the
state of California and throughout the Pacific Coast." The San Francisco–based Bay Area Council against Discrimination (BACAD), established in 1942, became the "prototype for the interracial societies." It
drew its leaders—including its first chairman, prominent black Berkeley attorney Walter Gordon—from cities all over the Bay Area. In keeping with the spirit of postwar egalitarianism, the BACAD was "committed to solving a broad spectrum of racial problems." It enjoyed
modest success in integrating some occupations but "faded quietly
from the scene" in mid-1944 because of "apathy and the lack of resources."[33]

The BACAD was replaced by the Council for Civic Unity (CCU),
which became the major interracial society. It was located in San Francisco and was led by Edward Howden, a white liberal and an Oakland
native. Beginning in 1952 the CCU produced "Dateline Freedom," a
weekly, fifteen-minute nationally broadcast radio program that informed
listeners about the state of race relations. The programs were enormously
popular in the Bay Area and represented what historian Albert Broussard has called the African American community's "fireside chats." In
1946 the Bay Area CCU became the California Council on Civic Unity

(CCCU) and gave birth to a statewide federation of interracial civic rights and civil liberties organizations known as the California Federation for Civic Unity (CFCU). This organization eventually broke away from the CCCU.[34]

As early as 1945 an interracial, prolabor, nonpartisan (but overwhelmingly Democratic) coalition known as the Richmond Better Government Committee won the support of the Richmond NAACP for its outspoken opposition to employment and housing discrimination. By 1946 Richmond residents had established the Richmond Council on Civic Unity (RCCU). The organization was headquartered in the YWCA building at Twelfth and Nevin Streets. Its first newsletter proclaimed: "We prefer civic unity to the disunity and setting up of race against race, religion against religion—in short, dividing the country so that the 'strong man' and his cohorts can step in almost unnoticed." The RCCU sponsored a number of meetings, panel discussions, and social events. In 1948 it was reorganized as the Richmond Council on Intergroup Relations (RCIR).[35]

The RCIR was eager to apply for membership in the California Federation for Civic Unity, realizing that "affiliation with the state organization will strengthen our local efforts considerably," but the group was hard-pressed to achieve affiliate status. The secretary of the RCIR noted: "Our membership is small and our funds are very limited so that we could not cover the minimum $25.00 fee at the present time." It appears that membership remained small even after a first-year recruitment drive that attracted a handful of religious, business, civic, and labor leaders from around the Bay Area. The predominantly white executive board was the heart of the organization. Whites appear to have made up the majority of the executive board during the five years of the RCIR's existence. The group's activities included creating a forum to "study state and national issues on intergroup relations as well as local conditions," running a speakers' bureau, and establishing publicity and outreach programs. It also sponsored a number of public meetings, school programs, and exhibitions on the effect of "fear and prejudice."[36]

The Richmond NAACP frequently collaborated with the RCIR. The passage of Richmond's fair employment practices ordinance in 1949 illustrates the attempts of black Richmondites to work within interracial coalitions. The outcome of the fight to pass the ordinance suggests the limitations of such alliances. The proposed ordinance, jointly authored by the NAACP and the RCIR, called for the creation of a commission of five members who would "hear complaints arising from any failure on the part of the city or companies having contracts with the city, to hire persons regardless of race, color or creed." The ordinance requested that the commission submit regular reports to the city council and work to persuade all employers to adopt hiring policies that "will coincide with the policy of the city on a voluntary basis." The RCIR/NAACP coalition requested that letters of endorsement be addressed to the city council but *mailed* to the RCIR and NAACP, "so that they may be submitted to the Council in a group." The NAACP and RCIR also sponsored a speakers' bureau that dispatched black and white members to answer questions about the ordinance at community and civic functions. On May 16, 1949, the city council unanimously passed Ordinance 1303, which banned racial, color, and religious discrimination as well as discrimination based on national origin or ancestry. The ordinance made "unlawful such discrimination by the city of Richmond and Persons hereafter acquiring city contracts." Violation of the ordinance was a misdemeanor, "punishable by a $500 fine or six months imprisonment or both." [37]

Ordinance 1303 appeared to be a victory for black Richmondites' coalition-building efforts. Four days after the law was enacted, Noah Griffin sent a congratulatory message to the Richmond NAACP: "We think the Richmond Branch deserves much credit for the part which it played in helping to get the city of Richmond to enact an FEPC law. I think it is safe to say this merely shows what can be done through cooperation of the various agencies that are interested in human uplift." Yet the victory was short-lived and caused some blacks to question the sincerity of their white allies. Blacks were alarmed by the ordinance's lack of enforcement provisions. To remedy this the RCIR, with the support of the NAACP, developed an addendum that would establish a five-member commission to "have the duty of supervision and investigating the enforcement and observance of Ordinance No. 1303." The city council rejected the addendum and in October 1961 repealed the entire ordinance. Years later city officials would explain that state legislation had preempted the municipal ordinance and that the "repeal was part of a general revision of city ordinances on that date." In 1961, however, many black Richmondites interpreted the reversal as a betrayal by whites who were not really committed to black progress and who feared growing black political strength. Two years after the passage of Ordinance 1303, a National Urban League report noted, "there has been some gradual incorporation of the Negro community into the body politic of Richmond" in the postwar era, but "this assimilation has been accompanied by considerable caution." For many black Richmondites the repeal of Ordinance 1303 underscored the validity of the league's observation. Cleophas Brown recalled that the ordinance "got away from us, it didn't have any teeth. . . . again, [they] divid[ed] and conquer[ed]." Margaret Starks noted: "it seemed like our hard work went down the drain. Even the so-called good white ones let us down."[38] The inability of municipal officials to implement legal remedies to employment and housing discrimination made black Richmondites skeptical of interracial alliances. Some believed that the repressive atmosphere of the Cold War made whites reluctant to commit themselves fully: "They thought it was a game, something to do with their time. Then they got scared of being smeared. They weren't in it for the long haul. Most of them just drifted away." Indeed by the early 1950s the RCIR had virtually disbanded. Winifred Sneddon, president of the RCIR, reported that "the organization wilted soon after" the new officers were elected in 1952. As McCarthyism checked activism of all kinds, groups like the RCIR and the NAACP retrenched or died off. The RCIR folded, but the NAACP remained; it ousted its radical faction and distanced itself from groups that were regarded as leftist. Blaming the political climate for the "coup" that drove black and white militants out of the NAACP, Cleophas Brown recalled: "That's when there was lots of red baiting." The more progressive ones "just got fed up and left."[39]

In 1952 the director of western field services for the National Urban League noted the changes in the Richmond branch: "The picture . . . is a much more calm one. The NAACP has undergone some reorganization and is beginning to reach real strength in membership and finance. The President and some of the members of the Executive Board are well informed, astute men, capable of running a sound program." By 1954 the "radical era" in the Richmond NAACP appears to have ended. That year president Lofton L. Fowler and secretary Hazel Hall rejected the membership applications of Cleophas Brown and his wife, Ursula (refunding their $6.50 membership fees and a $5.00 "contribution"), explaining: "Do to pass [sic] record of the Branch under your leadership as President, the Executive Committee voted unanimously to refund said money for the best welfare of the Branch [sic]." In 1956 Dr. Paul T. Robinson became president. He attempted to steer the organization in a new direction: "They were more interested in teas and banquets, being seen with white people."[40]

Even as black Richmondites attempted to form interracial alliances, they sometimes found themselves at odds with white supporters who

appeared to be patronizing and insensitive. The struggle for control of
the North Richmond Neighborhood House illuminates this dilemma.
The San Francisco branch of the American Friends Service Committee
(AFSC) had operated field missions in North Richmond since the late
1940s, working with the residents on upgrading housing and improving
living conditions. In 1950 the AFSC selected Percy Baker, an African
American social worker, to establish and serve as executive director of
the North Richmond Neighborhood House. Baker and his wife lived
and worked there for almost a year. The Neighborhood House became a
community fixture, providing a meeting place for a number of community organizations. For example, the City-Wide Mission, which "drew
support from most of the Negro Baptist and Methodist churches in
Richmond," maintained storage space in the Neighborhood House for
their sewing, mending, and charitable projects. The Neighborhood
House also offered after-school tutorial programs, prenatal programs,
and day-care facilities.[41]

However, the Neighborhood House met with opposition from some
black religious leaders who feared that its programs, dances, and other
coeducational activities would diminish youthful piety and supplant
their traditional influence among North Richmond residents. As a result,
a number of religious leaders and laypeople withheld support from the
Neighborhood House for ten years. The Neighborhood House encountered nonreligious opposition as well. Some North Richmond residents
believed that the center was "controlled by a bunch of outsiders," who
advocated postwar urban renewal policies that targeted African Americans. Therefore North Richmond residents demanded that the Neighborhood House's board of directors include community members.[42]

When illness eventually forced Percy Baker to resign, the executive
board appointed Edwin "Red" Stephenson, a "Caucasian converted
from his Southern background," to replace him. Dynamic and generally
sympathetic to the plight of African Americans, Stephenson refused to
live in the community with his family, which angered black residents: "I
didn't think North Richmond was a fit place for children to be growing
up." As he saw it, his job was "to help people obtain some of the same
choices in life that [his family] enjoyed." That included the ability to
"exercise our choice" not to "live . . . in North Richmond with our
kids." Black residents who had invested money, labor, and love in their
North Richmond homes found Stephenson's attitude offensive.[43]

Calls for community control of the Neighborhood House increased,
and in the 1960s Stephenson was forced to resign. Lucretia Edwards, a

former Neighborhood House social worker, recalled: "He forgot about involving people and the people of North Richmond threw him out." Margaret Starks recalled the mood of black Richmondites: "It was those black people who were fed up with taking second. Fired up and not going to take no more. You know, just like 'I'm black and I'm proud.' Way back in the forties and fifties." Cleophas Brown observed: "If it wasn't for us laying out on the line, nobody would have jumped on the band wagon."[44]

Despite their attempts at interracial coalition building, black Richmondites of all classes and economic statuses found that race contextualized virtually every important life decision in the postwar era. It became the central mobilizing factor for black postwar activism. Racial solidarity, though tenuous, resulted in some of the first breaches in Richmond's racial status quo. Nowhere was this assault on Jim Crow more evident than in the struggles waged by black Richmondites to live where they desired.[45] While new, segregated housing developments sprang up in and on the periphery of Richmond, the majority of black Richmondites continued to live in the cramped projects. African Americans were also being channeled into segregated housing like the Las Deltas project (built in 1949) in the unincorporated area of North Richmond or into the area known as the "Black Crescent" (located along the western edge of the city, separated from the main part of Richmond by the physical boundaries of the Eastshore Freeway, the Santa Fe Railroad spur, the Southern Pacific tracks, and the main line of the Santa Fe Railroad; see map 3). Others placed themselves on public housing waiting lists or left the city entirely. Black Richmondites, employing the "new street politics of the picket line" and drawing on their growing political clout, intensified their demands for fair housing. This issue prompted blacks to test Richmond's postwar political waters.[46]

California Voice columnist Louis Campbell noted that the "influx of gobs of new sepia citizens" translated into a "new complexion on things political around the Bay Area." Black votes could not be "sought (and bought) by the ancient method of 'greasing' a few white-haired 'Uncle Thomas' types who held lowly jobs around city hall." African Americans in Richmond and around the bay were now demanding a quid pro quo from white politicians in exchange for their increasingly valuable votes.[47]

Black Richmondites began to enter the political arena as the city experienced a decline in overall voter turnout. In 1947 Walter Freeman Jr. and labor activist Louis Richardson declared their candidacies for city

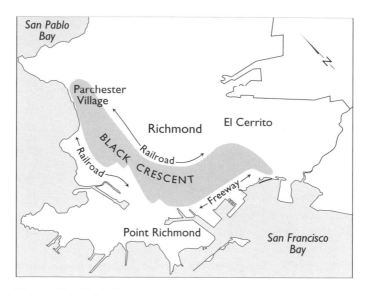

Map 3. The Black Crescent.

council because "It was time to put the colored side out. Housing was the main issue; jobs and everything like that." The *Richmond Independent* noted that of the five candidates running for the council, "two . . . are colored. The first time in the city's history that a person of the colored race has sought a council post." Moreover, Freeman and Richardson opposed each other in a primary contest that pitted an old-timer against a newcomer.[48]

The *Independent* characterized Richardson as a "newcomer to the city who has resided here for three years and who has the support of the left wingers." He ran on a platform that called for fair housing and employment practices, public control of Richmond's waterfront, and the elimination of the sales tax. Freeman was described as a "Richmond resident for 33 years who attended the local schools and who has the support of the right wing element in the colored section."[49] The *Independent*'s analysis of the candidates' bases of support oversimplified the differences between the two men, failing to take into account their numerous overlapping community affiliations and experiences. For example, both men belonged to local churches, were members of various social and benevolent organizations, were active members of the NAACP, and were outspoken opponents of employment and housing segregation. Most importantly, Freeman recalled, "we were both black and knew the score."

Of the 21,000 registered city voters, about 9,000 actually voted in the at-large primary. Richardson "made fifth place in a seven-man race," garnering 2,391 votes from "those precincts . . . in the area of the housing projects in the city." In the May runoff elections, James Kenny, Richardson's white union colleague, won a seat on the council, but Richardson did not. Walter Freeman Jr. polled only 852 votes, not enough to win a place on the ballot.[50]

Black voter response to the candidates shows how rapidly and profoundly black newcomers had been incorporated into the life of the community and how they now defined the postwar black community. Richardson's strongest support came from the predominantly black, politically ripe housing project residents. In the past the "traditionally influential group in city politics" tended to ignore project tenants "as participants in determining the future of housing in Richmond." The war boom changed this. The projects were now "political gold" for progressive candidates who could identify with and articulate black newcomers' aspirations. Black old-timers had become an irrelevant numerical minority in postwar Richmond. Walter Freeman Jr. recalled his difficulty in campaigning in the projects: "I gave a speech at one of the projects and people from the south side didn't know me. I told them how long I'd been in the city and they didn't believe me. I figured if they didn't believe me, wasn't no use in me running." He received votes "mostly from people who knew me before." The postwar black political voice had become the voice of the newcomers.[51]

Newcomer political potential was at the heart of the postwar deal making that resulted in the construction of new housing for black Richmondites. Parchester Village, a development built in northwest Richmond in 1949, was the first subdivision in the city where blacks could purchase homes. The deal that was struck was an attempt by black Richmondites to flex their political muscle, but it represented a compromise on the issue of residential desegregation. Louisiana migrant Guthrie John Williams, who had come to Richmond in 1942 to work as a joiner in the shipyards, was a principal player in the birth of Parchester Village. Williams, an accomplished carpenter whose application to the carpenters' union had been rejected when he arrived in Richmond, involved himself in a variety of activities dedicated to smashing segregation. In addition to founding and pastoring the Mt. Carmel Missionary Baptist Church in 1944 and presiding over the Interdenominational Ministerial Alliance, the Reverend Williams founded the Universal Non-Partisan League, which focused on desegregating Richmond's stores and businesses.[52]

In 1949 Williams made a bid for the city council but lost in the primary. His influence among black voters persuaded at least one white politician to court him, however. Amos Hinkley, incumbent council member and protégé of developer Fred Parr, eagerly sought the votes of blacks who had supported Williams. Hinkley approached Williams hoping to obtain the endorsement of the Universal Non-Partisan League and the Interdenominational Ministerial Alliance. In return, Williams and the Reverend Moses Bradford of the alliance extracted from Hinkley a promise to arrange a meeting with Parr to discuss the critical problem of black housing. Hinkley also agreed to give top priority to the issue of black housing upon his reelection to city council. Despite strong support from black voters, Hinkley was defeated but kept his commitment and introduced Williams and Bradford to Parr: "We were supposed to have 20 minutes with him and we wound up spending about an hour and 20 minutes. We talked about housing and jobs for minorities. . . . When I found out Parr was a Methodist, I told him, 'If you were a Baptist, I would have kept your head under water long enough where you would come up doing right.' That got a good laugh from him." Parr agreed to finance a housing development on sixty-seven acres of his unincorporated land near Point Pinole between the Santa Fe and Southern Pacific tracks "just across from the Richmond Golf Club." The development consisted of 409 houses and was advertised as an integrated "home community for all Americans."[53]

John and Gladys Jordan moved to Richmond in 1942 and were among the first residents of Parchester Village when it opened in 1950. The Jordans recalled that Parchester Village had been conceived initially as an integrated development because "black people who moved into the Village wouldn't have wanted to go into an all black community." They noted that some whites made deposits on the homes but withdrew them because they were not "ready to accommodate the dream of a multiracial community." Other black Richmondites explained that Parr and other developers had no intention of building an integrated community. Rather, the development was merely an attempt by white politicians and power brokers in Richmond to maintain residential segregation while appearing to appease black demands. Williams and Bradford "made the best of a bad situation."[54]

Whatever the circumstances, Parchester Village became home to middle- and working-class blacks who enthusiastically welcomed the housing. Some praised Parr as "a man who looks one hundred year[s] into the future." One resident even composed a poem. Parchester Village residents believed that the development was an oasis in an otherwise bleak housing situation. Resident Henry Hornsby recalled: "It was the realization of a dream for most, because homeowners in other neighborhoods signed restrictive covenants, banning them from selling to blacks."[55]

Many whites, however, doubted that Parchester residents were capable of handling the responsibilities of home ownership. Gladys Jordan recalled that "some people predicted [we] would live like animals there." John Jordan noted that the skeptics "underestimated our political sophistication. [We] made sure that we had access to these [government] people." From the beginning, the residents established internal leadership in the form of the Parchester Village Improvement Association, which comprised dues-paying homeowners who "put pressure" on the county for services (see figure 20). They successfully lobbied to obtain street lighting and sewage, telephone, and transportation services. In 1963 the residents voted for annexation to Richmond in order to receive services in Richmond instead of in the smaller city of San Pablo. Politically, Parchester Villagers were "conservative, content to work within the system" to get what they needed. They placed high priority on attending city and county government meetings to push for funding for their neighborhood. John Jordan explained: "Every time there was a City Council meeting, we packed the hall and let them know that we were the heaviest voting precinct."[56]

From the beginning, Parchester Village children had attended Lake and Bayview Elementary Schools, which were integrated. In 1959, the San Pablo school district, in which Parchester Village was located, proposed placing all Parchester Village children in Lake Elementary School. Parchester parents opposed the new plan, arguing that Lake would become a "de facto segregated school." They formed a citizens committee that met with the school board to study the issue during the summer of 1959. The pressure brought by Parchester Village parents persuaded the school board to adopt a plan that divided Parchester Village students between Lake and Bayview schools, thus preserving a racial balance in both.[57]

Parchester Village residents also initiated a number of community programs that reinforced their sense of collective strength and individual accomplishment. In 1950 the Parchester Veterans' Wives Club bought a house in the tract and converted it into a recreation center where residents held meetings, celebrated birthdays, and commemorated special anniversaries. The Parchester Hall of Fame in the recreation center honored the educational and career accomplishments of Parchester residents, paying special attention to the "generations coming up." Mary Simmons, an early Parchester resident and member of the Veterans' Wives Club, recalled that Parchester Baptist Church was the place "where a lot of those seeds of self worth got planted" for many black children. The church's activities insured that the "flowers of Parchester weren't left to grow wild."[58]

Thus, Parchester Village developed out of a bargain between politically awakened black Richmondites and white power brokers who had begun to court the black vote. While the collaboration did not end residential segregation, it represented an important milestone in which politically astute black Richmondites took "advantage of a bad situation and made something out of it." Many, like Cleophas Brown, believed that it "meant just the beginning of a new day." Clearly, Parchester Village represented much more than a place to live. It offered African Americans tangible proof of their strength as a community and of their expanding political relevance in the larger population.[59]

The exercise of political power was one strategy in black Richmondites' assault on Jim Crow. African Americans also tackled the problem individually, opening up new opportunities for all blacks. Wilbur and Vesper Wheat, who in 1950 were still living in an apartment in "that Harbor Gate shack," decided for the sake of their children to take matters into their own hands. They moved from the project to a spacious thirty-seven-hundred-dollar home in the white suburb of El Sobrante, adjacent to Richmond. Although Wilbur made no attempt to conceal his race, he was able to purchase the house only because the real estate agent and former owners "mistook [him] for someone else. They thought [he] was another race." Their white neighbors learned the truth, however, when "the guy that had been trying to buy the place" voiced his suspicions to the real estate agents after the transaction had been concluded. Whites "went down to the place and said 'why are you selling places to those damn niggers?'" The agents said, "'I don't think they're niggers. I think they're foreigners or something.' They said, 'hell no, they're niggers!'" The hostility escalated when the Wheats moved into their new home: "We had a little trouble. When the kids started into school they rocked my door. When the kids started at high school they had a few rounds over there." Undaunted, Wilbur and Vesper Wheat remained to raise their children and several grandchildren. Wilbur observed, "they never scared us out."[60]

In March 1952, former shipyard worker Wilbur Gary concluded that he, his wife, and seven children had "outgrown the four-room wartime housing project unit" in which they had lived for eight years. Gary, a contractor with a growing business, persuaded a white intermediary to negotiate the purchase of a three-bedroom house at 2821 Brook Way in the segregated Rollingwood district of Richmond. When the family arrived, their neighbors "watched in little curious groups while Gary and friends moved furniture into the white frame house" that they had purchased for $8,750. However, curiosity turned to violence as a mob of three hundred whites stood outside the residence shouting racial epithets and hurling bricks. Elton Brombacher, a white resident and co-founder (with the Reverend Fred Busher of Easter Hill Methodist Church) of Richmond's National Council of Christians and Jews recalled: "It was incredible. . . . hundreds of people surrounded the home to harass the family." The activity culminated with a cross burning on the lawn. Fearing for their safety but distrustful of local law enforcement officials (who had permitted the rioting to continue for two days), the Garys beseeched the NAACP for help.[61]

The Richmond NAACP organized twenty-four-hour guard vigils consisting of friends of the Gary family, NAACP members, members of the leftist Civil Rights Congress, and a few white neighbors. Wilbur Wheat, a vigil participant, recalled that "we all went down there to protect them. We had a big meeting down there to raise money too."[62] Elton Brombacher and Fred Busher joined in because "it was time the council stood up for the [Gary] family." The two men "went out and stood in front of the house that night." Busher carried the U.S. flag, and Brombacher held a flashlight so that he could read the preamble to the Constitution. Brombacher recalled: "I was so scared I couldn't hold the flashlight steady. The mobs were throwing rocks over our heads; they spat on us; they called us names."[63]

Noting the reluctance of local law enforcement authorities to respond, Franklin H. Williams, NAACP West Coast regional secretary, successfully prevailed upon Governor Earl Warren and state attorney general Robert W. Kenny to order the Richmond police and county sheriff's departments to provide the family with protection. The violence diminished, but white attitudes did not change. In an effort to "settle up the whole matter amicably" in a "calm and restrained way," the white Rollingwood Improvement Association offered to buy back the house from the Garys at a profit of over one thousand dollars. Wilbur Gary rejected the offer, declaring, "Money won't buy it. They made me the goat. I'm going to stick with it." Franklin H. Williams publicly invited the Rollingwood Improvement Association to file a lawsuit against the Garys or the house seller, so that the courts could reaffirm the "basic American principle established by the NAACP in our restrictive covenant cases that courts will not and cannot use their powers to maintain racially restrictive neighborhoods."[64]

A 1952 National Urban League study concluded that since the Gary incident "Negroes have been afraid to buy" where "homes have become available for Negroes in white areas." However, black Richmondites persisted in their fight for open housing. These struggles, so crucial to all African Americans, tended to erode the divisions between old-timers and newcomers. Cleophas Brown noted that "even people who may not have had the funds to move into those homes knew it was in their best interest to fight." Margaret Starks recalled: "Communists, Uncle Toms, preachers and everybody had to pull together. Where you were born wasn't the issue, but where you could go was the problem."[65]

Individual black Richmondites, in their quest for decent housing, opened up new opportunities for the entire black community, galvanized widespread support, and found a "strange but potent ally in the anti-Communist fervor that gripped the country." A report by the Richmond NAACP noted that the "Branch Officers fought for the right of the Gary family to live in the area and not be intimidated by people who don't believe in the American way of life, and not be miss lead by the Communist [*sic*]." Black Richmondites pressed their grievances through the courts and in the streets, invoking their constitutional guarantees within the context of the Cold War.[66]

Because race remained the overwhelming criterion by which whites evaluated and defined them, postwar black Richmondites, like eastern and midwestern blacks in the late nineteenth and early twentieth centuries, were forced to agitate for empowerment and advancement as *blacks* first, minimizing class or economic distinctions. Thus, black Richmondites functioned within two concurrent realities. The white reality, which imposed external restraints, saw only their skin color. Blacks also struggled with the reality of intraracial divisions that imposed their own constraints. Black Richmondites, desiring equal treatment in the larger society, chose the useful strategy of projecting the white view of them as racially monolithic.

This model only partially explains black activism in the postwar era, however. African American agency was an interplay of individualism and collectivism. Racial congregation was only one tactic in a range of resistance strategies employed by black people in Richmond. They engaged in racially based activities to legitimize their presence and affirm their worth in a society that devalued them as a group. However, in doing so they also created channels through which individual accomplishments could be nurtured and celebrated. Black institutions and activities gave men and women the opportunity to take pride in "a family well fed . . . , a congregation led joyfully in song[,] . . . a child graduated from high school," or a move to a new home. Thus, racial self-consciousness provided the context for group action and achievement, but it did not delimit individual possibilities. Margaret Starks noted: "We each had to do what we could. You put that little bit together, then you have something in this world."[67]

Black Richmondites came into political and social power in the 1960s, but the immediate postwar period proved to be the crucial "take off" period for their major political and social progress. Though modest compared to those of Oakland, Berkeley, and San Francisco, Richmond's professional base expanded during the 1950s as black teachers, lawyers, and doctors settled in the city alongside blue-collar residents.[68] Oklahoma native George Livingston came to Richmond as a teenager with his parents in 1952. He would become Richmond's first directly elected black mayor in the early 1960s, but he recalled that in the postwar period "black people did not talk about politics in the home because most assumed they wouldn't be able to enter into it." Livingston was also struck by the absence of black professional and middle-class role models in the city: "Back in Oklahoma we saw black teachers, doctors, lawyers, things like that. Here the only guys with suits on were white." Former state assemblyman John Knox, who came to Richmond in 1952 as a young attorney, found that "there were no blacks in banks, in retail outlets, in department stores. Their absence [was] especially noticeable in the retail industry." Elton Brombacher recalled, "there were no blacks in so-called 'cushy' positions. They were given jobs that whites didn't want."[69]

Young black people had few alternatives to the usual pastimes of "fighting on the weekend" with kids from other cities, going to church, or dancing in the local clubs. Joseph Griffin III recalled that the military presented an exciting alternative to some young black men: "A friend of mine we called Floopy Dupe was from out of town, back South. . . . He was staying out here in North Richmond . . . when I first ran into him in his uniform. . . . He just looked so good in his khaki uniform. I said that's what I wanted! I told my mama, 'it's the Airborne for me!' So me and my partner went. Boy and we did it, three years! And it was enjoyable, the paratroopers."[70]

Griffin recalled the racially unbalanced curriculum in the public schools he attended in the 1950s: "The teachers were all white. Education wise, we didn't know . . . anything that much about black history. The only thing they told us about was Columbus and how he discovered America, and you know, the Caucasians, whatever the nationality, but nothing about black history. I was really kept in the dark to it."[71]

This environment set the stage for the emergence of black entrepreneurial, professional, and middle classes in Richmond. Odis Cotright and Willie Mae Gilbert Cotright came from Louisiana to Richmond in 1944. Son of a Selma, Louisiana, sharecropper, Odis had studied biology at Southern University for almost three years. He had also gained practical business experience from years of working in dry cleaning establishments in Louisiana and Berkeley. In 1954 the Cotrights opened their grocery and variety store at Fifth and Barrett in Richmond, serving both black and white customers and taking in forty-five dollars the first day. It was the first black business to be opened in downtown Richmond.[72]

Unlike the family-oriented black concerns in prewar Richmond, the Cotrights' venture represented a shift in attitude toward the function and purpose of business ownership but echoed the philosophies of self-help and cooperation expounded several decades earlier by Booker T. Washington and Marcus Garvey. Odis Cotright regarded business ownership not only as a livelihood for individual black community members but also as a means of advancing the economic, social, and political fortunes of blacks in the city. Convinced that blacks with higher educational and technical training had the responsibility to share their knowledge with others in the community, Odis Cotright organized an unofficial black chamber of commerce, providing technical and financial assistance to would-be entrepreneurs. Through personal loans and technical assistance, he helped friends, residents, and former employees establish businesses ranging from pharmacies to dry cleaning establishments. For example, James McMillan, who was Richmond's first black pharmacist and later won a seat on the city council, "received invaluable support and aid" from Cotright before he opened his own practice downtown. McMillan recalled: "We all sort of looked at Odis as a father figure" who had the "technical expertise, financial generosity, and vision" for the entire community.[73]

The first black professionals entered the Richmond community during the 1950s and began to shape the expectations of all black Richmondites. Bay Area labor activist and civil rights leader Matt Crawford explained: "Beginning in the 1950s the community began to jell. They were influenced by the civil rights movement. The middle class developed.

Professionals got schooling. We got economic stability." The change appeared to be occurring in new and unheard-of areas in the city. For example, blacks were being hired in law enforcement for the first time as improved police-community relations became an increasingly higher priority in the postwar era. Officers Lonnie Washington and Douglas Ellison came on to the Richmond police force in 1946 and 1947, respectively, and were a source of community pride. However, the number of black police officers never exceeded more than seven out of a total force of over one hundred officers. In 1952 the Richmond school district hired fifteen black teachers, including two principals, most of whom taught in the city's predominantly black schools. The Richmond school board, which made personnel, policy, administrative, and promotion decisions, would remain all-white for the next three decades, except for a brief temporary appointment of a black board member, Terry Hatter, in the mid-1960s.[74]

The postwar era saw the growth of Richmond's black medical profession as well. Samuel Weeks, a graduate of Howard University Medical School, came to Richmond in 1946 and began his medical practice at nearby Brookside Hospital. For more than three months Weeks tried to obtain office space in downtown Richmond only to be stonewalled by real estate firms who "have agreed they will not rent or sell to a Negro in any of the downtown areas." An NAACP report noted that the Council on Civic Unity had "taken this as its task and [proposed] to find and secure an office for [Weeks]." In the meantime, Weeks shared an office with Dr. Ross, a "white woman physician" who agreed to "allow him to remain there until he can secure quarters." Through the intervention of white intermediaries and with pressure from the NAACP on city government, Weeks was able to set up private practice in downtown Richmond, where he served a racially integrated clientele.[75]

Within seven years Richmond gained another black physician. In 1953 Arkansas native and Meharry Medical College graduate Paul T. Robinson settled in Richmond to practice surgery at Brookside. In addition to running his medical practice, Robinson became active in community and civil rights affairs, eventually becoming president of the NAACP. In 1954 James McMillan left Portland, Oregon, where "black pharmacists were not being hired," and moved to Richmond, where he worked in Brookside and various county medical clinics. He went into practice with Dr. Weeks. With the help of a white colleague who acted as a go-between, McMillan was able to buy a downtown building in 1960, where he and Weeks practiced for a decade.[76]

Though black Richmondites found the road to the middle class and to professional occupations fraught with difficulty, it appears that black women (who slightly outnumbered men 6,855 to 6,519 in 1950) had even fewer options. Excluding teachers, black women in Richmond had few professional role models. They often had to struggle against racial and gender discrimination, with the latter sometimes emanating from their own race. As soon as the war was over the country shifted gears and the government waged a well-orchestrated propaganda campaign to persuade millions of "Rosie the Riveters" to turn in their hard hats and welding gear for frying pans and baby bottles. Radio and magazine advertisements, popular fiction, motion pictures, and even medical advice commanded women to relinquish their jobs to returning veterans and content themselves with hearth and home.

While millions of women acquiesced, a significant portion of married women with children, compelled by economic necessity, continued to work outside the home, thus changing the face of the American workforce indelibly. Economic and social circumstances made postwar hearth and home propaganda unrealistic if not undesirable for the majority of black women. Compared to white women, black women continued in the workforce in greater numbers. In 1950 one-third of married black women worked outside the home, compared to one-quarter of all married women in the population as a whole. Historian Jacqueline Jones has noted that "to most black women, regardless of class, work seemed to form an integral part of the female role." [77]

Yet it appears that in Richmond some black men, motivated by a desire to regulate the quality and degree of women's participation in the postwar labor force, expressed a racially modified version of the government's propaganda. They objected not to women's working outside the home but to their seeking employment in areas outside traditional spheres of black female labor. Historically, the dual toil of black women enriched the "supply of cheap labor" in the marketplace and sustained "their own kin groups" in the home. World War II had given black women options that were now being threatened in the postwar period. Margaret Starks explained: "Black women have always worked. Washing clothes for white people, cooking, cleaning. But after the war jobs got tight again and some of these men got crazy again." Some black women in Richmond "had to fight their husbands, boyfriends and fathers who most times wanted them to just work at certain jobs." Citing her own situation as typical of that of many others, Starks recalled, "[My husband] didn't want me to work in the shipyards" and "didn't like me trying to publish a newspaper either. I had to work and I wasn't going to work as no maid! Not here!" [78]

In truth, black women in postwar Richmond, like black men, found themselves forced back into unemployment or low paying domestic and service jobs as war industries shut down and postwar recession hit. Black women in Richmond settled into a postwar cycle of "day work" in the homes and kitchens of whites or worked seasonal cannery and factory jobs. However, some found ways to break out of this pattern. Margaret Starks recalled that after the war a number of women "wanted to go to nursing school" but could not persuade their husbands or fathers. "Some couldn't afford it, and then you might not get hired if they did." One woman overcame these impediments by using her earnings as a proprietor of a brothel and after hours club in North Richmond to finance her education. She "put herself through nursing school and sent her daughter to nursing school." Eventually both women were hired as practical nurses at Brookside Hospital. They were "good nurses, some of the best Contra Costa [County] ever had too and her husband didn't have a word to say."[79]

Vera Beratta became a postwar businesswoman, deriving a comfortable income from a small grocery store she owned in North Richmond. In addition to running that enterprise, Beratta bought the Pink Kitchen, which did a brisk business as a nightspot and eatery and an even brisker one renting out "the cottages she had out in back" to people who "needed a place to stay." The cottages, "rented by the hour," were rumored to cater to prostitutes and their clients. Minnie Lue Nichols became an influential and politically connected businesswoman as the owner of a successful nightclub and restaurant in North Richmond. Her establishment became a meeting place for musicians, politicians, and even the black Interdenominational Ministerial Alliance.[80]

In the postwar era, civil rights groups like the NAACP and the Congress of Racial Equality (CORE) stepped up their legal attacks on the separate-but-equal doctrine that had been in place since 1896. Their cases comprised the litigation that resulted in the 1954 *Brown v. Board of Education of Topeka, Kansas,* ruling that ordered the desegregation of the nation's public schools. The winds that blew through the nation's consciousness, sweeping aside old notions of racial superiority, gradualism, and separation, were propelled by the deliberate and systematic efforts of thousands of determined black Americans. These winds swept through Richmond as well. Black Richmondites joined their national counterparts and at times stood at the forefront of postwar transformations. Cleophas Brown identified *Brown v. Board of Education* as the point at which "black folks in Richmond saw the light" and really began to "believe they could break through."[81]

Benefiting from an increased black population, a rising tide of Democratic voter registration, and support from white progressives around the Bay Area, black Richmondites began to break the grip that the white establishment exerted on the city's political life.[82] Black voter registration became a grassroots, community-wide effort, involving individuals and community institutions: "The Chlora Hayes Sledge Club was the focal point. Then the Elks. They all branched out. We all worked. As I say, we registered so many voters that at poll time all the people hadn't voted. It was two o'clock the next afternoon before all those folks got to vote!"[83]

Political fervor, Democratic demographics, and the optimism of the civil rights movement inspired several black Richmondites to enter politics. George Livingston attributed a 1963 visit to Richmond by Dr. Martin Luther King Jr. to his decision to seek a city council seat. Livingston, a twenty-nine-year-old shipyard worker and member of the city planning commission, sought King's advice and was encouraged to run. Livingston was defeated in his 1963 bid but was elected to the council in 1965, where he served for twelve years. He attributed his victory to "hard work by whites and blacks." Livingston recalled that the "time was right for blacks to challenge the political waters." Subsequently, three other black Richmondites were elected to the city council.[84]

The political career of George Carroll, a cum laude graduate of Brooklyn Law School who moved to Richmond in 1952 to practice law, symbolized the hopes of most black Richmondites. Carroll's rise focused attention on black postwar demands and helped close intraracial conflict. His election to the city council represented a synthesis of old and new and mirrored the optimism of the integrationist phase of the civil rights movement. In the course of his career, Carroll served as a legal representative in union desegregation cases, participated in the NAACP, and worked with black youth: "I became involved partly because I felt I'd give back to my community some of the great opportunities I had as a young man growing up." In 1959 George Carroll made his first run for city council. He recalled that "the ministers and other leaders in the black community got together for the first time then to put up a united front in backing a candidate for the council. . . . The choice came down to the Rev[erend] Wilbur Johnson, a Methodist minister, and myself. I was chosen, and I ran and lost."[85]

Two year later in 1961, the thirty-eight-year-old Carroll became the second black person voted onto a Bay Area city council. He campaigned on a platform that emphasized human rights and inspired the enthusiasm of African Americans and the cautious approval of whites, who characterized him as "scholarly, articulate and soft spoken." An array of black clergy (including the Richmond Interdenominational Ministerial Alliance, the Baptist Union, and the Greater Richmond Interfaith Program) endorsed him, calling for his election from Sunday morning pulpits and collecting special offerings for his campaign. Carroll recalled: "They were very active. They gave me money and workers and had people out walking precincts for me."[86] Margaret Starks campaigned for him: "Oh my God, he was a shoo-in! Everybody loved him. We just worked, honey. We hit the streets, went door-to-door, saw that everybody was registered. We went all over the county. On election day we went and knocked on doors and brought the people to the polls in cars."[87]

George Carroll came into office on the rising tide of a strong Democratic coalition that swept three Republican incumbents from office and ushered in an era of liberal coalition politics in Richmond. Although the new Democratic coalition did not make explicit policy commitments to blacks, white political liberals understood Carroll's unique position as liaison to the vote-rich, heavily Democratic black community. Moreover, Carroll's achievements eased intraracial divisions in the community. An easterner, he was accepted by longtime black residents as "someone with culture and education." Black newcomers found him to be "like neutral territory because [he] was from New York, the East. Someone who didn't have no ax to grind." His demonstrated commitment to community concerns and his impeccable professional credentials made him an "equalizer" who was "loyal to blacks but could handle whites on their own level." Margaret Starks explained that he "knitted everyone together. . . . Everyone knew that he was honest, educated, and good. You had confidence in him."[88]

George Carroll's key contribution while a councilman was the creation of the Richmond Commission on Human Relations. One of the first municipal bodies of its kind in the country, the commission in 1964 led the fight against California's Proposition 14 initiative, which called for a special election to repeal the Rumford Fair Housing Act, which had struck down racial discrimination in housing. Despite strong opposition from the commission and an array of civic and political organizations, 56 percent of Richmond voters voted for Proposition 14. Three years later, after a long legal battle, Proposition 14 (which had become Article 1, Section 26 of the California Constitution) was overturned by the state supreme court, whose ruling was upheld by the United States Supreme Court.[89]

George Carroll's election represented a synthesis of newcomer energy, black activism, and political maturity. It spoke to the egalitarian, integrationist vision most black Richmondites came to embrace in the decades following World War II. In 1964 the city council unanimously elected George Carroll to serve as Richmond's first black mayor (a position he held until he resigned to accept a judgeship in Richmond's Bay Municipal Court in 1965). In his mayoral address Carroll framed his political achievements within the optimism of the civil rights movement: "I view this as another step in the unfolding drama in America where a man is judged on his work as an individual and not on the color of his skin." [90]

In 1963, two years after George Carroll's election, a Democratic coalition won control of the city council. It appeared that black Richmondites had finally won a place on the civic agenda and would now be in a position to shape it. Margaret Starks recalled: "Before all the riots and before they killed Dr. King," black people "thought that just to get elected was a major breakthrough and would make a difference for all." They believed that "If *nobody* did it, you can go to the polls and do what you want to do. Don't talk about it. Just go in there and do it!" Cleophas Brown noted: "That song they sung, Ain't Gonna Let Nobody Turn Me 'Round, that was how the colored people really felt, keep on walking [and] talking!" [91]

African Americans' wartime gains and the postwar demobilization that threatened to erode those gains spurred black Richmondites to challenge the system that barred them from full economic and political participation. They employed the language and tactics of the civil rights movement to press their demands. In 1963, two years before the Los Angeles ghetto of Watts exploded with the rage of people frustrated by the glacial pace of progress, three years before fights among black and white high school students ignited rioting throughout Richmond, and five years before Martin Luther King Jr.'s assassination virtually extinguished hope for a "Beloved Community," most black Richmondites were willing to maintain, at least temporarily, faith in the civil rights vision that was transforming the nation. [92]

CHAPTER 5

Traditions from Home

Now Richmond, California is a great little town
And I live there and, Jack, I gets around.
If you ever go there and you want to jump for joy,
I'll tell you where to go that's the Club Savoy.
Jimmy McCracklin,
"Club Savoy"

World War II dispersed African Americans throughout the country and disseminated African American cultural expressions in the larger society. As black men and women entered the urban industrial workforce via the war and became residents of the Golden State, they were sustained by cultural traditions, most of them deeply rooted in the southern agrarian matrix. Folk healing, blues and gospel music, Pentecostal or "Holy Ghost" religious styles, social clubs based on regional origin, and participation in sports became the cultural fabric of the black community in Richmond. Black working-class cultural expressions transformed the African American community and were themselves transformed in the process. The cultural evolution reflected changes in black political and social realities in Richmond and the nation.

African American migrants to Richmond came looking for the California dream, which promised economic advancement and greater freedom. However, few were willing to abandon their cultural and social traditions. The traditions were anchored in an African and African American southern ethos that valued communality, spontaneity, and individual expressiveness. Historian Herbert G. Gutman has suggested that cultural traditions and institutions, far from being curious carryovers or anachronistic survivals of an earlier time, represent a kind of resource that workers have drawn upon in their struggle against employers and others who would deny them equal treatment. "Traditions from home" provided black Richmondites with culturally sanctioned channels through which they could confront and unravel new urban complexities and contradictions just as they had done in the Jim Crow South. The processes of migration and urbanization did not lead to a breakdown of African American primary groups or social mores. Rather, the black community was sustained and invigorated by cultural resources that gave them access to power, even as the larger society attempted to render it powerless.[1]

The newcomers' retention of folk healing practices illustrates the role and function of culture in their transition to life in California. Of necessity, many blacks resorted to folk healing traditions, despite the availability of professional medical treatment for shipyard employees and their families, because racist policies barred them from local hospitals and physicians. Beryl Reid was forced to take her son to a hospital in Martinez, twenty miles away, "to have a two-inch wooden splinter removed from his foot" because the local hospital "would not treat blacks." Similarly, Vesper Wheat recalled: "There weren't any black [doctors]. . . . All we had here was Richmond Hospital but you couldn't go there. I took my little girl there when she was three or four, with blood shooting out, but they turned me around at the door." The situation presented a special problem for pregnant women. Because they were not allowed to receive prenatal care or deliver in Richmond hospitals, most African American women turned to other community women to see them through their pregnancies. They "had their babies at home like they were used to [doing] anyway," usually attended by a midwife. Midwives appear to have enjoyed an elevated status among black Richmondites and derived income for services that were in high demand. Georgie Wheat Bonaparte was regarded as an experienced midwife whose skills rivaled those of an obstetrician. Georgie assisted her sister-in-law Vesper Wheat in the home delivery of Vesper and Wilbur Wheat's first child: "She knew a lot about how to handle it because she was from Louisiana. When [the doctor] finally came, the thing was already born. He just cut the navel and said bye-bye." However, home delivery and midwifery faded away when "black doctors finally came to Richmond." Margaret Starks recalled: "The women who helped out with having babies were still around but people didn't call for them anymore. That was too old fashioned. They couldn't make money from that anymore." Thus the medicalization of birth rendered a southern agrarian black tradition virtually obsolete as black physicians moved to Richmond and gained access to medical facilities. Ironically, increased opportunities for black male professionals in Richmond eliminated a uniquely female cultural tradition and economic resource.[2]

Black newcomers were suspicious of other types of professional medical treatment, however. Some feared that the nurses who dispensed inoculations in the North Richmond clinic (which operated in the home of prewar black resident Emma Jarret) were poisoning their children (see figure 21). Margaret Starks recalled: "The people didn't realize [that inoculations were beneficial]. Some of these people were from rural places and never had typhoid shots, measles shots, tuberculosis, nothing." After a "lot of education," they finally accepted the clinic. Nonetheless, black newcomer parents continued to draw on a rich folk pharmacopoeia to treat their children and themselves. For example, many newcomer parents plied their children with horehound candy as a precaution against worms. Some mothers washed their babies' faces in urine-soaked diapers to insure a smooth complexion and to prevent rashes. Others insisted that nosebleeds could be controlled by reading a specific passage from the Bible in a darkened room, and some contended that the "lick of a dog" could heal cuts and scrapes.[3]

Massive doses of "castor oil, salts, calomel and quinine" served as traditional cures for syphilis. The patent medicine Black Draught, touted as a cure for everything from the common cold to impotence, could be found in the medicine cabinets of many black Richmondites. Black longtime residents tended to disparage the folk prescriptions as "old timey" but did not dismiss their effectiveness absolutely. Walter Freeman Jr. noted: "Those folks didn't know any better and had to make do. Some of those country things work, though. Doctors today use lots of them." While reliance on folk treatments was a result of economic necessity, at a deeper level the retention of traditional healing practices allowed black newcomers some control over their environment.[4]

Folk remedies might heal the body, but African American musical traditions from home ministered to the souls of black newcomers. The southern agrarian tradition through which much of black American music has been filtered flows from an older and broader musical context. Black American music is essentially derived from African musical traditions and aesthetics that value communal improvisation, spontaneity, and movement. The fact of slavery altered the African context, scattering African peoples to all points in the New World, but black music retained certain fundamentally African conceptual approaches to creating and performing. The African musical ethos combined with the African American experience to produce black secular and religious music that embraced blues, rhythm and blues, jazz, soul, spirituals, and gospel. Music, the most vital and enduring component of African American culture, represents the most accessible cultural indicator of the state of mind and condition of the black community.

Composer Olly Wilson has suggested that black Americans have managed to "retain some semblance of a unique identity," despite countervailing historical and sociological pressure, by continually "tapping into a basic store of African ways of creating music." These cultural resources lie "buried deep in the [black] collective psyche." This revitalizing process sustained waves of black migrants, from those dispersed in the African diaspora to those who arrived in Richmond, California, in the 1940s and 1950s.[5]

The first wave of black migration during the World War I era and the 1920s transformed black agrarian workers into urban industrial laborers. The music these migrants brought with them evolved from "walking behind a mule way back in slavery times" and was characterized by a strong sense of time and place. Country blues musicians viewed the world in personal terms but represented the sensibilities of all rural black people enmeshed in a system that offered few options. Blues performers served as secular priests/priestesses who received ordination from the people for whom they performed. As a result, the blues developed as a communal expression, dependent on audience participation to validate it, shape it, and pass it along. At the core of the blues tradition was an acceptance of all life's vicissitudes with dignity and style.[6] Migration also urbanized the country blues as blues musicians, serving northern urban audiences, now sang about urban concerns and incorporated amplified guitars, "crying harps," drums, and bass into their repertoires in order to be heard in the larger, noisier big-city dance halls.[7]

African American men and women were equally important as repositories of black culture, both urban and southern rural. When they migrated to California during the World War II era, they transported blues traditions with them. Ironically, blacks arrived in the state in such large numbers that neither housing nor recreational facilities could be built rapidly enough to accommodate California's code of racial separation. While housing discrimination posed the most serious problem, blacks and whites often rubbed elbows in California's night spots. In the Bay Area for example, Slim Jenkins's popular night club and café on Seventh Street in Oakland drew middle-class blacks and whites. Such social mingling may account for the deemphasis of blues content in the styles and repertoires of the black performers who played in clubs like these.[8]

However, black newcomers to Richmond steadfastly demanded the undiluted urban blues. North Richmond's blues clubs were "rough places that catered to a hard-drinking, fast-living black clientele." Many Bay Area blacks regarded them as "honky tonks," "juke joints," and "buckets of blood." Clubs like Tappers Inn, the Savoy Club, the 341, the Brown Derby, the Dew Drop Inn, the Down Beat, the Pink Kitchen, and Minnie Lue's served an array of needs. Besides providing entertainment, food, and drink, some offered personal services like hairdressing and barbering, which were not readily available to blacks elsewhere in the city.[9] Most became as well known for their wide-open atmosphere as for their food and entertainment. Local newspapers blamed the North Richmond clubs for the upsurge of prostitution, gambling, and other crimes. As a teenager, Bill Thurston sneaked into Tappers Inn and was accidentally shot in the leg when a fight broke out. He recalled, "you could do anything you wanted out there. . . . Gambling and all kind of illegal activity went on and people knew about it but there wasn't anything you could do." The formerly quiet, interracial neighborhood taverns of North Richmond were quickly supplanted by the blues clubs where "they'd start cutting up each other. You'd see more people get killed." Margaret Starks who worked as a "peacekeeper" in Tappers Inn, carried a .38 revolver: "We used to have to check the guns and knives just like we did hats and coats." Longtime black residents generally regarded Richmond's blues clubs as unsavory and devoid of middle-class respectability. Nevertheless, middle-class African Americans from around the Bay Area were drawn to them. Ivy Reid Lewis explained: "That's where you went if you wanted to hear good music. Tappers Inn that's where I went. Everybody came to Tappers Inn." Some made surreptitious visits to the North Richmond clubs. Bill Thurston recalled: "If someone of some kind of stature went out there they'd generally have to sneak to go out there."[10]

The Savoy Club on Chesley Street was one of the city's most popular blues spots. After moving to the Bay Area, Oklahoma-born blues guitarist Lowell Fulson did an "extensive residency" at the Savoy in the 1940s and 1950s. He recalled that the club was a "one-room country shack" that sometimes accommodated three hundred people a night. The Savoy was owned and operated by Willie Mae "Granny" Johnson, an Arkansas migrant and sister-in-law of Missouri-born pianist and singer Jimmy McCracklin. Its decor resembled that of an "old road house" with "oil-cloth tablecloths" on wooden tables. The room-length bar served beer and wine, and Granny Johnson served home-cooked meals of greens, ribs, chicken, and other southern cuisine. A house band composed of Bay Area–based musicians alternated with and frequently backed performers such as B. B. King, Charles Brown, L. C. "Good Rocking" Robinson, and Jimmy McCracklin. In addition to the music, dancing, and food, patrons could try their luck at the card and dice games that were fixtures in the club.[11] Jimmy McCracklin paid homage to the Savoy Club in a postwar recording:

Now Richmond, California is a great little town. And I live there and, Jack, I gets around. If you ever go there and you want to jump for joy, I'll tell you where to go that's the Club Savoy. . . . Now everybody goes there to have some fun 'cause the joint really jumps from nine to one. Around midnight everybody is high and in the mood. 'Cause the band starts playing them dirty blues.[12]

Tappers Inn was the most popular night spot in North Richmond from the time it opened in 1941 until its demise in the mid-1950s. Located on Chesley Street, Tappers Inn was owned by East Indian entrepreneur George Bally, known to North Richmond residents as "the Hindu." The club offered a variety of services including round-the-clock barber and beauty shops, a service station that operated all night, and a restaurant that served "southern style" food (see figure 22). Patrons recalled that Tappers Inn was a "very lavish place." The brilliantly polished rectangular bar was twenty-five feet long and fronted a tall mirror that reflected multicolored lights. Red leather booths and tables spread with white linen tablecloths ringed the dance floor, which at times held over six hundred people. Margaret Starks, who booked talent for the club, recalled: "It got so crowded on weekends that we had to take the bar stools out and the people just stood three and four deep at the bar." Patrons jitterbugged and "slow dragged" out on the dance floor to the well-stocked jukebox or to live music played by musicians like Charles Brown, Jimmy Witherspoon, B. B. King, Mabel Scott, and Ivory Joe Hunter. Others engaged in card games like "tonk," poker, and craps or played the slot machines that were set up in the back room.[13]

Minnie Lue Nichols's self-named club also became a blues staple in North Richmond. Before coming to Richmond, Nichols had moved from her native Atlanta to New York, where she worked as a cook in various restaurants in the early 1940s and perfected her culinary skills. She became acquainted with North Richmond while visiting relatives there during the war. In 1948 Nichols moved to North Richmond permanently, where she approached Mr. Brown, the proprietor of a North Richmond restaurant, and asked for a cooking job. He offered to lease her his sagging business for ninety dollars a month, but Nichols, lacking the funds, struck a deal, promising to cook there for three days and improve profits. In return she would gain the lease. She explained: "I didn't have any money to start with and I didn't have anything to lose." Relying only on her talent for cooking and her outgoing personality, Nichols filled the restaurant with "customers [who] kept the jukebox going day and night." In three days the jukebox brought in sixty dollars, more than the owner had "collected from that box in a month previously." This persuaded the owner to advance Nichols forty dollars to "buy the food she needed" to continue operating the restaurant. She opened her own place shortly afterward, and it immediately caught on with black Richmondites (see figure 23). Minnie Lue's featured "home cooking" like "chitterlings, greens, chicken, and sweet potato pies." In addition to "downhome cooking" the club showcased local blues musicians and national celebrities like B. B. King, Bobby "Blue" Bland, Sugar Pie DeSanto, Charles Brown, Jimmy McCracklin, Ray Charles, and James Brown. She kept the jukebox stocked with "all the latest" records.[14]

In the early 1950s Nichols purchased a larger lot and built a new place. She expanded her menu to include "spaghetti and other things" and added a patio for open-air dining. In 1958 Minnie Lue's became the first black establishment in Richmond to obtain a full liquor license. Minnie Lue's remained a community fixture until Nichols's death in 1983, but by the mid-1960s, a new political climate had translated into dwindling audiences for the blues. Nichols recalled that whites who came to her club during that period were intimidated by "black militants, members of the Black Panther Party. They ran all the whites out and really hurt my business." Younger, urban African Americans, calling for black power and cultural nationalism, began to drift away from the musical tradition that had sustained their elders.[15]

Attempts by black Richmondites to achieve power and community control predated the rise of the black power movement, however. Black Richmondites were voicing objections to white entry in and control of their neighborhoods as early as the 1940s. North Richmond was a magnet to many whites, who were drawn by the music, illicit activities, and the "exoticism" of African American life. The blues clubs appear to have been one area in which blacks could exercise authority and achieve a measure of power and economic autonomy, that is, by regulating white access to the cultural and other commodities that were available in North Richmond. Black club owners and operators established the rules by which whites could partake of these things. Margaret Starks recalled: "Well, the whites were scared to come out there. The blacks didn't allow them out here [just] anytime. If they came out, they said they were Mexicans. A taxi couldn't bring them. I didn't allow a white taxi cab company out there because they were prejudiced. . . . When whites came, I told them to come 'round through the back."[16]

This control was evident in the function of the clandestine after hours clubs that usually operated in private homes in North Richmond. After-hours-club "jams" featured local and national musicians and attracted a select clientele. Patrons could purchase home-cooked meals, liquor flowed, and gambling and prostitution were often available. Although most after hours clubs served a racially mixed clientele, some catered to whites only. White men could indulge in sexual liaisons with prostitutes of various races.[17] On a visit to a North Richmond after hours club, Margaret Starks observed members of the Last Man's Club, a social group comprised of white World War I veterans: "It was nice. Nice little furniture and everything. It had a bar and one of these Magnavox things. They'd come there and party. Sometimes they had live music. I was there one time and I saw all these Last Men, all these married men, lawyers and doctors so I never did go back."[18]

North Richmond's blues clubs also served as racial enclaves and staging grounds for outside activities. Like the urban saloons that catered to the European immigrants who poured into the United States in the nineteenth and early twentieth centuries, the blues clubs helped orient African American newcomers to their new urban industrial environment, provided them with a cultural sanctuary, and nurtured their political consciousness. For example, Margaret Starks published the city's first black newspaper, the *Richmond Guide,* from her wartime project apartment on South Thirty-third Street in 1943 but subsequently transferred operations to the clubs she managed in North Richmond. She moved the paper to Tappers Inn at 701 Chesley Street and later to the Blue Haven Cafe at 513 Grove. Starks relocated the newspaper to the clubs because "everybody knew where to find me if they needed something or had something to tell me. Everyone came through those clubs."[19]

Many black newcomers were introduced to their first social activism in the blues clubs. Black Richmondites' wartime campaigns against auxiliary unions germinated in the blues clubs. In 1943 members of the ad hoc committee Shipyard Workers against Discrimination (SWAD) were "meeting over beers" at Tappers to develop their attack on the shipyard auxiliaries. After the Richmond NAACP evolved from SWAD in 1944, Margaret Starks served as secretary of the NAACP from 1944 through 1947 and conducted much of the chapter's business from her clubs. She recalled: "We plotted many strategies there." Similarly, Minnie Lue's became a meeting place for the NAACP and the Richmond Interdenominational Ministerial Alliance in the postwar era.[20]

The blues clubs held another appeal for some African American women in Richmond who found the choice between the shipyards or "somebody's kitchen" still too restrictive. A few enterprising women found avenues of independence in the clubs. Although Richmond's blues clubs and turn-of-the-century white immigrant saloons served similar functions for their patrons, the white saloons, or "working men's clubs," generally restricted women to rigidly defined, subservient roles. In contrast, North Richmond's blues clubs were relatively free of gender constraints. Not only did black women participate as patrons and performers in the clubs but a few also could become owners and managers. These women pushed beyond the limitations of race and gender, employing skills traditionally applied to "women's work." Minnie Lue Nichols recalled: "It was just easier to take care of a club, give them music in a club, than it was to work all day and night in the yards, then turn around and work at home taking care of babies. Besides, if women were going to cook, they could make some real money off it" (see figure 24).[21]

The exact number of blues and after hours clubs owned and/or operated by women in North Richmond is impossible to ascertain given the transitory and often illicit nature of some of the enterprises and the paucity of materials documenting the African American experience in Richmond. The Savoy Club, Minnie Lue's, the B and L Club, Tappers Inn, and perhaps as many as three or four other clubs were owned and/or operated by women.

Too little is known about these black female entrepreneurs to draw a composite profile, but it appears that the most well known shared some common characteristics. For example, all had migrated from the South during the war or immediate postwar period, coming from Texas, Arkansas, and Georgia. All had been employed in traditional female domestic or service work in their home states. Some had worked in the

Richmond shipyards prior to starting their clubs. Most were or had been married. At least one, Billye Strickland, married into a prewar black Richmond family. Billye, whose migrant status is unclear, owned and operated the B and L Club (a club and motel operation) with her husband, Lawrence Strickland, whose family had resided in Richmond since 1916. When Lawrence was drafted and sent overseas, Billye took over as sole proprietor. Although a man owned Tappers Inn, Margaret Starks managed it and booked talent there and in several other venues.[22]

Like millions of African American newcomers to the Golden State, the blues club women of North Richmond resolved that "they weren't going into some white woman's kitchen and make five dollars a week. They said they did that back home and they weren't going to do that out here." Thus, the clubs enabled them to step outside the roles dictated by racism and sexism and attain a greater measure of economic and personal autonomy. Willie Mae "Granny" Johnson's position as owner of the Savoy Club required more than cooking skills. She was the chief executive officer, controlling booking, purchasing, and all executive decisions, including "hiring and firing." Her husband, Deacon, worked a "day job . . . and didn't have anything to do with it." Margaret Starks's career as a concert promoter and local political force evolved from her blues club activities. Minnie Lue Nichols became an astute businesswoman and community leader as a result of her club ownership. One Richmond woman translated the managerial and clerical skills she had gained as a bookkeeper in an after hours club and brothel chain into her own "legitimate bookkeeping service and made a good living." Others put themselves through nursing school.[23]

The blues club women often served as employment referral agents and power brokers in their communities. The clubs, catering as they did to newcomer cultural tastes, had a substantial economic impact on the larger African American community as well. As the shipyards and other wartime industries began to pull out of Richmond, this fact became even more crucial. Although assistance from club owners could not begin to meet the need, on a small scale the clubs provided employment for a cross section of black workers, including musicians, bartenders, cooks, clerical workers, custodians, and security guards. Minnie Lue's "kept some fellows with money in their pockets" by giving them "little sweeping up jobs and things like that." Moreover, female club owner/operators, who had to contend with obtaining liquor licenses, building permits, and bank loans, gained access to the larger white community and acquired a considerable amount of expertise in dealing with the white business and financial establishment. Thus, blues club women often were called upon to negotiate financial and governmental bureaucracies not only for themselves but also for the inexperienced and less well connected members of their community.[24]

Although blues club women represented only a small minority of Richmond's African American female workforce, their mere presence attests to the profound transforming impact World War II had on the lives of working-class black women. Their activities illustrated, as Margaret Starks noted, that the "whole world had changed."[25]

In addition to serving political and economic functions, the blues clubs were the place where the link between power and culture was most evident. Blues music provided African American newcomers and old-timers with a cultural means to reaffirm their value and dignity—commodities not highly prized in the urban industrial marketplace. The clubs functioned as sanctuaries and safety valves where frustrations could be vented in traditionally sanctioned and defined ways:[26] "Those people didn't have too much, so they weren't about to let go of the music and good times they were used to. It made them feel better. I remember one lady from Louisiana, had gold all in her mouth, told me that she loved to hear that music because listening to that music in Tappers made her forget all that stuff in the shipyards. She always felt better when she left."[27]

Though some African Americans agreed with the statement of one black newcomer who declared "The blues ain't nothing but a nigger with the wants," the majority of newcomers to Richmond had a higher regard for the music. It imparted a solidarity among patrons and performers that transcended entertainment. Minnie Lue Nichols recalled: "Well, if you've never felt the blues, I can't hardly explain. You know how it *feels*. . . . It was a blues crowd, a beautiful crowd. When the house is full and they're rocking with members of the band, you enjoy it." Patrons responded to the musical messages with shouts of "Sing your song!" or "Tell it!" One Louisiana newcomer declared: "I would follow a [blues] guitar player to hell!"[28] Blues clubs provided black newcomers with a welcome refuge from the racial hostility that permeated the world in which they earned their livelihoods.[29]

The clubs also provided many working-class African Americans with an environment where, in contrast to the outside world, the rules were straightforward and consistent. The prevailing blues club etiquette dictated that "it didn't matter what you did outside on your jobs or who you were, if you acted right, nobody was better than anybody else."[30]

Club protocol also blunted some of the intraracial friction that pitted black newcomers against black longtime residents. Old-timers might resent and ridicule black newcomers' "country ways," but they were compelled to interact with them on an equal footing when they entered the clubs. Blues club etiquette dictated equality regardless of income, length of residency, or family background. Behavior that violated this unwritten code included "signifying" (ridiculing someone's looks or family lineage, sometimes referred to as "playing the Dozens" or, on the West Coast, as "cutting" or "chopping"), bragging about one's money, "poor-mouthing" (never having money to spend), and refusing to reciprocate gifts of drinks or meals. Failing to acknowledge a greeting or neglecting to inquire about family members appear to have been serious lapses. However, the high demand for bouncers and "peacekeepers" in the clubs indicates that patrons did not scrupulously honor the blues club code.[31]

By the mid-1950s new attitudes had begun to emerge in the black community. The speed of events brought an ever changing face to the world in which black people now lived. In a cotton field or an isolated rural cabin, for example, change might seem slow and hard to discern in anything other than seasons or weather. In the city things were different. By the mid-1950s, black Richmondites numbered between sixteen and twenty thousand. Almost 5 percent of the black population was under age twenty-five and too young to have had any direct experience with the rural South. Moreover, the Supreme Court's 1954 ruling that overturned the Jim Crow doctrine of separate but equal appeared to signal a significant rupture with the past. These factors contributed to the feeling that "the past was falling away" and that life's fundamentals had indeed been altered. No matter how frustrating the realities of city life might be, many blacks believed that "where there was change there was hope." Winds of change were sweeping through the United States and would touch every facet of African American life, including black musical expression and North Richmond's blues clubs.[32]

Urban blues, with its southern agrarian base, now seemed anachronistic in the fast-paced, industrialized cities of the postwar United States. The quickened beat, amplified volume, and commercial lyrics of rhythm and blues (R&B) music now seemed to point to the future. Blues musicians who had been staples in North Richmond's clubs either adapted to these new sensibilities and "cleaned up their act" or waned in popularity by the end of 1950s.[33] The R&B musicians who emerged in the postwar period were younger and tended to be urban born or urbanized early in their lives. With their more flamboyant attire, polished stage presentation, horn sections, "honking" saxophones, and louder instruments, their music seemed to announce new black aspirations and assertiveness. Guitarists like Aaron "T-Bone" Walker and Bo Diddley often played their instruments behind their backs, over their heads, or with their teeth, as if to proclaim their fearlessness of and mastery over modern technology and the complexities of urban life.

The new musical genre still functioned within the African American ethos of communalism and spontaneity, however, and patrons in the North Richmond clubs insisted that the R&B musicians still supply a "beat that could move you." Margaret Starks recalled: "They always would come out and be with the people. Sometimes we would have drinks together after the gig. People liked to see they were just regular people." People "always treated the musicians like they were part of the family. They'd let them know if they didn't like something they were putting down."[34]

By the mid-1960s, however, R&B was being supplanted by a new musical genre. As the integrationist phase of the civil rights movement waned and more-militant articulations of black power and black pride emerged, African American popular music began to reflect these changes as well. Even R&B seemed distant to a younger generation that was completely comfortable in the urban setting and had begun to formulate broader definitions of power and community. These changes diminished the dominance of the R&B "honkers and shouters" and eroded the importance of the North Richmond clubs as cultural refuges. The postwar goals of urban industrial black America now found a voice in the polished, sophisticated sounds of soul. Soul music, performed by artists in dazzling formal attire who executed intricately choreographed dance routines, symbolized the aspirations of an upwardly mobile black population. Soul performers like the Motown artists who burst on the scene in the early 1960s usually bypassed the blues club venues to perform for thousands in large concert halls across the country and around the world. In addition to the impact of new political sensibilities, technology also accelerated the demise of the clubs as record companies and television now disseminated African American music to a wider, younger crossover audience, which was even farther removed from the blues roots of the music. These factors took their toll on the blues and on North Richmond's blues clubs. The final blow came when a police crackdown on vice and gambling in North Richmond shut down many of the remaining establishments. By the mid-1960s only a few remained. The Savoy closed in the early 1970s. Minnie Lue's continued through the early

1980s, more as a neighborhood tavern and café than as a venue for music.[35]

Ollie Freeman, owner of Jazzland Records, a popular North Richmond record store, explained the decline of blues in Richmond: "People are seeking a little different class of night life. . . . Today there has come a different trend in music. People watch TV and accept a different class of entertainment. If they can't go out and find this type of excitement for themselves, they don't want this other thing. They label it lowbrow. 'I don't want my kid to listen to that crud,' they will say. 'That blues sickens me. I don't want no blues.'"[36]

In the process of adapting to changing times, an African American musical tradition from home was adopted by the larger society. The musical voice of working-class black men and women became an inextricable part of the cultural fabric of the United States. Ironically, by the end of the 1960s rock and roll, the offspring of blues and R&B, had become the voice of a generation of white American youth.[37]

Sanctified (Holy Ghost or Pentecostal) churches and gospel music were the religious equivalents of blues clubs and blues music in Richmond. During the war the number of Sanctified storefront churches mushroomed in the city as thousands of black newcomers poured in. The black devout transported a preference for this emotionally expressive worship style and music with them and energized the black community by doing so. Despite its newcomer origins and the lower class label attached to storefront churches, Sanctified services had been present in Richmond for more than two decades. The city's first Sanctified church, the Church of God in Christ (COGIC) was established in the 1920s. Louis and Georgie Wheat Bonaparte, founding members of the COGIC (which became McGlothen Temple in the 1940s), informed Wilbur Wheat upon his arrival in 1942: "You ain't nothing if you ain't Church of God In Christ." Even though newcomers' religious traditions were given a warmer reception than their secular musical preferences, some black old timers tended to disdain the "disorganized" and "primitive" quality of the storefront churches that sprang up in the housing projects and empty buildings along Cutting Boulevard.[38]

The storefront churches were constructed much like the newcomers' homes—with few resources and much ingenuity. Often a small congregation pooled their money and rented a store or some other retail structure. Others met in private homes or held tent services. Mildred Slocum noted that the new churches "really weren't that much to look at." The emotionally charged worship style and exuberant gospel music of the newcomers' churches reflected "a cumulative expression" of the African American urban experience yet retained the "traditional values of black folk life as it has evolved since slave days."[39]

Thus storefront churches provided devout black newcomers with a "nonworldly" communal experience compatible with their religious beliefs and cultural ethos. Sanctified behavior such as shouting, arm waving, "dancing," and speaking in tongues expressed a religious vitality sprung from an African religious aesthetic that had been filtered through the prism of the African-American southern agrarian experience.[40]

Many black newcomers believed this ethos was diluted in the staid, mainline Baptist and Methodist churches. Margaret Starks recalled: "You didn't go into any of those little storefront churches if you didn't want to dance and shout. That may have been too much for some people." In Sanctified church services, black youth found excitement rivaling the blues club experience. Joseph Griffin III recalled that McGlothen Temple always incorporated "drums, horns, guitar and organ" into its services because "the Bible say 'make a joyful noise unto the Lord.' The joint be jumping!"[41]

Like worship style, gospel music was also fueled by religious piety that found expression in dramatic emotionalism. Unlike its secular blues and R&B counterparts (much of which had been appropriated and commercialized by white musicians), gospel managed to retain its relatively autonomous position. It was "first and foremost a product and symbol of Black religion," which is a repository of spiritual and ethnic group values.[42] Gospel superstars like Mahalia Jackson, the Golden Gaters, the Soul Stirrers, and Clara Ward performed in churches around the Bay Area, but black Richmondites recalled that "some good gospel came right out of the churches [in Richmond]." Black Richmondites tended to "make the music themselves," relying on the time-honored tradition of group improvisation to shape it. Songwriter Bob Geddins recalled that "in some of those churches they never did the song the same way twice. They'd have the notes wrote down or get one of my gospel records and learn the song, but that's all. They made the song."[43] However, some black Richmond residents, such as Charles Henry Thurston, disapproved of this type of improvisation. His son recalled: "Yeah, my daddy couldn't stomach that. When he sang, he wanted to sing the song the way whoever wrote it, as opposed to North Richmond. He hated quartets too, because quartets didn't sing, they'd holler and shout. So North Richmond started drifting in that direction."[44]

Richmond's churches gained a reputation in the Bay Area for being

"wild and emotional." Charles Henry Thurston eventually left the vener-
able North Richmond Missionary Baptist Church, convinced that it
had become "just too rough for him." He switched to Beth Eden Baptist Church in Oakland, seeking "more of the subdued, non-ritualistic
folks [who] didn't do a lot of shouting and this kind of thing. [The]
Preacher didn't holler in Beth Eden, whereas the preacher would holler
in some of the others."[45] Richmond's storefront and mainline churches
became associated with the uneducated, lower classes, even though black
Richmondites (newcomers and old-timers) compared favorably in education and income to blacks throughout the Bay Area. Margaret Starks
explained: "Richmond just wasn't filled with the folks that counted in
society; no doctors or lawyers, just plain working people." Yet by the
early 1960s Richmond's gospel choirs had transcended their humble
storefront origins, participating in choir competitions in the Bay Area
and around the country. Now most mainline black churches in the Bay
Area included at least one gospel choir in their musical repertoire.[46]
Thus, another newcomer tradition from home had become a dominant
cultural expression of Richmond's black community and had influenced
African American communities around the Bay Area.

The newcomers' churches, like the blues clubs, functioned as social
safety valves for black newcomers and longtime residents, who often
found their paths to advancement blocked within the established church
hierarchies that restricted positions of authority to a hand-picked few.
The flexible structure of newcomer churches offered black Richmondites more mobility. Thus, newcomer churches accommodated the ambitions of disgruntled old-line church members, who frequently "jumped
ship" to join the new churches and rise through the ecclesiastical ranks.
Louis H. Narcisse's Mt. Zion Spiritual Temple, while atypical of newcomer churches in many respects, exemplifies the energy and social mobility that attracted so many black Richmondites to newcomer churches.
Narcisse, a Louisiana migrant and former shipyard worker, first established Mt. Zion Spiritual Temple in Oakland in 1945 and opened a Richmond branch in the early 1950s. It was an eclectic mixture of Catholic,
Baptist, and Sanctified religion, liberally laced with an activist social gospel. Its motto was "It's nice to be nice." Narcisse's church became a force
in the Bay Area, establishing food, employment, and educational programs and winning endorsements from mainline clergy and political
leaders. Narcisse, a self-appointed "bishop," was eventually crowned
king of the church. Members were designated "saints" and were able to
quickly ascend to higher positions by contributing their time and finan-

cial resources to the church and its programs. Royal titles such as prince, princess, and queen mother (along with crowns and silk robes) denoted their progress in the church hierarchy.[47]

Margaret Starks, who attended numerous services in the Richmond and Oakland temples, noted: "All you needed to do was get involved in the programs, no hard rules, no tests." In Richmond, "people were leaving those other churches right and left" to join Mt. Zion Spiritual Temple. By the late 1950s King Narcisse was delivering weekly radio broadcasts and had opened branches of the church in Sacramento and Detroit. At its peak in the 1960s, church membership was estimated at two hundred thousand nationwide, but it declined sharply in the 1970s. Thus Mt. Zion Spiritual Temple and other newcomer churches provided the means by which black newcomers could regulate the degree, quality, and pace of assimilation into the urban environment. Their religious traditions eventually became institutionalized in the community and furnished black Richmondites another cultural avenue for cohesion and empowerment.[48]

The popularity of state clubs in Richmond also attests to the functionalism of African American traditions in the new urban industrial environment. State clubs were social organizations composed of black migrants from the same state, town, or parish. Although one state club predated the war, the number of clubs increased during the war and in the immediate postwar period. Through state clubs black Richmondites attempted to retain their regional identities while adapting to their new homes in California.

Some of the clubs were quite specific in their membership requirements. Bill Thurston recalled: "They used to have a Mississippi Club and a Vicksburg, Mississippi Club. They have in Vallejo right today a Vicksburg, Mississippi Club." At least one club expanded its scope, reaching out to the alumni of a predominantly black southern college: "There's a Jackson [Mississippi] State College Alumni Club now. [They] get together all over the country. Might even have a newsletter. Which is more sophisticated, where say folks from Mississippi would just gather at some time." Despite the perception of exclusivity, however, state clubs were open to anyone if "they behaved themselves and wanted to have a good time."[49]

Thus state clubs served a dual purpose in Richmond. They affirmed black southern cultural traditions and facilitated positive interaction among black newcomers and old-timers. Bill Thurston recalled: "The people probably were a bit homesick and wanted to hear news from home and be around homefolks." Irene Malbrough Batchan, former resident of St. Landry Parish, Louisiana, in "the heart of Zydeco country," described the sanctuary the state clubs represented to black newcomer children who were made to feel like outsiders because of their speech: "We were a curiosity when we came. The teachers would call roll and when they heard us talk, because we had this little French accent, people would laugh." The state club "was just like family; everybody talked like that. Everybody ate home food. Food on food!"[50]

In the early 1960s some of the state clubs faded out as people "began to move away from Richmond and began to feel more comfortable with living in such a diverse society." However, a few endured. As a youth, Bill Thurston attended "a picnic or something" sponsored by the Arkansas Club in the wartime housing projects. Decades later, in the seventies, said Thurston, "I went to this club where I hadn't been since the forties and it's still going on. Some of the old people, older than I am . . . doing Christmas or something at the Arkansas Club. Some of the people I had seen as a kid, as a teenager." Eventually, some state clubs merged with other Bay Area organizations to sponsor huge yearly regional gatherings, complete with southern cuisine, dancing, and the gamut of African American music. In the 1970s the meeting of the St. Landry's Parish Club became a yearly event, drawing hundreds of people from all over California. Joseph Malbrough and Irene Malbrough Batchan recalled: "One year it got so big we held it in the Richmond Auditorium and we had quite a good crowd."[51] Richmond's state clubs reinforced group solidarity and celebrated individuality in a society that tended to regard African Americans as a faceless, cultureless, monolithic reserve-labor pool. Irene Malbrough Batchan noted: "We were proud of our music, dances, things like that. You can't just let them think you haven't done anything, or you don't amount to anything. After all we were the town too."[52]

Like state clubs and blues clubs, baseball was an important cultural channel that muted intraracial conflict, enhanced group cohesiveness, and underscored African Americans' connection to the nation's mass culture. Unlike the other traditions from home, sports, particularly baseball, was an established feature of African American life in Richmond before World War II. The war highlighted its significance to the community.

Historian Rob Ruck has shown that the all-black sandlot baseball teams that developed in Pittsburgh, Pennsylvania, during the early 1900s helped unify and empower the community by providing it with an autonomous means for self-organization, creativity, and expression within the sometimes grim urban experiences of work and neighborhood.[53] Baseball served a similar function for black Richmondites. Charles Reid, a star pitcher for the semiprofessional Pierce Colored Giants and later North Richmond's recreation director, noted that "black youth had something to offer themselves and their community" and that sports "could bring all that out." Unlike eastern teams, however, many of Richmond's prewar sandlot teams were interracial. In the 1920s Walter Freeman Jr. played baseball with the "Italian and Portuguese boys" who were his North Richmond neighbors. Joseph Malbrough was paid to play for a team sponsored by a lumber company in Slopes, Nevada, during his "layoff" season from Pullman: "When the season was down, I worked . . . in the spring at the sawmill playing baseball for the camp. You see, they had a baseball camp and all you had to do was play baseball and they would pay you like you were working." Malbrough became the "first colored to ever play American Legion Baseball. It was an all-white team and I was on it. I had to be good to be on an all-white team in 1931."[54]

The influx of blacks to Richmond during the war resulted in an increase in the number of all-black baseball teams. Teams like the North Richmond Spiders, sponsored by community contributions of money and equipment, were composed of newcomers and longtime residents. The baseball teams provided enjoyment for the entire community. Ivy Reid Lewis recalled: "Every Sunday that was the entertainment. I mean hundreds of people would come [from] all over to see the games. We were like cheerleaders." Black Richmondites rooted for several all-girl teams, including the Spiderettes, a very popular softball team during the 1940s and 1950s (see figure 25). Housing project teams like the all-girl Canal Queens were also popular among black Richmondites. However, some prewar black residents regarded project teams as rowdy because they were composed primarily of newcomer children. Matches involving project teams sometimes bristled with class antagonisms. Ivy Reid Lewis, a player for the Spiderettes, recalled a game with a team from the Eastshore housing project: "We beat them. But all the black people came out of the housing project and started throwing rocks at us and ran us home."[55]

More often baseball inspired a sense of racial solidarity and provided a forum for "symbolic political assertion." Bill Thurston noted: "Once those uniforms went on, they had to learn to be a team. All these things, clubs, teams were just as necessary. They gave unity, pride which were almost prerequisite before blacks could really become political in Richmond." Through competitive excellence on the playing field, black

Richmondites proclaimed their capabilities and potential far beyond the realm of sports. Sports became the "great leveler" for many blacks. Participation in sports offered a socially sanctioned passage into the American mainstream and underscored black Richmondites' link to the common culture: "Blacks who were here could use baseball or boxing as a passport. What could be more all-American than baseball?" Black Richmondites, like their counterparts around the country, understood that Jackie Robinson's demolition of the color bar in professional baseball in 1947 transcended the playing field. His accomplishments spoke to the aspirations of all African Americans and symbolized their determination to realize victory over Jim Crow in the postwar United States. Minnie Lue Nichols explained: "Every time a colored boy did good in a ball game, it was just like we were saying 'I'm here.'" [56]

By the first decade after the war African Americans who had come to work in Richmond's war industries were no longer newcomers. Their determination had helped to revitalize Richmond's black community and had contributed to the dismantling of racial barriers. Their experiences underscore how profoundly World War II transformed the individual and collective lives of African Americans. Folk medicine, blues and gospel music, storefront churches, state club activities, and sports were weapons in the cultural arsenal of black Richmondites in their combat against some of the harshest aspects of their transition from the South to their new homes in the Golden State. The cultural resources, broad based and flexible enough to adapt to the complexities of urban life, retained their African American roots and left an indelible imprint both on the black community and on the larger community.

However, black traditions from home were themselves transformed by life in California. The southern agrarian flavor of black cultural expressions was diminished, despite the care black newcomers took to retain it. On trips back to Louisiana, Irene Malbrough Batchan and Joseph Malbrough were acutely aware of "how different we had become. . . . Now *they* would tease *us*. Too California!" Former shipfitter Henry Debney and his family went back to Texas after the shipyards closed only to return because "they found they had become used to California—Richmond in particular." Charles Henry Thurston "might leave to go back home, but he wouldn't desert that California living." [57] In this respect, however, the adaptability of black Richmondites' cultural traditions remained true to the African ethos from which they flowed. That ethos valued transformation, improvisation, and reinvention—qualities that were at the core of the African American cultural tradition and the California dream.

CHAPTER 6

Epilogue
Community, Success, and Unfulfilled Promise

We didn't think the streets were paved with gold or anything,
but we thought in California we could mix and mingle and
get along.

Wilbur Wheat, 1987

Today, in the late 1990s, Richmond's population of more than 90,000 represents a substantial increase over its 1940 total of approximately 24,000 but a notable decline from its wartime high of over 100,000. According to the 1990 census figures, African Americans (38,260) now comprise the city's majority. Blacks played an active role in Richmond's history and the history of African Americans in the urban industrial United States. However, the efforts and accomplishments of the people and their institutions have gone virtually unrecognized in most of the city's official records and accounts. Thus, today one might conclude that black people were inconsequential to the development of events. In reality, black Richmondites are the living repositories of the deeds and aspirations that transformed the city, the state, and the nation. Mildred Slocum explained, "the people are the history." [1]

Although black Richmondites underwent a process of proletarianization similar to that experienced by African Americans in other cities, an array of economic, social, and cultural factors made Richmond both similar and different from other black communities in the United States. Despite black agency and the persistence of a culture of expectation that enabled them to challenge and dismantle the overt manifestations of racism, Richmond's promise went largely unfulfilled for most of its black residents.[2] Lee Howard, former president of the Richmond NAACP, observed that black Richmondites have always known that "there was no parking place here."[3]

Within the Bay Area, Richmond has been regarded as a bad place to be in many respects. Wayne Thompson, the city manager in the postwar period, admitted that his "knottiest problem is how to make Richmond a good place to live." Today, that problem still confronts city officials. Many Richmond streets and neighborhoods are scarred with abandoned buildings and litter-strewn lots. The downtown that once bustled with purpose and activity during the 1940s went into decline, despite the desperate efforts of city officials to retain the shipyards and a viable economic base. A revitalized downtown remains an elusive goal today. The fires that burn in the Chevron Oil Refinery's flare stacks surrounding North Richmond illuminate grimy factories, railroad tracks, weathered houses, and polluted air. The blues clubs, cafés, and nightspots that operated as social and cultural oases for thousands of African Americans have disappeared. The religious, social, and benevolent institutions that once comprised the hub of black community life and group solidarity have lost much of their influence in the community. Black Richmondites continue to struggle against racial discrimination, unemployment, substandard housing, poverty, crime, and an image that has characterized them as socially and culturally inferior.[4]

The story of African Americans in Richmond is not a success story as success has commonly come to be measured in the late-twentieth-century United States. For black Richmondites, economic and material attainment could never be the sole criteria of success. For many, residency in the Golden State signaled a degree of progress and achievement that transcended economic accomplishment. They regarded themselves as part of a larger social and cultural milieu that was uniquely California.[5] Like other residents of the state, black Richmondites perceived a freedom to reinvent themselves and start anew.[6] Their transplanted cultural expressions provided a surrogate world in which self-respect, civility, and identity could be maintained, but even these were transformed in the new atmosphere of California.[7]

The "experiential dimension" derived from migration, community building, and participation in the diversity of the city and state represented black Richmondites' "guiding complex of beliefs," a complex that resulted in a positive assessment of themselves, their environment, and their achievements.[8] This ethos frequently placed them in the forefront of social and political activism that belied their small numbers and defied the stigma of deficiency with which other black communities branded them. Margaret Starks observed: "We were small, honey, but nothing got past us. We were involved in everything. FEPC, the march on Washington, everything. So many things we were doing no one ever gives [us] credit. No one wants to place our deeds in the right light. But we were there and did it."[9]

Their efforts to abolish Jim Crow and discrimination in their city corresponded to civil rights campaigns by black Americans across the country. In the 1940s, before the southern civil rights movement captured the public's attention in the 1950s and 1960s, black Richmondites were putting their bodies on the line and standing on their constitutional rights as American citizens in demanding equal treatment. Before *Brown v. Board of Education,* before black students braved howling mobs in Little Rock, and before 250,000 black and white Americans marched on Washington with their dream of universal equality, working-class black women and men on the West Coast were proving that the times were indeed changing, even in small California cities like Richmond.[10]

However, while the possibilities of life in California energized black Richmondites, the reality disappointed and frustrated them.[11] Wilbur Wheat noted that his version of the California dream, where "Colored, white, Mexican . . . [were] all living along so," fell short of the reality. He concluded: "But I guess that was wrong too."[12]

In the mid-1960s housing and employment discrimination, school segregation, police brutality, and official indifference continued to plague black residents.[13] These frustrations culminated in an outbreak of racial violence that gripped the city in 1966, when fist fights broke out among black, Mexican American, and white students at Richmond Union High School. For two weeks the city was racked by violence and racial tension as escalating rumors of black retaliation, inflammatory articles in the local press, and a massive show of force by the police exacerbated an outbreak of looting, rock throwing, and arson in the downtown area.[14]

The vision of integration and racial equality that had sustained a generation of black Richmondites virtually evaporated as black frustration and anger at the slow pace of change exploded in the city. Thus, the experiences of the black community in Richmond can be seen as a microcosm of the experiences, ideologies, and tensions that attended the urbanization of African Americans across the country. Black Richmondites were part of a broader story of migration, urbanization, and industrialization that began at the turn of the twentieth century and was expedited by World War II. The history of black Richmondites reveals that from the beginning black working-class women and men were actively engaged in shaping these processes in order to elevate their status in a society that underestimated their capabilities and consistently attempted to confine them to its periphery.

In addition, the history of the African American community in Richmond illuminates some of the issues that confront urban black communities today. Black Richmond's present-day dilemmas have national implications and are rooted in history. The problems that black people face today in Richmond and in other American cities—high unemployment, continuing racial discrimination, poor education, crime, and disintegrating families—were addressed but not resolved in the struggles of black Richmondites in the prewar and wartime periods. As the nation is transformed by postindustrial cyber technologies and global economies, African Americans are once again called upon to master the complexities and contradictions of a new age. We are challenged to develop new strategies for survival and advancement that will renew a sense of community and revitalize the institutions and affiliations that have served as stabilizing, regulatory, and creative forces in black communities from Africa to the Pacific Coast of the United States.

Notes

Introduction

1. In 1940 the number of African Americans living in the Mountain and Pacific states numbered almost 171,000, with California containing 124,306, in a total population of nearly 7,000,000. By 1950 the population of these states had swelled to almost 20,000,000, with African Americans comprising over 570,000 of the total; and in California blacks represented over 460,000 of the Golden State's 10,586,163 residents. See U.S. Department of Commerce, Bureau of the Census, "Population by Race, by States, 1930 to 1950," no. 45 in *Statistical Abstract of the United States* (Washington, D.C.: GPO, 1960), 30. See also Gerald D. Nash, *The American West Transformed: The Impact of the Second World War* (Bloomington: Indiana University Press, 1985), 88–106; Marilynn S. Johnson, *The Second Gold Rush: Oakland and the East Bay in World War II* (Berkeley: University of California Press, 1993), 51–54, 197–201.

2. Florette Henri, *Black Migration: Movement North, 1900–1920* (Garden City, N.Y.: Anchor Books, 1976); James Borchert, *Alley Life in Washington, D.C.: Family, Community, Religion, and Folklife in the City, 1850–1970* (Urbana: University of Illinois Press, 1980); Peter Gottlieb, *Making Their Own Way: Southern Blacks' Migration to Pittsburgh, 1916–1930* (Urbana: University of Illinois Press, 1987); James R. Grossman, *Land of Hope: Chicago, Black Southerners, and the Great Migration* (Chicago: University of Chicago Press, 1989); Carole Marks, *Farewell—We're Good and Gone: The Great Black Migration* (Bloomington: Indiana University Press, 1989); Joe William Trotter Jr., *Black Milwaukee: The Making of an Industrial Proletariat, 1915–1945* (Urbana: University of Illinois Press, 1985); Rob Ruck, *Sandlot Seasons: Sport in Black Pittsburgh* (Urbana: University of Illinois Press, 1987); Katrina Hazzard-Gordon, *Jookin': The Rise of Social Dance Formations in African-American Culture* (Philadelphia: Temple University Press, 1990); Nicholas Lemann, *The Promised Land: The Great Black Migration and How It Changed America* (New York: Alfred A. Knopf, 1991);

Burton W. Peretti, *The Creation of Jazz: Music, Race, and Culture in Urban America* (Urbana: University of Illinois Press, 1992); Elizabeth Clark-Lewis, *Living In, Living Out: African American Domestics in Washington, D.C., 1910–1940* (Washington, D.C.: Smithsonian Institution, 1994).

3. Eleanor Ramsey, "Allensworth: A Study in Social Change" (Ph.D. diss., University of California, Berkeley, 1977); Keith E. Collins, *Black Los Angeles: The Maturing of the Ghetto, 1940–1950* (Saratoga, Calif.: Century Twenty-One Publishing, 1980); Quintard Taylor, *The Forging of a Black Community: Seattle's Central District from 1870 through the Civil Rights Era* (Seattle: University of Washington Press, 1994); Sucheng Chan, Douglas Henry Daniels, Mario T. Garcia, and Terry P. Wilson, eds., *Peoples of Color in the American West* (Lexington, Mass.: D.C. Heath and Company, 1994); Elizabeth Jameson and Susan Armitage, *Writing the Range: Race, Class, and Culture in the Women's West* (Norman: University of Oklahoma Press, 1997); Lawrence P. Crouchett, Lonnie G. Bunch III, and Martha Kendall Winnacker, *Visions toward Tomorrow: The History of the East Bay Afro-American Community, 1852–1977* (Oakland: Northern California Center for Afro-American History and Life, 1989); Douglas Henry Daniels, *Pioneer Urbanites: A Social and Cultural History of Black San Franciscans* (Berkeley: University of California Press, 1990); Albert S. Broussard, *Black San Francisco: The Struggle for Racial Equality in the West, 1900–1954* (Lawrence: University Press of Kansas, 1993); Johnson, *The Second Gold Rush;* Delores Nason McBroome, *Parallel Communities: African Americans in California's East Bay, 1850–1963* (New York: Garland Publishing, 1993); Gretchen Lemke-Santangelo, *Abiding Courage: African American Migrant Women and the East Bay Community* (Chapel Hill: University of North Carolina Press, 1996).

4. Gretchen Lemke-Santangelo has argued that African American female migrants to the Bay Area during World War II were the primary culture bearers. See her *Abiding Courage,* 133–52.

5. For "traditions from home," see Shirley Ann Wilson Moore, "Traditions from Home: African Americans in Wartime Richmond, California," in *The War in American Culture: Society and Consciousness during World War II,* ed. Lewis A. Erenberg and Susan E. Hirsch (Chicago: University of Chicago Press, 1996), 263–83. For "California lifestyle," see Mildred Slocum, interview with author, November 17, 1987. For a discussion of the "promised land," see Grossman, *Land of Hope,* 103. Taylor, *The Forging of the Black Community,* 13–45.

6. Wilbur Wheat and Vesper Wheat, interview with author, January 24, 1987; Wilbur Wheat, telephone conversation with author, January 26, 1987.

7. Earl Lewis, "Expectations, Economic Opportunities, and Life in the Industrial Age: Black Migration to Norfolk, Virginia, 1910–1945," in *The Great Migration in Historical Perspective: New Dimensions of Race, Class, and Gender,* ed. Joe William Trotter Jr. (Bloomington: Indiana University Press, 1991), 22–45.

Chapter 1.   Richmond before the War

1. For "Wonder City," see F. J. Hulaniski, ed., *History of Contra Costa County, California* (Berkeley, Calif.: Elms Publishing Company, 1917), 337 (see also pp. 35, 336). See also Joseph C. Whitnah, *A History of Richmond, Califor-*

nia: The City That Grew from a Rancho (Richmond: Chamber of Commerce, 1944), 8, 18–31, 46–48, 78; Eleanor Mason Ramsey, "Richmond, California, between 1850–1940: An Ethnohistorical Reconstruction," draft submitted to California Archaeological Consultants, Inc., February 15, 1980, 7–15, photocopy in author's possession; Susan D. Cole, *Richmond: Windows to the Past* (Richmond: Wild Cat Canyon Books, 1980), 51–52; *The Richmond Independent,* "The Woman's Edition," a special edition published by the Richmond Historical Association (hereafter cited as "The Woman's Edition"), 1910, Richmond Museum, 8, 15, 17, 21; Burg Brothers Real Estate Company, "Burg Brothers Real Estate Company for the Pullman Townsite, Burg Brothers Exclusive Agents," 1910, pamphlet, miscellaneous pamphlet collection, Richmond Museum; Hubert Owen Brown, "The Impact of War Worker Migration on the Public School System of Richmond, California, from 1940 to 1945" (Ph.D. diss., Stanford University, 1973), 18.

2. U.S. Department of Commerce, Bureau of the Census, *Thirteenth Census of the United States, 1910* (hereafter cited as 1910 Census), vol. 2 (Washington, D.C.: GPO, 1911), 184, table 4; U.S. Department of Commerce, Bureau of the Census, *Sixteenth Census of the United States, 1940* (hereafter cited as 1940 Census), vol. 2 (Washington, D.C.: GPO, 1943), 610, table 32; U.S. Department of Commerce, Bureau of the Census, *Special Census of Richmond, California: September 1943,* ser. P-SC, no. 6 (Washington, D.C.: GPO, 1943); Richmond Department of Health, "Vital Statistics Report," January 2, 1945, Government Documents Library, University of California, Berkeley (the document is stamped "Bureau of Public Administration Library, Jul. 29, 1949, University of California"); W. Miller Barbour, *An Exploratory Study of Socio-Economic Problems affecting the Negro-White Relationship in Richmond, California* (Pasadena, Calif.: United Community Defense Services, Inc., and the National Urban League, 1952), 3; U.S. Department of Commerce, Bureau of the Census, *Special Census of Richmond, 1947,* ser. P-28, no. 280 (Washington, D.C.: GPO, 1941), 18. See also Robert Wenkert, John Magney, and Fred Templeton, *An Historical Digest of Negro-White Relations in Richmond, California* (Berkeley: Survey Research Center, University of California, February 1967, rev. September 1967), 18.

3. Charles Wollenberg, *Golden Gate Metropolis: Perspectives on Bay Area History* (Berkeley: Institute of Governmental Studies, University of California, Berkeley, 1985), 5, 31; Cole, *Richmond,* 7.

4. Wollenberg, *Golden Gate Metropolis,* 53–61; Ramsey, "Richmond, California, between 1850–1940," February 15, 1980, 2–6; Cole, *Richmond,* 17, 19.

5. Whitnah, *A History of Richmond,* 19–31; Ramsey, "Richmond, California, between 1850–1940," February 15, 1980, 7–14.

6. Whitnah, *A History of Richmond,* 29.

7. Ramsey, "Richmond, California, between 1850–1940," February 15, 1980, 12–15; Whitnah, *A History of Richmond,* 27–31. The name "Richmond" appears to predate actual incorporation by more than fifty years. Edmund Randolph, originally from Richmond, Virginia, represented the city of San Francisco when California's first legislature met in San Jose in December 1849, and he became state assemblyman from San Francisco. His "loyalty to the town of his birth" caused him to persuade a federal surveying party mapping the San Francisco Bay to place the names "Point Richmond" and "Richmond" on an 1854 geodetic

coast map which was the geodetic map at the terminal selected by the San Joaquin Valley Railroad; and by 1899 maps made by the railroad carried the name
"Point Richmond Avenue," designating a county road that later became Barrett Avenue, a central street in Richmond. Whitnah, *A History of Richmond*, 28.

8. Ramsey, "Richmond, California, between 1850–1940," February 15, 1980,
14–15; Whitnah, *A History of Richmond*, 46–48.

9. Whitnah, *A History of Richmond*, 8; Cole, *Richmond*, 51–52. For other
cities' attitudes toward industrialization, see Robert A. Slayton, *Back of the
Yards: The Making of a Local Democracy* (Chicago: University of Chicago Press,
1986), 15–38; John Bodnar, *Immigration and Industrialization: Ethnicity in an
American Mill Town, 1870–1940* (Pittsburgh: University of Pittsburgh Press,
1977), 3–21, 102–26; John Bodnar, Roger Simon, and Michael P. Weber, *Lives of
Their Own: Blacks, Italians, and Poles in Pittsburgh, 1900–1960* (Urbana: Univer-
sity of Illinois Press, 1982), 13–25; Jane Addams, *The Spirit of Youth and the City
Streets* (1909; reprint, Urbana: University of Illinois Press, 1972), xxvi, 128–31;
Alan Trachtenberg, *The Incorporation of America: Culture and Society in the
Gilded Age* (New York: Hill and Wang, 1982), 80–81, 121–39.

10. 1910 Census, 2:118, 582–614.

11. U.S. Department of Commerce, Bureau of the Census, *Fourteenth Census of the United States, 1920* (hereafter cited as 1920 Census), vol. 3 (Washington,
D.C.: GPO, 1921), 118–19; U.S. Department of Commerce, Bureau of the Census, *Fifteenth Census of the United States, 1930* (hereafter cited as 1930 Census),
vol. 3 (Washington, D.C.: GPO, 1931), pt. 1, 261; 1940 Census, 2:610. Also see
Wenkert, Magney, and Templeton, *An Historical Digest of Negro-White Relations*, 11–16.

12. Among this group of influential professionals and executives were Henry
Creeger, Edward Downer, and John Galvin. Creeger was the manager of American Standard Company and served on the Richmond High School board of
trustees and on the Richmond Chamber of Commerce. He also was a member
of the Richmond Elks club and sat on the blue-ribbon wartime committee established to attract war industries to the city. Edward Downer was the founder
and president of the Mechanics Bank of Richmond, and John Galvin was publisher of the *Richmond Independent*, the town's leading newspaper. Brown,
"The Impact of War Worker Migration," 38–40.

13. *Richmond Independent*, January 30, 1939; Brown, "The Impact of War
Worker Migration," 37.

14. Brown, "The Impact of War Worker Migration," 37.

15. Hulaniski, *History of Contra Costa County*, 335; Whitnah, *A History of
Richmond*, 78; "The Woman's Edition," 8. See also Burg Brothers Real Estate
Company, "Burg Brothers Real Estate Company for the Pullman Townsite."

16. Hulaniski, *History of Contra Costa County*, 335–36; Brown, "The Impact
of War Worker Migration," 18; "Richmond's Greatest Industry," in "The
Woman's Edition," 21.

17. "The Pullman Shops," in "The Woman's Edition," 17. Hulaniski, *History of Contra Costa County*, 336.

18. Burg Brothers Real Estate Company, "Burg Brothers Real Estate Company for the Pullman Townsite"; Ramsey, "Richmond, California, between
1850–1940," 16.

19. Hulaniski, *History of Contra Costa County*, 336; Brown, "The Impact of War Worker Migration," 18.

20. "Richmond Past and Present," in "The Woman's Edition," 15.

21. Whitnah, *A History of Richmond*, 84–85.

22. Brown, "The Impact of War Worker Migration," 30; Cole, *Richmond*, 56–57.

23. Evan Griffins, "Early History of Richmond, Contra Costa County, California," December 1938, suppl., December 1939, 5–6, Richmond Museum; Brown, "The Impact of War Worker Migration," 37.

24. Wenkert, Magney, and Templeton, *An Historical Digest of Negro-White Relations*, 5, 9, 53–55; Whitnah, *A History of Richmond*, 53–55; "The Woman's Edition," 6.

25. Wenkert, Magney, and Templeton, *An Historical Digest of Negro-White Relations*, 3–9 (quotation on p. 8).

26. "The Woman's Edition," 37; Stanley Nystrom, interview with author, July 31, 1986.

27. The material on Richmond's nonblack minority groups has been summarized from interviews conducted by the author and Eleanor Mason Ramsey with Japanese American residents of Richmond and Native American employees of Santa Fe Railroad yards, July–November 1980. Also see Eleanor Mason Ramsey, "Richmond, California, between 1850–1940," chap. 5 in "Investigation of Cultural Resources within the Richmond Harbor Redevelopment Project 11-A, Richmond, Contra Costa County, California," 5.11–5.16, 5.23–5.33, prepared by California Archaeological Consultants, Banks and Orlins, March 1981, San Francisco, bound typescript, Richmond Collection, Richmond Public Library. Brown, "The Impact of War Worker Migration," 38–40.

28. Brown, "The Impact of War Worker Migration," 39; Japanese American residents of Richmond and Native American employees of Santa Fe Railroad yards, interview; Ethel Rogoss, interview by Eleanor Mason Ramsey, Richmond, Calif., July 7, 1980; also Ramsey, "Richmond, California, between 1850–1940," March 1981, 5.24–5.28.

29. Brown, "The Impact of War Worker Migration," 40; Japanese American residents of Richmond, interview by Eleanor Mason Ramsey, November 9, 1980.

30. "The Woman's Edition," 18; U.S. Department of Commerce, Bureau of the Census, *Thirteenth Census of the United States, 1910*, vol. 19, township 15, enumeration district 177 (Washington, D.C.: National Archives Administration, n.d.), microcopy T624, reel 75, California: Contra Costa and Fresno Counties (hereafter cited as 1910 Manuscript Census). Prewar black Richmond resident Harry Williams recalled that in the 1930s the Fong Wong Shrimp camp was located at the foot of Third Street in Richmond: "They had these big vats. They would just take them all out in the back, to get their net or whatever, and they poured them in these vats, and they're steaming vats." Harry Williams and Marguerite Williams, "Reflections of a Longtime Black Family in Richmond," an oral history conducted in 1985 by Judith R. Dunning, Regional Oral History Office, Bancroft Library, University of California, Berkeley, 1990, 13–14.

31. Edward E. France, "Some Aspects of the Migration of the Negro to the San Francisco Bay Area since 1940" (Ph.D. diss., University of California, 1962), 18–19; Kenneth G. Goode, *California's Black Pioneers: A Brief Historical Sur-*

vey (Santa Barbara, Calif.: McNally and Loftin, 1971), 109; Lawrence P. Crouchett, Lonnie G. Bunch III, and Martha Kendall Winnacker, *Visions toward Tomorrow: The History of the East Bay Afro-American Community, 1852–1977* (Oakland: Northern California Center for Afro-American History and Life, 1989), 9–10, 17.

32. 1910 Manuscript Census; W. Sherman Savage, "The Negro in the Westward Movement," *Journal of Negro History* 25 (1940): 533–34; Goode, *California's Black Pioneers*, 25, 62–66; Robert F. Heizer and Alan F. Almquist, *The Other Californians: Prejudice and Discrimination under Spain, Mexico, and the United States to 1920* (Berkeley: University of California Press, 1977), 120–28.

33. 1910 2:118, 614. Additional information regarding migration was obtained from interviews conducted by the author with Richmond residents Joseph Malbrough and Irene Malbrough Batchan, August 18, 1985; William Malbrough and Irene Malbrough Batchan, September 14, 1985; Walter Freeman Jr. and Joseph Griffin III, November 28, 1987; Mildred Slocum, November 17, 1987; George Johnson, August 13, 1985. For a review of African American migration, see Joe William Trotter Jr., "Black Migration in Historical Perspective: A Review of the Literature," in *The Great Migration in Historical Perspective: New Dimensions of Race, Class, and Gender,* ed. Joe William Trotter Jr. (Bloomington: Indiana University Press, 1991), 1–21. See also, Shirley Ann Moore, "Getting There, Being There: African American Migration to Richmond, California, 1910–1945," in *The Great Migration in Historical Perspective: New Dimensions of Race, Class, and Gender,* ed. Joe William Trotter Jr. (Bloomington: Indiana University Press, 1991), 106–26. For analyses of African American migration to the Midwest and Northeast, see Florette Henri, *Black Migration: Movement North, 1900–1920* (Garden City, N.Y.: Anchor Books, 1976), esp. 49–80, 133–73; James R. Grossman, *Land of Hope: Chicago, Black Southerners, and the Great Migration* (Chicago: University of Chicago Press, 1989); Carole Marks, *Farewell—We're Good and Gone: The Great Black Migration* (Bloomington: Indiana University Press, 1989); Nicholas Lemann, *The Promised Land: The Great Black Migration and How It Changed America* (New York: Alfred A. Knopf, 1991).

34. Freeman and Griffin, interview.

35. Ibid.; Joseph Malbrough and Irene Malbrough Batchan, interview.

36. Peter Gottlieb, *Making Their Own Way: Southern Migration to Pittsburgh, 1916–1930* (Urbana: University of Illinois Press, 1987), 7, 12–13; James Borchert, *Alley Life in Washington, D.C.: Family, Community, Religion, and Folk Life in the City, 1850–1970* (Urbana: University of Illinois Press, 1980), ix–xii; Earl Lewis, "Afro-American Adaptive Strategies: The Visiting Habits of Kith and Kin among Black Norfolkians during the First Great Migration," *Journal of Family History* 12, no. 4 (winter 1987): 407–20.

37. Wilbur Wheat and Vesper Wheat, interview with author, January 24, 1987.

38. Slocum, interview.

39. Freeman and Griffin, interview; William Malbrough and Irene Malbrough Batchan, interview.

40. 1910 Manuscript Census; Freeman and Griffin, interview.

41. William Malbrough and Irene Malbrough Batchan, interview; Joseph Malbrough and Irene Malbrough Batchan, interview; Freeman and Griffin, interview. See also Williams and Williams, "Reflections," 4–5.

42. Williams and Williams, "Reflections," 19; Joseph Malbrough and Irene Malbrough Batchan, interview.

43. I am indebted to Susan E. Hirsch for sharing some of her research on black workers and labor unions in the Pullman Company. See Susan E. Hirsch, "No Victory in the Workplace: Women and Minorities at Pullman during World War II," in *The War in American Culture: Society and Consciousness during World War II,* ed. Lewis A. Erenberg and Susan E. Hirsch (Chicago: University of Chicago Press, 1996), 241–62; and Hirsch, untitled manuscript on the Pullman Company, esp. chaps. 2 and 4, Loyola University of Chicago, Chicago, Ill. "Proceedings of the Meeting between the Pullman Company and the Pullman Company Employees Association of the Repair Shops," August 1940, box 39-250, 46, Pullman Company Papers, Newberry Library, Chicago, Ill.

44. "The Woman's Edition," 17; *Oakland Tribune,* February 8, 1925; Joseph Malbrough and Irene Malbrough Batchan, interview.

45. Joseph Malbrough and Irene Malbrough Batchan, interview.

46. Ibid.

47. William Malbrough and Irene Malbrough Batchan, interview; 1910 Manuscript Census; Freeman and Griffin, interview; Slocum, interview.

48. Freeman and Griffin, interview; Johnson interview. George and Ida Johnson moved to California in 1918 and the Bay Area in 1919. They settled in Richmond in the mid-1930s. For an overview of domestic service in general and African American domestic workers in particular, see David M. Katzman, *Seven Days a Week: Women and Domestic Service in Industrializing America* (Urbana: University of Illinois Press, 1981), 24–26, 46, 55, 65–94; 221–22, 266–79; and Borchert, *Alley Life in Washington,* 168–95.

49. Joseph Malbrough and Irene Malbrough Batchan, interview.

50. Williams and Williams, "Reflections," 9–10; Joseph Malbrough and Irene Malbrough Batchan, interview; Ivy Reid Lewis, interview with author, July 29, 1987. For over ten years, beginning in 1947, Claude Blair operated a "tailing off" machine for the Filice and Perrelli Cannery in Richmond. His stepdaughter, Bessie Clemons, worked on the cannery floor on the conveyer belt and briefly on the "pitter." The cannery employed up to a "thousand people a shift." Mr. Blair recalled that after the war many blacks worked with him in the warehouse as "lumpers" loading crates of fruit onto the loading platform. Claude A. Blair and Bessie Clemons, interview with author, July 29, 1980.

51. Lewis, interview.

52. 1910 Census, 2:644–45; Brown, "The Impact of War Worker Migration," 32.

53. Lewis, interview.

54. William Malbrough and Irene Malbrough Batchan, interview; Freeman and Griffin, interview.

55. *Western Outlook,* July 24, 1925; *Oakland Independent,* December 14, 1929.

56. *Pacific Coast Appeal,* ca. January 3, 1905.

57. William Malbrough and Irene Malbrough Batchan, interview.

58. Ibid.; Joseph Griffin III, telephone conversation with author, November 11, 1987; Slocum, interview.

59. Kenneth Kusmer, *A Ghetto Takes Shape: Black Cleveland, 1870–1930* (Urbana: University of Illinois Press, 1980), 77–78, 80–84, 103–5, 140–44, 191–95,

243–44. For a good overview of the social and economic dynamics and business entrepreneurship in California's major urban black communities, see Keith E. Collins, *Black Los Angeles: The Maturing of the Ghetto, 1940–1950* (Saratoga, Calif.: Century Twenty-One Publishing, 1980); Crouchett, Bunch, and Winnacker, *Visions toward Tomorrow;* Donald Hausler, "Blacks in Oakland," monograph, 1987, Oakland Public Library History Room, Oakland, Calif.; Douglas Henry Daniels, *Pioneer Urbanites: A Social and Cultural History of Black San Franciscans* (Berkeley: University of California Press, 1990); Albert S. Broussard, *Black San Francisco: The Struggle for Racial Equality in the West, 1900–1954* (Lawrence: University Press of Kansas, 1993).

60. Tilghman Press, *Colored Directory of the Leading Cities of Northern California, 1916–1917* (Oakland, Calif.: Tilghman Press, 1917), 70; 1910 Manuscript Census; 1910 Census, 2:184, table 4; 1920 Census, 2:119, table 10; Joseph Malbrough and Irene Malbrough Batchan, interview; "Opportunities in Richmond, California, Where Rail and Sail Meet!" *Western Appeal,* June 8, 1921.

61. Williams and Williams, "Reflections," 4–15; *Western American,* June 25, 1926; France, "Some Aspects of the Migration of the Negro."

62. "Walls Addition to the City of Richmond," 1909, pamphlet, Richmond Pamphlets Collection, Bancroft Library, University of California, Berkeley. Also see *Western American,* April 29, 1927, 1; *West [Contra Costa] County Times,* January 20, 1986.

63. California's first restrictive covenant case decided prior to 1915 involved a Chinese-owned laundry in San Diego in 1892. See *Gondolfo v. Hartman,* 49 Fed. 181 (C.C.S.C., California); *Los Angeles Inv. Co. v. Gary,* 181 Cal. 680 (1919); *Janss Investment Co. v. Walden,* 196 Cal. 653 (1925); *Wayt v. Patee,* 205 Cal. 46 (1928). For a discussion of restrictive covenants in California, see Heizer and Almquist, *The Other Californians,* 92–137. For a discussion of restrictive covenants nationally, see Tom C. Clark and Philip B. Perlman, *Prejudice and Property: An Historic Brief against Racial Covenants, Submitted to the Supreme Court* (Washington, D.C.: Public Affairs Press, 1948), 6, 11–21, 39–67, 87; Loren Miller, "The Power of Restrictive Covenants," *Survey Graphic* 36, no. 1 (January 1947): 46; Franklin N. Williams, "Keepers of the Wall," *Frontier: The Voice of the New West* (April 1960): 9–11. For a discussion of segregated housing patterns nationally, see C. Vann Woodward, *The Strange Career of Jim Crow* (New York: Oxford Press, 1955), esp. chap. 3; Borchert, *Alley Life in Washington,* 7–8; E. Franklin Frazier, *The Negro in the United States* (New York: Macmillan, 1957), 126–27, 232–34; Kusmer, *A Ghetto Takes Shape,* 46–47. For a discussion of violence reinforcing segregation, see Grossman, *Land of Hope,* esp. chap. 1 and pp. 13–19; Shawn Lay, ed., *The Invisible Empire in the West: Toward a New Historical Appraisal of the Ku Klux Klan of the 1920s* (Urbana: University of Illinois Press, 1992).

64. Joseph Malbrough and Irene Malbrough Batchan, interview; E. P. (Edwin P.) "Red" Stephenson, "Transition: White Man in a Black Town, 1950–1967," an oral history conducted 1975, in "Bay Area Foundations History: Oral History Transcripts/Interviews, 1971–75," vol. 5, Regional Oral History Office, Bancroft Library, University of California, Berkeley, 1971, 27–28; Lewis, interview; Sherrill David Luke, "The Problems of Annexing North Richmond to the

City of Richmond" (master's thesis, University of California, Berkeley, 1954), 3; Brown, "The Impact of War Worker Migration," 41; Lee Hildebrand, "North Richmond Blues," *The East Bay Express: The East Bay's Free Weekly,* February 9, 1979, 1, 4; William Sokol, "From Workingman's Town to All American City: The Socio-Political Economy of Richmond, California, during World War II," June 1971, Richmond Collection, Richmond Public Library, 34; Wenkert, Magney, and Templeton, *An Historical Digest of Negro-White Relations,* 21–22.

65. Kusmer, *A Ghetto Takes Shape,* 45–52; Borchert, *Alley Life in Washington,* 7, 29–56; Bodnar, Simon, and Weber, *Lives of Their Own,* 70–82; Lewis, interview; Joseph Malbrough and Irene Malbrough Batchan, interview; Stephenson, "Transition," 28.

66. Tilghman Press, *Colored Directory, 1916–1917,* 70; *Western American,* April 29, 1927, 1; Joseph Malbrough and Irene Malbrough Batchan, interview; Lewis, interview; *West [Contra Costa] County Times,* January 20, 1986; Williams, "Keepers of the Wall," 9–10; Nystrom, interview; Brown, "The Impact of War Worker Migration," 88–95.

67. Nystrom, interview.

68. Freeman and Griffin, interview.

69. Lawrence Crouchett, telephone conversation with author, October 6, 1987; Freeman and Griffin, interview. For a detailed analysis of similar Klan activities in another small California town, see Christopher N. Cocoltchos, "The Invisible Empire and the Search for the Orderly Community: The Ku Klux Klan in Anaheim, California," in *The Invisible Empire in the West: Toward a New Historical Appraisal of the Ku Klux Klan of the 1920s,* ed. Shawn Lay (Urbana: University of Illinois Press, 1992), 97–120.

70. Freeman and Griffin, interview.

71. *Richmond Independent,* June 16, 1922, 1. See also Whitnah, *A History of Richmond,* 67–68.

72. Benevolent and Protective Order of Elks, Richmond Lodge, No. 1251, "Golden Anniversary, 1911–1961," n.d., commemorative booklet, Richmond Museum; Hiram Evans, "Klan's Fight for Americanism," *North American Review* 123 (March–May 1926): 33–63; Evans, quoted in Leon Litwack and Winthrop D. Jordan, *The United States: Becoming a World Power,* 7th ed. (Englewood Cliffs, N.J.: Prentice-Hall, 1991), 2:614; Lay, *The Invisible Empire in the West,* esp. 6–9, 97–120; Kusmer, *A Ghetto Takes Shape,* 74–189; Leon Litwack, "The Blues Keep Falling," in Berkeley Art Center, *Ethnic Notions: Black Images in the White Mind* (Berkeley, Calif.: Berkeley Art Center, 1982), 15–19; Slocum, interview.

73. Freeman and Griffin, interview; Margaret Starks, interview with author, April 2, 1988; Slocum, interview; Brown, "The Impact of War Worker Migration," 37.

74. W. E. Burghardt DuBois, "The Function of the Negro Church," in *The Black Church in America,* ed. Hart M. Nelsen, Raytha L. Yokley, and Anne K. Nelsen (New York: Basic Books, 1971), 77; E. Franklin Frazier, *The Negro Church in America* (New York: Schocken Books, 1964), 44–45.

75. Lewis, interview.

76. Williams and Williams, "Reflections," 34–35. Lewis, interview. Peter

Gottlieb describes similar intraracial "color" discrimination in some African American churches of Pittsburgh during the Great Migration. See Gottlieb, *Making Their Own Way,* 197–98.

77. North Richmond Missionary Baptist Church, "Sixtieth Anniversary Program," May 27, 1979, in the personal papers of Mildred Slocum. I am indebted to Mrs. Emma Clark, head of reference at the Richmond Public Library, and longtime member of McGlothen Temple, Church of God in Christ, in Richmond for her assistance in my research on African Americans in Richmond. Her information on home church services was invaluable (Clark, conversation with author, October 15, 1987). For a discussion of similar home church worship among African American alley residents of Washington, D.C., see Borchert, *Alley Life in Washington,* 199–201.

78. North Richmond Missionary Baptist Church, "Sixtieth Anniversary Program."

79. Ibid.; Williams and Williams, "Reflections," 34; William Malbrough and Irene Malbrough Batchan, interview; Freeman and Griffin, interview.

80. Lewis, interview; First African Methodist Episcopal Church (AME), bulletin no. 3, collection of Sunday bulletins, Bancroft Library, University of California, Berkeley; miscellaneous California black newspapers, 1903–1929, Bancroft Library, University of California, Berkeley; *Western American,* December 14, 1928; Joseph Malbrough and Irene Malbrough Batchan, interview.

81. *Western Appeal,* June 22, 1921.

82. Ibid.; *Western Appeal,* November 16, 1921. The program for the sixtieth anniversary celebration reported that the "third session of the Negro Baptist Missionary Associates convened with the North Richmond Missionary Baptist Church October 18–22, 1922. Rev. Holmes was presented with $3.00, the Sunday School with $2.00 and the church with $5.00." The "executive board of the Negro Baptist Associates met with North Richmond Missionary Baptist Church July 27, 1922 and raised $14.00. North Richmond was also present on November 12–16, 1925 at the first annual session of the California Missionary Baptist Convention." North Richmond Missionary Baptist Church, "Sixtieth Anniversary Program," 1.

83. Freeman and Griffin, interview.

84. Ibid.; Slocum, interview.

85. Slocum, interview; Freeman and Griffin, interview.

86. Freeman and Griffin, interview. Zora Neal Hurston described the black Baptist tradition of "bearing up" in her book *The Sanctified Church* (Berkeley, Calif.: Turtle Island, 1983), 84. See also Lawrence Levine, *Black Culture and Black Consciousness: Afro-American Folk Thought from Slavery to Freedom* (New York: Oxford University Press, 1977), 42–44, 174–89; Albert J. Raboteau, *Slave Religion: The Invisible Institution in the Antebellum South* (New York: Oxford University Press, 1980), 4–42, 55–92, 212–88.

87. Freeman and Griffin, interview. For a discussion of emotional worship styles in other prewar African American communities, see Borchert, *Alley Life in Washington,* 197–99; Grossman, *Land of Hope,* 156–57; Gottlieb, *Making Their Own Way,* 200–203.

88. Grossman, *Land of Hope,* 94–95, 131, 156–60; Gottlieb, *Making Their*

Own Way, 197–204; Kusmer, *A Ghetto Takes Shape,* 207–8; Frazier, *The Negro in the United States,* 352–55.

89. Lewis, interview; Freeman and Griffin, interview; Slocum, interview; William Malbrough and Irene Malbrough Batchan, interview; Walter Freeman Jr. and Annie Mae Freeman, interview with author, January 14, 1988; Raboteau, *Slave Religion,* 133–50, 231–39; Leon Litwack, *Been in the Storm So Long: The Aftermath of Slavery* (New York: Vintage Books, 1980), 24–25, 465–71.

90. Slocum, interview; Lewis, interview; Freeman and Griffin, interview.

91. Slocum, interview.

92. Freeman and Griffin, interview; William Malbrough and Irene Malbrough Batchan, interview; Slocum, interview; North Richmond Missionary Baptist Church, "Sixtieth Anniversary Program."

93. For a discussion of secular institutions promoting leadership and self-help, see August Meier, *Negro Thought in America, 1880–1915: Racial Ideologies in the Age of Booker T. Washington* (Ann Arbor: University of Michigan Press, 1988), 4, 6–8, 86–99, csp. 100–118, and for an interpretation of Booker T. Washington and the impact of his concept of self-help, 208–47. Also see W. E. Burghardt DuBois, *The Souls of Black Folk: Essays and Sketches* (1903; reprint, Greenwich, Conn.: A Fawcett Premier Book, 1961), 42–54. For a discussion of the role and function of black women's clubs, see Paula Giddings, *When and Where I Enter: The Impact of Black Women on Race and Sex in America* (New York: Bantam Books, 1984), 95–117; "The History of the National Association of Colored Women's Clubs," *Western American,* July 30, 1926; W. A. Lowe and V. A. Clift, eds., *Encyclopedia of Black America* (New York: McGraw Hill, 1981), 863; Shirley Ann Wilson Moore, "Your Life Is Really Not Just Your Own: African American Women in Twentieth Century California," unpublished manuscript, 5; Darlene Clark Hine, ed., *Black Women in America: An Historical Encyclopedia* (New York: Carlson Publishing, 1993), 2:895–97.

94. Frances Mary Albrier, "Determined Advocate for Racial Equality," an oral history conducted 1977–78 by Malca Chall, Regional Oral History Office, Bancroft Library, University of California, Berkeley, 228a; Margaret Marlowe Nottage, ed., *Woman's Journal: California Association of Colored Women's Clubs* (n.p., 1945), 13, Bancroft Library, University of California, Berkeley; "The Exchange Program, Women's Arts and Crafts, California Federation of Colored Women's Clubs, Northern Section," *Western American,* June 25, 1926.

95. Nottage, *Woman's Journal,* 13; "The Exchange Program, Women's Arts and Crafts"; Moore, "Your Life Is Really Not Just Your Own," 6.

96. *Western American,* June 25, 1926, December 14, 1928; *Oakland Independent,* December 14, 1929.

97. Freeman and Freeman, interview; Ashler Lodge No. 35, "Centennial Yearbook of the Most Worshipful Prince Hall Grand Lodge Free Accepted Masons, California and Jurisdiction," Richmond, Calif., at the Centennial Communication of the Grand Lodge, San Francisco, July 17–21, 1955; Tilghman Press, *Colored Directory, 1916–1917,* 70.

98. Freeman and Freeman, interview; Williams and Williams, "Reflections," 7, 36; Ashler Lodge No. 35, "Centennial Yearbook."

99. Freeman and Freeman, interview.

100. Ibid.

101. Ibid.

102. Walter Freeman Jr. joined Ashler lodge in 1934. He recalled that the new lodge was located on Fifth Street between Macdonald and Bissell in downtown Richmond. For information on the location of the lodge, see *Oakland Independent,* December 14, 1929.

103. William Malbrough and Irene Malbrough Batchan, interview.

104. Joseph Malbrough and Irene Malbrough Batchan, interview.

105. Hurston, *The Sanctified Church,* 62–63.

106. Katrina Hazzard-Gordon, *Jookin': The Rise of Social Dance Formations in African American Culture* (Philadelphia: Temple University Press, 1990), 76–119; Slocum, interview; Freeman and Griffin, interview; Lewis, interview.

107. Lewis, interview.

108. Freeman and Griffin, interview. See also Helen Richards, "Crichetts Opened First Business Here," [*Richmond Independent?*], n.d., Richmond Collection, Richmond Public Library. This article reports that in 1902 city founders staged bullfights in the "new town of Richmond" because "citizens felt an urgent need for local excitement and lively entertainment" and to "advertise the town." An arena was built on the "flats between Point Richmond hills and the Santa Fe shops." The arena was named "plaza del Torres [*sic*]" and "matadors and picadors were transported from Mexico." The plaza was lighted by electricity furnished by a "private concern. With all the light needed for illumination of the arena and stands, the plant couldn't produce enough for the local homes, so it was a case of sitting home in darkness or smell lamp-light or attending the bullfights, so a crowd was present for all events." The first bullfights were staged August 4–10, 1902.

109. Lewis, interview.

110. Ibid.; Joseph Malbrough and Irene Malbrough Batchan, interview; Freeman and Griffin, interview; Williams and Williams, "Reflections," 17.

111. Slocum, interview; Lewis, interview.

112. Walter Freeman Jr., telephone conversation with author, January 16, 1989. See also Hausler, "Blacks in Oakland," 93–94; *Oakland Sunshine,* February 25, 1922; Raoul C. Peterson, "Garveyism in California: A Lady Remembers," *Core,* fall/winter 1973, 20–22; Crouchett, Bunch, and Winnacker, *Visions toward Tomorrow,* 32–33;

113. Brown, "The Impact of War Worker Migration," 43; Minutes, Richmond City Council, September 8, 1941; Lewis, interview.

114. *Western Appeal,* November 16, 1921. See also Kusmer, *A Ghetto Takes Shape,* 35–52; Gilbert Osofsky, *Harlem: The Making of a Ghetto, Negro New York, 1880–1930* (New York: Harper and Row, 1971); Allen Spear, *Black Chicago: The Making of a Negro Ghetto* (Chicago: University of Chicago Press, 1967); August Meier and Elliott M. Rudwick, *From Plantation to Ghetto: An Interpretive History of American Negroes* (New York: Hill and Wang, 1966), 189–220; Trotter, "Black Migration in Historical Perspective," 1–17.

115. Freeman and Griffin, interview.

116. Ibid.

117. Ibid.; Luke, "The Problem of Annexing North Richmond," 10.

118. William Malbrough and Irene Malbrough Batchan, interview; Joseph Malbrough and Irene Malbrough Batchan, interview.

119. Sanborn Insurance Company, *Sanborn Insurance Map* (New York: Sanborn Insurance Company, 1930, amended 1957), 1:101–2, 108, 111, 113, 116, 402, 417; Freeman and Griffin, interview.

120. Slocum, interview.

121. Freeman and Griffin, interview.

122. Johnson, interview.

123. Frazier, *The Negro in the United States*, 599–600; Studs Terkel, *Hard Times: An Oral History of the Great Depression* (New York: Pocket Books, 1970), 21.

124. 1920 Census, 3:119; 1930 Census, vol. 3, pt. 1, 261.

125. J. McFarline Ervin, *The Participation of the Negro in the Community Life of Los Angeles* (1931; reprint, Los Angeles: R & E Research Associates), 14.

126. Whitnah, *A History of Richmond*, 116; Freeman and Griffin, interview.

127. Brown, "The Impact of War Worker Migration," 23.

128. Whitnah, A *History of Richmond*, 116–17. Richmond's major shipping terminal, Parr-Richmond, spent over two million dollars on advertising its facilities nationwide. The *Independent* editorialized in favor of the city's willingness to guarantee relocating industries a placid business climate free of "industrial strife" and no political interference "unfriendly to industrial growth." As proof, Richmond declined to join other Bay Area cities in antipollution suits against canneries, on the grounds that the offending businesses provided employment to many Richmond residents. *Richmond Independent*, November 22, 1939, February 9, 1940; Freeman and Griffin, interview; William Malbrough and Irene Malbrough Batchan, interview.

129. Joseph Malbrough and Irene Malbrough Batchan, interview.

130. Philip S. Foner, *Organized Labor and the Black Worker, 1619–1981*, 2d ed. (New York: International Publishers, 1982), 215–37 (quote on p. 216). For a discussion of the Communist Party's attempts to attract African Americans during the 1930s through the Workers Alliance of America and the National Unemployed Councils, see Lizabeth Cohen's study of workers in Chicago, *Making a New Deal: Industrial Workers in Chicago, 1919–1930* (New York: Cambridge University Press, 1990), 261–67.

131. Brown, "The Impact of War Worker Migration," 24–25; *Richmond Independent*, March 6, 1940. Richmond resident Cleophas Brown was a black union and civil rights activist who was an active member in the Workers Alliance and the Communist Party. In 1946 he was summoned before House Un-American Activities Committee to testify about his political activities. Cleophas Brown, telephone conversation with author, October 18, 1987; William Malbrough and Irene Malbrough Batchan, interview.

132. Brown, "The Impact of War Worker Migration," 24–25; *Richmond Independent*, March 6, 1940; William Malbrough and Irene Malbrough Batchan, interview.

133. Joseph Malbrough and Irene Malbrough Batchan, interview.

134. Freeman and Griffin, interview.

135. Lewis, interview; Williams and Williams, "Reflections," 14–15.

136. Lewis, interview; Williams and Williams, "Reflections," 36.

137. 1940 Census, 2:610, 637.

138. Lewis, interview.

139. Ernestine Green, interview with author, August 18, 1985; Joseph Malbrough and Irene Malbrough Batchan, interview; William Malbrough and Irene Malbrough Batchan, interview.

Chapter 2.   Shipyards and Shipbuilders

1. Franklin D. Roosevelt, Executive Order No. 8802, June 25, 1941, and Executive Order No. 9346, "Further Amending Executive Order No. 8802 by Establishing a New Committee on Fair Employment Practice and Defining Its Powers and Duties," May 24, 1943, box 7, entry no. 85, General Records 1941–45, Records of the President's Committee on Fair Employment Practice, record group 228, National Archives, Pacific Sierra Region (region 12), San Bruno, Calif. (hereafter cited as FEPC Records); W. Miller Barbour, *An Exploratory Study of Socio-Economic Problems affecting the Negro-White Relationship in Richmond, California* (Pasadena, Calif.: United Community Defense Services, Inc., and the National Urban League, 1952), 5, table 2, and 68, table 4; Richard Pollenberg, *War and Society: The United States, 1941–1945* (Westport, Conn.: Greenwood Press, 1972), 104–5.

2. Alyce Mano Kramer, "The Story of the Richmond Shipyards," 1945, ser. 15, carton 288, folder 5, pp. 6, 13–16, 21, Henry J. Kaiser Papers, Bancroft Library, University of California, Berkeley (hereafter cited as Kaiser Papers); "Todd Shipyards Sever Kaiser Link," *Brooklyn Eagle,* February 25, 1942, ser. 18, vol. 77, "Richmond Shipyards, January–April 1942, Scrapbook," Kaiser Papers; and "Big Shipbuilders End Affiliation," *New York Times,* February 25, 1942, ser. 18, vol. 77, "Richmond Shipyards, January–April 1942, Scrapbook," Kaiser Papers; William Sokol, "From Workingman's Town to All American City: The Socio-Political Economy of Richmond, California, during World War II," June 1971, Richmond Collection, Richmond Public Library, 12; Joseph C. Whitnah, *A History of Richmond, California: The City That Grew from a Rancho* (Richmond: Chamber of Commerce, 1944), 117–18; Gerald D. Nash, *The American West Transformed: The Impact of the Second World War* (Bloomington: Indiana University Press, 1985), 27, 66–70; Mark S. Foster, *Henry J. Kaiser: Builder in the Modern American West* (Austin: University of Texas Press, 1989), 68–89.

3. Kramer, "The Story of the Richmond Shipyards," 13–16; Foster, *Henry J. Kaiser,* 63–71; "Todd Shipyards Sever Kaiser Link."

4. Kramer, "The Story of the Richmond Shipyards," 13–16, 21, 29, 37; Whitnah, *A History of Richmond,* 119; Hubert Owen Brown, "The Impact of War Worker Migration on the Public School System of Richmond, California, from 1940–1945" (Ph.D. diss., Stanford University, 1973), 1; James McVittie, *An Avalanche Hits Richmond* (Richmond: Office of City Manager, 1944), 9.

5. "Testimony of Thomas M. Carlson, City Attorney for Richmond," 835–36, "Testimony of J. A. McVittie, City Manager of the City of Richmond," 836–41, and "Testimony of Walter T. Helm, City Superintendent of Schools,

Richmond, Calif.," 884–89, in House Subcommittee of the Committee on Naval Affairs Investigating Congested Areas, *Hearings before the United States House Committee on Naval Affairs,* 78th Cong., 1st sess., April 12–17, 1943 (hereafter cited as *Congested Areas Hearings*); Nash, *The American West Transformed,* 69; McVittie, *An Avalanche Hits Richmond,* 141; "Richmond Took a Beating," *Fortune Magazine,* February 1945, 265–67; "Report, May 13, 1942," see esp. chart entitled "Distribution of Employees," ser. 15, carton 288, folder 7, Kaiser Papers; "Report, February 1943," see esp. section entitled "Distribution of Payroll by Location," ser. 15, carton 288, folder 6, Kaiser Papers; Stanley Nystrom, "A Family's Roots in Richmond: Recollections of a Lifetime Resident," an oral history conducted in 1985 by Judith R. Dunning, Regional Oral History Office, Bancroft Library, University of California, Berkeley, 1990, 44–46, 48–56; Ivy Reid Lewis, interview with author, July 29, 1987.

6. "Richmond Took a Beating"; *Richmond Independent,* March 16, 1941; "Testimony of J. A. McVittie," *Congested Areas Hearings,* 836–41; "Testimony of Walter T. Helm," *Congested Area Hearings,* 887; "Testimony of Thomas M. Carlson," *Congested Areas Hearings,* 835; Joseph Fabry, *Swingshift: Building the Liberty Ships* (San Francisco: Strawberry Hill Press, 1982), 150; "Testimony of Arthur A. Hall, Richmond, California, Local Manager of the United States Employment Services Operating under the Manpower Commission, Richmond, Calif.," *Congested Areas Hearings,* 859.

7. Nash, *The American West Transformed,* 8–10, 17–19, 25–27, 66–70; John E. Wiltz, *From Isolation to War, 1931–1941* (New York: Thomas Y. Crowell Company, 1968), 67–97; Sokol, "From Workingman's Town to All American City," 12; Whitnah, *A History of Richmond,* 117–18.

8. Lewis Campbell, "Look Before You Leap," *California Voice,* August 1, 1941; *California Voice,* March 6, 1942.

9. Cy W. Record, "Characteristics of Some Unemployed Negro Shipyard Workers in Richmond, California" (Berkeley: Library of Economic Research, University of California, Berkeley, September 1947), 11, Intergovernmental Studies Library, University of California, Berkeley; Nash, *The American West Transformed,* 98; Kaiser Industries, *The Kaiser Story* (Oakland, Calif.: Kaiser Industries, Corp., 1968), 27, 31, ser. 15, carton 288, Kaiser Papers. In discussing the inexperience of the workers and the technological innovations at the Richmond yards, Alyce Mano Kramer referred to the shipbuilders as "these novices, these upstarts, these madmen," who in November 1942 turned out a ship in "the world's record time of four and a half days to launching." On average, 241 days were required to build a ship the old way, but "standardization, prefabrication, and welding reduced this average at the height of mass production to little more than a month." Kramer, "The Story of the Richmond Shipyards," 29, 37–39. See also David A. Oppenheim, *Pre-Fab. Ship S.S. Robert E. Peary* (Richmond: Permanente Metals Corporation, November 15, 1942), ser. 15, carton 288, folder 19; "Log of Events for Minute-by-Minute Building Progress," ser. 15, carton 288, folder 22, Kaiser Papers; Kaiser Company, Inc., *Richmond Shipyard Number Three—An Employee Handbook,* 1943, ser. 15, carton 288, folder 26, p. 13, Kaiser Papers; "Subject: Prefabrication at Richmond Shipyard Number Two," December 17, 1942, ser. 15, carton 289, folder 11, p. 2, Kaiser Papers; "Model

Manual for Richmond Yards," *People's World,* March 14, 1942; "Shipyards Start 7-Day-Week on Sun., March 15," *Richmond Independent,* March 7, 1942; "A Splendid Example," *New York Times-Herald,* March 10, 1942, ser. 18, vol. 77, Kaiser Papers.

10. Kaiser Industries, *The Kaiser Story,* 27; Kramer, "The Story of the Richmond Shipyards," 56; Sokol, "From Workingman's Town to All American City," 30; Kaiser Permanente, "Serve Your Country and Yourself: Help Build War-Winning Ships at Richmond, California," ca. 1943, ser. 15, carton, 288, folder 3, Kaiser Papers.

11. Kaiser Permanente, "Serve Your Country and Yourself."

12. *California Voice,* July 16, 1943; Lewis, interview; "Shipbuilding Richmond-Transportation and Housing Requirements 1942," ser. 15, carton 288, folder 7, Kaiser Papers; "The Transportation and Housing Problem as it Affects Labor Turnover in the Richmond Shipyards, Report, February 1943," ser. 15, carton 288, folder 6, Kaiser Papers; Harre W. Demoro, "Old Shipyard Railway Recalled," *Oakland Tribune,* September 13, 1970.

13. Harry Williams and Marguerite Williams, "Reflections of a Longtime Black Family in Richmond," an oral history conducted in 1985 by Judith R. Dunning, Regional Oral History Office, Bancroft Library, University of California, Berkeley, 1990, 110, 113; Mildred Slocum, interview with author, November 17, 1987.

14. "Testimony of Thomas M. Carlson," 835–36, "Testimony of J. A. McVittie," 836–41, and "Testimony of Walter T. Helm," 884–89, in *Congested Areas Hearings;* Nash, *The American West Transformed,* 69; McVittie, *An Avalanche Hits Richmond,* 141; "Richmond Took a Beating," 265–67; "Report, May 13, 1942"; "Report, February 1943"; Nystrom, "A Family's Roots in Richmond," 44–46, 48–56; "Testimony of Arthur A. Hall," *Congested Areas Hearings,* 860–61; Edward Rutledge to Sam Kagel, June 12, 1944, box 11, entry no. 68, FEPC Records; Sam Kagel (signed by A. L. Sharee) to Edward Rutledge, memorandum, June 9, 1944, attached statistical reports, "An Analysis of Non-White Employment in Richmond, California, May 1, 1944" and "Employment Figures Taken from Richmond ES-270 Reports, May 1, 1944," box 11, entry no. 68, FEPC Records; *California Voice,* July 16, 1943.

15. Nash, *The American West Transformed,* 37–42; "Testimony of Arthur A. Hall," *Congested Areas Hearings,* 854–55; House Subcommittee of the Committee on Military Affairs, *Hearings on Labor Shortages in the Pacific Coast and Rocky Mountain States,* 78th Cong., 1st sess., April 12–17, 1943, 4. Lawrence W. Cramer, "Available and Needed Workers Have Been Barred from Employment" (speech delivered at the regional meeting of the National Conference of Social Work, New York, March 11, 1943), in "U.S. Committee on Fair Employment Practice, Miscellaneous Publications," typeset manuscript, n.d., 1–11, Doe Library, University of California, Berkeley; "Statement of Henry J. Kaiser, Oakland, Calif., before the House of Representatives Committee on Labor, Regarding the Labor Shortage and Possible Restrictions on Movement from War Essential Jobs and Absenteeism," ca. 1943, ser. 8, carton 148, folder 1, Kaiser Papers; Sokol, "From Workingman's Town to All American City," 20.

16. "Industrial Relations Department Report 1943," D. J. Robertson to J. J.

Boney, memorandum, January 6, 1943, ser. 2, carton 20, folder 32, Kaiser Papers; William Martin Camp, *Skip to My Lou* (New York: Doubleday, Doran and Company, 1945), 107–8.

17. Kramer, "The Story of the Richmond Shipyards," 57; "Testimony of Arthur A. Hall," *Congested Areas Hearings*, 855; Kaiser Permanente, "Serve Your Country and Yourself"; Robertson to Boney, memorandum, January 6, 1943.

18. Permanente Metals Corporation, *A Booklet of Illustrated Facts about the Shipyards at Richmond, California* (Oakland, Calif.: Permanente Metals Corporation, 1944), 32; Charles H. Day, file memorandum, January 19, 1943, ser. 2, carton 20, folder 32, Kaiser Papers; Kaiser Industries, *The Kaiser Story*, 31; Helen Smith Alancraig, "Cordonices Village: A Study of Non-Segregated Public Housing in the San Francisco Bay Area" (master's thesis, University of California, Berkeley, 1953), 30, 35; Cy W. Record, "The Negro-White Issue in California," *Labor and Nation*, May–June 1948, 25–27.

19. Kramer, "The Story of the Richmond Shipyards," 57–58; see "Labor Turnover 1942," graphic, in "Construction Progress Reports, Richmond Yard, 1942–1943, vol. 1," ser. 18, vol. 68, Kaiser Papers; William Beck, [Kaiser Shipyards] Industrial Relations Department, "Reports Contract Recruits Section, 1943," ser. 2, carton 20, folder 32, Kaiser Papers; "Men Recruited and Transportation Advanced," in the same report; W[illia]m Beck to Chas. H. Day and James C. Egan, March 1, 1943, D. J. Robertson to James C. Egan, December 29, 1942, Robertson to Boney, January 6, 1943, and W[illia]m Beck to C. H. Day and J. C. Egan, March 23, 1943, all in ser. 2, carton 20, folder 32, Kaiser Papers; Jean Johnson to J. C. Egan, memorandum, March 9, 1943, ser. 2, carton 20, folder 32, Kaiser Papers; Jean Johnson to William Beck, memorandum, February 13, 1943; Jean Johnson to James C. Egan, memorandum, February 7, 1943; Charles H. Day, file memorandum, January 19, 1943, all in ser. 2, carton 20, folder 32, Kaiser Papers.

20. Kaiser Industries, *The Kaiser Story*, 31; Sokol, "From Workingman's Town to All American City," 20; E. P. (Edwin P.) "Red" Stephenson, "Transition: White Man in a Black Town, 1950–1967," an oral history conducted in 1975, in "Bay Area Foundations History: Oral History Transcripts/Interviews, 1971–75," vol. 5, Regional Oral History Office, Bancroft Library, University of California, Berkeley, 1971, 25; Kramer, "The Story of the Richmond Shipyards," 57–58.

21. "Testimony of Arthur A. Hall," 860–62. Edward E. France, *Some Aspects of the Migration of the Negro to the San Francisco Bay Area since 1940* (Ph.D. diss., University of California, Berkeley, 1962), 21;

22. Margaret Starks, interview with author, April 2, 1988; William H. McKinney, interview with author, June 18, 1991. Also see Kaiser Permanente, "Serve Your Country and Yourself"; Alancraig, "Cordonices Village," 30, 35; Record, "The Negro-White Issue in California," 25–27.

23. Robert Wenkert, John Magney, and Fred Templeton, *An Historical Digest of Negro-White Relations in Richmond, California* (Berkeley: Survey Research Center, University of California, Berkeley, February 1967, rev. September 1967), 17–18; *California Eagle*, June 9, 1933, 38–40; Keith E. Collins, *Black Los Angeles: The Maturing of the Ghetto, 1940–1950* (Saratoga, Calif.: Century Twenty-One Publishing, 1980), 90, 11–12, 25; Starks, interview.

24. Bill Thurston, interview with author, September 10, 1983.

25. Ibid.

26. Wilbur Wheat and Vesper Wheat, interview with author, January 24, 1987. See also James R. Grossman, *Land of Hope: Chicago, Black Southerners, and the Great Migration* (Chicago: University of Chicago Press, 1991), 66–74, 110; Cameron-Stanford House, *Oakland's Sleeping Car Porters* (Oakland, Calif.: Cameron-Stanford House, 1979); Lawrence P. Crouchett, Lonnie G. Bunch III, and Martha Kendall Winnacker, *Visions toward Tomorrow: The History of the East Bay Afro-American Community, 1852–1977* (Oakland: Northern California Center for Afro-American History and Life, 1989), 9–10.

27. Wheat and Wheat, interview.

28. Thurston, interview; Record, "Characteristics of Some Unemployed Negro Shipyard Workers," 9, 31. For the role of kinship and friendship correspondence in European immigration, see Herbert G. Gutman, *Work, Culture, and Society in Industrializing America: Essays in American Working-Class and Social History* (New York: Vintage Books, 1976); John Bodnar, Roger Simon, and Michael. P. Weber, *Lives of Their Own: Blacks, Italians, and Poles in Pittsburgh, 1900–1960* (Urbana: University of Illinois Press, 1982), 41–42. Thomas Bell's novel *Out of This Furnace* (Pittsburgh: University of Pittsburgh Press, 1976) provides a fictionalized but historically accurate account of life and kinship ties among Slovak immigrants in Pennsylvania's steel industries. See esp. pp. 3–258.

29. Nicholas Lemann, *The Promised Land: The Great Black Migration and How It Changed America* (New York: Alfred A. Knopf, 1991), 3–7, 48–51; "Revolution in Cotton," *Colliers,* July 21, 1945; Bruce Nelson, "Organized Labor and the Struggle for Black Equality in Mobile during World War II," *The Journal of American History* 80, no. 3 (December 1993): 952–88; Record, "Characteristics of Some Unemployed Negro Shipyard Workers," 31.

30. Record, "Characteristics of Some Unemployed Negro Shipyard Workers," 31.

31. "Testimony of Arthur A. Hall," *Congested Areas Hearings,* 857, 860–61; North Richmond Neighborhood House report, in Roy M. Hamachi, "Postwar Housing in Richmond, California: A Case Study of Local Housing Developments in the Postwar Period" (master's thesis, University of California, Berkeley, 1954), 27–28, carton 6, "Subject Files, California, Richmond," Catherine Bauer Wurster Papers, Bancroft Library, University of California, Berkeley; Record, "Characteristics of Some Unemployed Negro Shipyard Workers," 30.

32. Miriam Frank, Marilyn Ziebarth, and Connie Field, *The Life and Times of Rosie the Riveter: The Story of Three Million Working Women during World War II* (Emeryville, Calif.: Clarity Educational Productions, 1982) 17; Margaret Starks, telephone conversation with author, June 29, 1988.

33. Starks, interview. See also Charles S. Johnson, *The Negro War Worker in San Francisco* (San Francisco: n.p., 1944), 2, 5, 7. For a discussion of the importance of including gender issues in examining African American migration, see Darlene Clark Hine, "Black Migration to the Urban Midwest: The Gender Dimension, 1915–1945," in *The Great Migration in Historical Perspective: New Dimensions of Race, Class, and Gender,* ed. Joe William Trotter Jr. (Bloomington:

Indiana University Press, 1991), 127–46; Gretchen Lemke-Santangelo, *Abiding Courage: African American Migrant Women and the East Bay Community* (Chapel Hill: University of North Carolina Press, 1996), 49–68; Frank, Ziebarth, and Field, *The Life and Times of Rosie the Riveter,* 17; Frances Mary Albrier, "Determined Advocate for Racial Equality," an oral history conducted 1977–78 by Malca Chall, Regional Oral History Office, Bancroft Library, University of California, Berkeley, 1978, vi, 132–33.

34. Starks, interview; Record, "Characteristics of Some Unemployed Negro Shipyard Workers," 9, 31.

35. Kramer, "The Story of the Richmond Shipyards," 59. Richmond City Attorney T. M. Carlson estimated that at least 90,000 shipyard workers were employed by Kaiser in "U.S. Sees Parley for Sale of Shipyards, City Seeks Land for Industry to Use Unemployed," *Richmond Record Herald,* March 12, 1946, ser. 2, carton 27, folder 26, Kaiser Papers. By May of 1944 total employment in all four shipyards had dropped to 75,099, and the nonwhite employment figure had fallen to 6,508, or approximately 9 percent of the total workforce. See "Employment Figures for Richmond Shipyards, May 1, 1944," in Kagel (signed by Sharee) to Rutledge, memorandum, June 9, 1944; Will Maslow to Edward Rutledge, memorandum, March 28, 1945, box 7, entry no. 85, General Records 1941–1945, FEPC Records (in which Maslow estimates that of the approximately ninety thousand African Americans in the Bay Area, forty thousand worked in Bay Area shipyards); Fabry, *Swingshift,* 231; Barbour, *An Exploratory Study of Socio-Economic Problems,* 6–7; Wenkert, Magney, and Templeton, *An Historical Digest of Negro-White Relations,* 17; Kaiser Industries, *The Kaiser Story,* 21, 27.

36. Whitnah, *A History of Richmond,* 199; Brown, "The Impact of War Worker Migration," 11; Johnson, *The Negro War Worker in San Francisco,* 2, 5, 7.

37. McKinney, interview, June 18, 1991. See also Bodnar, Simon, and Weber, *Lives of Their Own,* 31–37; Carter G. Woodson, *A Century of Negro Migration* (1918; reprint, New York: Russell and Russell, 1969), 11, 21, 46–91; Clyde Kiser, *Sea Island to City: A Study of St. Helena Islanders in New York City* (1932; reprint, New York: AMS Press, 1969), 149–52; see Thomas Roy Peyton, *Quest for Dignity: An Autobiography of a Negro Doctor* (Los Angeles: Warren F. Lewis Publishing, 1950), esp. 96–109, for an account black middle- and professional-class migration to the West during World War II. See also Record, "Characteristics of Some Unemployed Negro Shipyard Workers," 19–22, 26, 32.

38. U.S. Department of Commerce, Bureau of the Census, *Special Census of Richmond, California: September 1943,* ser. P-SC, no. 6 (Washington, D.C.: GPO, 1943), and U.S. Department of Commerce, Bureau of the Census, *Special Census of Richmond, California, 1947,* ser P-28, no. 280 (Washington, D.C.: GPO, 1947); Wenkert, Magney, and Templeton, *An Historical Digest of Negro-White Relations,* 16.

39. Peter Gottlieb, *Making Their Own Way: Southern Blacks' Migration to Pittsburgh, 1916–1930* (Urbana: University of Illinois Press, 1987), 5–7, 12–13; Joe William Trotter Jr., *Black Milwaukee: The Making of an Industrial Proletariat, 1915–1945* (Urbana: University of Illinois Press, 1985), xii, 54.

40. Barbour, *An Exploratory Study of Socio-Economic Problems,* 4–11; International Brotherhood of Boilermakers, Iron Shipbuilders, and Helpers of Amer-

ica, Local No. 513, *Arsenal of Democracy* (Berkeley, Calif.: Tam Gibbs Co., Printers, 1947), 45; *Richmond Record Herald,* July 15, 1941; Johnson to Egan, memorandum, March 9, 1943; Fabry, *Swingshift,* 97, 186; Nystrom, "A Family's Roots in Richmond," 28; Camp, *Skip to My Lou,* 103.

41. Fabry, *Swingshift,* 186.

42. Starks, interview; Lewis, interview; Albrier, "Determined Advocate," 125; "Testimony of Ivan W. Hill," *Congested Area Hearings,* 883; Camp, *Skip to My Lou,* 103; Barbour, *An Exploratory Study of Socio-Economic Problems,* 9.

43. Roosevelt, Executive Order No. 9346; *Fortune,* June 1943, 43–44; Philip S. Foner, *Organized Labor and the Black Worker, 1619–1981,* 2d ed. (New York: International Publishers, 1982), 238–47; Cramer, "Available and Needed Workers Have Been Barred from Employment." Cramer noted in the speech that "prior to Pearl Harbor . . . Defense training courses were often administered to exclude Negroes, Jews, Spanish-Americans, aliens, foreign born citizens and members of certain religious denominations were on the unwanted lists" (3, 5–7). Malcolm Ross, "Testimony before the House Labor Committee," *Hearings on H.R.* 3986, 78th Cong., 2d sess., 6; McKinney, interview, June 18, 1991.

44. Robert C. Goodwin, Executive Director, USES, to F. W. Hunter, Regional Director, USES, June 18, 1945, box 7, entry no. 85, FEPC Records.

45. Foster, *Henry J. Kaiser,* 79–82; Foner, *Organized Labor and the Black Worker,* 247–49; Clarence R. Johnson to George H. Johnson, "Employment-Richmond Shipyards," June 11, 1943, box 14, entry no. 70, Closed Cases 1941–46, FEPC Records; Charles Wollenberg, *Marinship at War: Shipbuilding and Social Change in Wartime Sausalito* (Berkeley, Calif.: Western Heritage Press, 1990), 74–75; Edward Rutledge to Will Maslow, "Discrimination against Minority Group in Northern California," March 28, 1945, box 7, entry no. 85, General Records 1941–45, FEPC Records; USEA quoted in Brown, "The Impact of War Worker Migration," 173.

46. Kagel (signed by Sharee) to Rutledge, "Non-White Employment—ES-270 Reports, Richmond, California," memorandum, June 9, 1944; Clay P. Bedford to All Yard Assistant Managers, All Yard Superintendents, The Department of Industrial Relations, "Equal Employment Opportunities for All Workers," memorandum, December 11, 1943, box 7, entry no. 85, General Records 1941–45, FEPC Records; F. W. Hunter to Robert C. Goodwin, "USES Violations of the Non-Discrimination Program," memorandum, June 18, 1945, box 7, entry no. 85, FEPC Records; Wollenberg, *Marinship at War,* 72; Bartley C. Crum to Lloyd E. Mabon, January 19, 1945, box 11, entry no. 68, Active Cases 1941–46, FEPC Records; Bartley C. Crum to Edward Rutledge, January 25, 1945, box 11, entry no. 68, Active Cases 1941–46, FEPC Records; Samuel D. Hudson and Marcellus Knox, "Complaint against Steamfitters & Helpers Union, Local 590, Case Number 12-UR-92" (also see "Work History of Samuel Hudson" and "Work History of Marcellus Knox" appended to complaint), January 8, 1945, box 11, entry no. 68, Active Cases 1941–46, FEPC Records; Edward Rutledge to Bartley C. Crum, January 24, 1945, box 11, entry no. 68, Active Cases 1941–46, FEPC Records; memorandum to [Edward] Rutledge, re: WMC reports from "Miss Pierce" on "USES orders re steamfitters," January 9, 1945, box 11,

entry no. 68, Active Cases 1941–46, FEPC Records; J. L. Thompson to Sam Kagel, December 30, 1944, box 11, entry no. 68, Active Cases 1941–46, FEPC Records; David F. Selvin to Walter White, January 19, 1943, carton 23, Cottrell. L. [C. L.] Dellums Papers, Bancroft Library, University of California, Berkeley.

47. Record, "Characteristics of Some Unemployed Negro Shipyard Workers" 19–22, 26, 32.

48. Trotter, *Black Milwaukee,* 54.

49. Thurston, interview; Wheat and Wheat, interview.

50. Kaiser Shipyards, "Chronological History of Kaiser Company, Inc., Shipyard Number Three Richmond, California," n.d., 1, 11, 12, ser. 15, carton 289, folder 11, Kaiser Papers.

51. Kaiser Industries, *The Kaiser Story,* 27, 31; Sam Kagel to Edward Rutledge, April 9, 1945, box 7, entry no. 85, General Records 1941–45, FEPC Records; Edward Rutledge to Will Maslow, March 28, 1945, box 7, entry no. 85, General Records 1941–45, FEPC Records; Kaiser Permanente, "Serve Your Country and Yourself."

52. Kaiser Industries, *The Kaiser Story,* 33; Brown, "The Impact of War Worker Migration," 42–43; Record, "Characteristics of Some Unemployed Negro Shipyard Workers," 43–45 (see esp. p. 45, table xii); Thurston, interview.

53. President's Committee on Fair Employment Practice, press releases, November 5, 1943, and November 10, 1943; Clarence R. Johnson to George M. Johnson, June 11, 1943, box 14, entry no. 70, Closed Cases 1941–46, FEPC Records. Regarding Dellums's union's support of Sylvester White's cause, see C. L Dellums to Roger Cramer [*sic*], March 24, 1942, box 14, entry no. 70, Closed Cases 1941–46, FEPC Records; Clarence R. Johnson to Dr. Robert C. Weaver, "Complaint filed by Sylvester White against Welder's Local 681," May 19, 1942, box 14, entry no. 70, Closed Cases 1941–1946, FEPC Records; Robert C. Weaver to Lawrence W. Cramer, May 25, 1942, box 14, entry no. 70, Closed Cases 1941–46, FEPC Records; USES director quoted in Brown, "The Impact of War Worker Migration," 173.

54. Isaiah Brooks, Affidavit, State of California, County of Alameda, October 4, 1941, box 14, entry no. 70, Closed Cases 1941–46, FEPC Records; C. L. Dellums to Laurence [*sic*] Cramer, November 18, 1941, box 14, entry no. 70, Closed Cases 1941–46, FEPC Records.

55. Kramer, "The Story of the Richmond Shipyards," 61; "Women on Payroll by Months and Crafts 1942 Total All Kaiser Shipyards," graphic, ser. 18, vol. 68, n.p., Kaiser Papers; Kagel (signed by Sharee) to Rutledge, "Non-White Employment—ES-270 Reports, Richmond, California," memorandum, June 9, 1944; Rutledge to Kagel, June 12, 1944.

56. Kenneth Ferrell, "Copy of Note" to R. Brown, September 18, 1942; George M. Johnson to Flora Hilliard, October 27, 1942; Flora M. Hilliard to George M. Johnson, November 3, 1942, box 14, entry no. 70, Closed Cases 1941–46, FEPC Records.

57. Mrs. Elmira Ake to President Ro[o]sevelt, October 24, 1942, box 14, entry no. 70, Closed Cases, 1941–46, FEPC Records; George M. Johnson to Mrs. Elmira Ake, November 20, 1942, box 14, entry no. 70, Closed Cases 1941–46, FEPC Records.

58. William R. Brown to Franklin D. Roos[e]velt, December 26, 1944, box 7, entry no. 85, General Records 1941–1945, FEPC Records.

59. Albrier, "Determined Advocate," vi, 130–32.

60. Ibid., 134.

61. Thurgood Marshall, "Negro Status in the Boilermakers' Union," *Crisis,* March 1944, 78; Foner, *Organized Labor and the Black Worker,* 247; David F. Selvin to Walter White, January 19, 1943, 2–3, carton 23, Cottrell. L. [C. L.] Dellums Papers, Bancroft Library, University of California, Berkeley. In the same letter, Selvin also reported that trainees and journeymen in Bay Area auxiliaries, including Local A-36, paid monthly dues of $2.50 and $2.95, respectively, while trainees and journeymen in regular locals paid monthly dues of $3 and $3.50, respectively. The difference in payment between the auxiliaries and the regular locals lay in the different insurance policies blacks and whites were given. Auxiliary members were "given an insurance policy which provides a death benefit of $166 in the first year in the event of death, $333 in the second year, $500 in the third and thereafter." Regular members received a policy which "provides a death benefit in the first year of $333, $666 in the second year, and $1000 in the third and thereafter."

62. Selvin to White, January 19, 1943.

63. George M. Johnson to Clarence R. Johnson, memorandum, "Employment-Richmond Shipyards," June 11, 1943, box 14, entry no. 70, Closed Cases, 1941–46, FEPC Records; "Auxiliary Lodge Number 36 of the International Brotherhood of Boilermakers, Iron Shipbuilders, and Helpers of America (Local A-36)," in Tilghman Press, *We Also Serve: Ten Percent of a Nation Working and Fighting for Victory* (Berkeley, Calif.: Tilghman Press, 1945), 25.

64. "Auxiliary Lodge Number 36," 30; Thurston, interview.

65. McKinney, interview, June 18, 1991.

66. Cleophas Brown, telephone conversation with author, October 18, 1987; Matt Crawford, telephone conversation with author, October 18, 1987.

67. Brown to Franklin D. Roos[e]velt, December 26, 1944.

68. Cleophas Brown, interview by Judith Dunning for "On the Waterfront: An Oral History of Richmond, California," March 1, 1985, audiotapes in the personal collection of Mrs. Ursula Brown (hereafter cited as Brown, Dunning interview); Cleophas Brown, telephone conversation.

For an incisive account of the *James v. Marinship* battle and the struggle of black workers against union discrimination in the Bay Area, see Albert S. Broussard, *Black San Francisco: The Struggle for Racial Equality in the West, 1900–1954* (Lawrence: University Press of Kansas, 1993), 157–65; Wollenberg, *Marinship at War,* esp. chap. 7, pp. 70–84; Shirley Ann Moore, "Getting There, Being There: African-American Migration to Richmond California, 1910–1945," in *The Great Migration in Historical Perspective: New Dimensions of Race, Class, and Gender,* ed. Joe William Trotter Jr. (Bloomington: Indiana University Press, 1991), 106–26. See also Nash, *The American West Transformed,* 92–93; Brown, "The Impact of War Worker Migration," 176; Foner, *Organized Labor and the Black Worker,* 248–49; Charles Wollenberg, *Golden Gate Metropolis: Perspectives on Bay Area History* (Berkeley: Institute of Governmental Studies, University of California, Berkeley, 1985), 249.

69. Ursula Brown, interview with author, August 28, 1993; Cleophas Brown, telephone conversation.

70. Brown, Dunning interview.

71. Brown, "The Impact of War Worker Migration," 175–76; Starks, interview; *Richmond Independent,* April 14, 1947; Louis Campbell, "Our Town," *California Voice,* April 13, 1951; "Labor Man Nominated in Richmond," *Labor Herald,* April 22, 1947, carton 16, folder "O.A. Correspondence Branch, Richmond 1946–1947," Records of the National Association for the Advancement of Colored People, West Coast Region, 1946–1970, Bancroft Library University of California, Berkeley (hereafter cited as NAACP Records); Brown, Dunning interview.

72. Katherine Archibald, *Wartime Shipyard: A Study in Social Disunity* (Berkeley: University of California Press, 1947), 3–4; Harry L. Kingman to Will Maslow, "Life Magazine Project," memorandum, February 1, 1945, box 7, entry no. 85, General Records 1941–45, FEPC Records.

73. Fabry, *Swingshift,* 186, 190, 231; Johnson to Egan, memorandum, March 9, 1943.

74. Barbour, *An Exploratory Study of Socio-Economic Problems,* 6, 9; Wilbur Wheat, telephone conversation with author, January 26, 1987.

75. For a general discussion of black and white assimilation in the urban industrial workforce, see Bodnar, Simon, and Weber, *Lives of Their Own,* 237–41; Brown, "The Impact of War Worker Migration," 121; "Richmond Took a Beating," 267; Kaiser Company, Inc., *Richmond Shipyard Number Three,* 91; Robertson to Boney, memorandum, January 6, 1943; James Nobel Gregory, *American Exodus: The Dust Bowl Migration and Okie Culture* (New York: Oxford University Press, 1989).

76. Albrier, "Determined Advocate," 131.

77. Wheat and Wheat, interview.

78. Richmond Shipyard Number Two, *Full Ahead,* 26; Kramer, "The Story of the Richmond Shipyards," 61–63; Frank, Ziebarth, and Field, *The Life and Times of Rosie the Riveter,* 84; Albrier, "Determined Advocate," 131; Sokol, "From Workingman's Town to All American City," 36; Wheat and Wheat, interview.

79. Permanente Metals Corporation, *A Booklet of Illustrated Facts,* 30, 35; Sokol, "From Workingman's Town to All American City," 36; Wheat and Wheat, interview; Permanente Metals Corporation, Kaiser Company, Inc., Kaiser, Inc. "How We're Cared For," *Fore 'n' Aft* 4, no. 15 (April 4, 1944): 20–21, ser. 15, carton 288, folder 3, Kaiser Papers; Kramer, "The Story of the Richmond Shipyards," 58, 70–71; Charles S. Day to file memorandum, January 19, 1943, ser. 2, carton 20, folder 32, Kaiser Papers; Kaiser Permanente, Inc., "Where Does Our Dough Go?" *A Health Plan for Employees of the Richmond Shipyard, Richmond, California,* 1942, 22–23, ser. 15, carton 288, folder 3, Kaiser Papers.

80. Brown, "The Impact of War Worker Migration," 176; Tilghman Press, *We Also Serve,* 8; *Oakland Tribune,* April 14, 1944. See program for launching of S.S. *Fisk Victory,* ser. 15, carton 288, folder 18, "Shipbuilding Richmond Yard 2, Launching Program," Kaiser Papers.

81. Kaiser Industries, *The Kaiser Story,* 27; Stanley Nystrom, interview with

author, July 31, 1986; Fabry, *Swingshift,* 189; Barbour, *An Exploratory Study of Socio-Economic Problems,* 8–9; Wheat, telephone conversation.

82. Augusta H. Clawson, *Shipyard Diary of a Woman Welder* (New York: Penguin Books, 1944), 8.

83. Sokol, "From Workingman's Town to All American City," 81 n. 15; J. Edgar Hoover to T. A. Bedford, January 28, 1943, ser. 15, carton 288, folder 22, Kaiser Papers.

84. Kaiser Richmond Shipbuilding Corporation, "Craft Work Descriptions—Richmond Shipyards," 1944, ser. 2, carton 10, n.p., Kaiser Papers; Patricia Cooper, *Once a Cigar Maker: Men, Women, and Work Culture in American Cigar Factories, 1900–1919* (Urbana: University of Illinois Press, 1987), 2, 41–74, 65–66; Wheat and Wheat, interview; Starks, interview; Joseph Malbrough and Irene Malbrough Batchan, interview with author, August 18, 1985.

85. First four quotations in text come from Wheat, telephone conversation. For "extremely high," see Beck to Day and Egan, memorandum, March 31, 1943. See also Sokol, "From Workingman's Town to All American City," 52, for twenty thousand monthly turnover figure.

86. Sokol, "From Workingman's Town to All American City," 38–39, 52–53; D. J. Robertson to J. C. Egan, memorandum, February 2, 1943; William Beck to C. H. Day and J. C. Egan, memorandum, March 31, 1943; William Beck to Dave Olson and S. D. Raudenbush, March 10, 1943; M. M. Spencer to D. H. Olson, S. D. Raudenbush, and J. C. Egan, memorandum, March 20, 1943, all in ser. 2, carton 20, folder 32, Kaiser Papers.

87. Wheat and Wheat, interview.

88. International Brotherhood of Boilermakers, Iron Shipbuilders, and Helpers of America, Local No. 513, *Richmond, Arsenal of Democracy,* 100; Subcommittee of House Committee on Merchant Marine and Fisheries, *Hearings on Shipyard Profits,* 78th Cong., 2d sess., 1944, 5:856; "Testimony of Arthur A. Hall," *Congested Areas Hearings,* 865–66; Sokol, "From Workingman's Town to All American City," 51–52; Nash, *The American West Transformed,* 39; Henry J. Kaiser, memorandum, n.d., "Lets Talk about *Presenteeism,*" ser. 8, carton 148, folder 1, Kaiser Papers; Hall Babbitt to Henry J. Kaiser, March 30, 1943, ser. 8, carton 148, folder 1, Kaiser Papers; "Statement of Henry J. Kaiser, Oakland, California," galley proof of testimony before the House Committee on Labor, n.d., ser. 8, carton, 148, folder 1, Kaiser Papers.

89. Gutman, *Work, Culture, and Society in Industrializing America,* esp. pt. 1, 3–117; House Committee on Merchant Marines and Fisheries, *Hearings on Shipyard Profits,* 5:856; Beck to Day and Egan, memorandum, March 31, 1943; "Labor Turnover 1942," graphic. African Americans were not the only shipyard workers who were dissatisfied with shipyard discipline in the Richmond yards. Kaiser officials reported in general that

the type of men who have been coming in from the south are of a very different character than those from the Middle West. A great many of these men have come to us immediately upon arrival to state that they don't like it here and want us to send them home or they want their wives brought out immediately or they won't stay; in other words, they are homesick. Either the Southerners are more sentimental than the Northerners or their wives treat them better.

See Johnson to Egan, memorandum, March 9, 1943; Starks, telephone conversation.

90. For some of the Kaiser-sponsored activities and amenities, see Richmond Shipyard Number Two, *Full Ahead,* 26; Kaiser Permanente, "Serve Your Country and Yourself"; Kramer, "The Story of the Richmond Shipyards," 61–62. For a discussion of African Americans and social obligations, see Trotter, *Black Milwaukee,* 62; Albrier, "Determined Advocate," 125.

91. Henry J. Kaiser, memorandum, n.d.; Babbitt to Kaiser, March 30, 1943; "Statement of Henry J. Kaiser, Oakland, California," galley proof, n.d.; Wheat and Wheat, interview.

92. Starks, telephone conversation.

93. Williams and Williams, "Reflections," 110; Albrier, "Determined Advocate," vi, 132–33; Starks, telephone conversation.

94. Bob Geddins, interview with author, May 8, 1987; Bob Geddins, "Living Blues Interview: Bob Geddins," interview by Tom Mazzolini, *Living Blues Magazine,* September/October 1977, 19–30.

95. Joseph Malbrough and Irene Malbrough Batchan, interview.

Chapter 3.   Boomtown

1. "Richmond Took a Beating," *Fortune,* February 1945, 269.

2. Hubert Owen Brown, "The Impact of War Worker Migration on the Public School System of Richmond, California, from 1940–1945" (Ph.D. diss., Stanford University, 1973), 113; "Testimony of Arthur A. Hall, Local Manager of the United States Employment Services Operating under the Manpower Commission, Richmond, Calif.," Subcommittee of the House Committee on Naval Affairs Investigating Congested Areas, *Hearings before the United States House Committee on Naval Affairs,* 78th Cong., 1st sess., April 12–17, 1943 (hereafter cited as *Congested Areas Hearings*), 859; "Richmond Took a Beating," 269; "Richmond: A City of High Hopes and Big Headaches," *Fortnight: The News Magazine of California* 3, no 12 (December 19, 1947): 18; "Testimony of J. A. McVittie, City Manager of the City of Richmond," *Congested Areas Hearings,* 836.

3. "Testimony of Arthur A. Hall," *Congested Areas Hearings,* 859; "Testimony of J. A. McVittie," *Congested Areas Hearings,* 836.

4. "Testimony of Walter T. Helm." *Congested Areas Hearings,* 887; "Richmond Took a Beating," 264.

5. Brown, "The Impact of War Worker Migration," 110–13; "Richmond Took a Beating," 262, 264.

6. Brown, "The Impact of War Worker Migration," 100–113, 128; "Richmond Took a Beating," 264; Richard Reinhardt, "Richmond—Boom That Didn't Bust," *San Francisco Chronicle,* August 16, 1953; *Richmond Independent,* March 16, 1941; "Testimony of J. A. McVittie," *Congested Areas Hearings,* 836–41; "Testimony of Walter T. Helm," *Congested Areas Hearings,* 887; "Testimony of Thomas M. Carlson, City Attorney for Richmond," *Congested Areas Hearings,* 835.

7. Richard Pollenberg, *War and Society: The United States, 1941–1945* (Westport, Conn., Greenwood Press, 1972), 140–45; Lowell Juilleard Carr and James Edson Stermer, *Willow Run* (New York: Harper, 1952; reprint, New York: Arno Press, 1977), 62–86; Robert J. Havighurst and H. Gerthon Morgan, *The Social History of a War Boom Community* (New York: Longmans Greene, 1951), 23–87; Gerald D. Nash, *The American West Transformed: The Impact of the Second World War* (Bloomington: Indiana University Press, 1985), 68–69.

8. "Testimony of Walter T. Helm," *Congested Areas Hearings,* 871, 888. See also Richmond Chamber of Commerce, "Richmond, California—On the San Francisco Bay," in W. Miller Barbour, *An Exploratory Study of Socio-Economic Problems affecting the Negro-White Relationship in Richmond, California* (Pasadena, Calif.: United Community Defense Services, Inc., and the National Urban League, 1952), 3; James A. McVittie, *An Avalanche Hits Richmond* (Richmond: Office of the City Manager, 1944), 141; "Richmond Took a Beating," 265, 267; and Brown, "The Impact of War Worker Migration," 156–57.

9. Brown, "The Impact of War Worker Migration,"

10. *Richmond Independent,* June 24, 1943; "Richmond Took a Beating," 267; Brown, "The Impact of War Worker Migration," 110–13, 194–97, 232; "Testimony of Walter T. Helm," *Congested Areas Hearings,* 884–89; Roy M. Hamachi, "Postwar Housing in Richmond, California: A Case Study of Local Housing Developments in the Postwar Period" (master's thesis, University of California, Berkeley, 1954), 4, 15–16, carton 6, "Subject Files, California, Richmond," Catherine Bauer Wurster Papers, Bancroft Library, University of California, Berkeley.

11. "Testimony of John A. Miller, Area Coordinator of National Defense for Contra Costa County, Calif.," *Congested Areas Hearings,* 866–67; "Testimony of L. E. Jones, Chief of Police of the City of Richmond" (see report read by James A. McVittie for Charles R. Blake, health officer of the city of Richmond and McVittie's comments), *Congested Areas Hearings,* 880–82; "Testimony of Ivan W. Hill, Director of Recreation, Richmond, Calif.," *Congested Areas Hearings,* 882–84.

12. "Testimony of John A. Miller," *Congested Areas Hearings,* 867; Brown, "The Impact of War Worker Migration," 121; Harry Williams and Marguerite Williams, "Reflections of a Longtime Black Family in Richmond," an oral history conducted in 1985 by Judith R. Dunning, Regional Oral History Office, Bancroft Library, University of California, Berkeley, 1990, 48.

13. Bill Thurston, interview with author, September 10, 1983; "Testimony of C. E. Miller, Production Engineer, Kaiser Shipyards," 754–55, and "Testimony of John A. Miller," 867, *Congested Areas Hearings;* Williams and Williams, "Reflections," 48; *Oakland Tribune,* September 30, 1970. See also "Transportation and Housing Requirements," May 13, 1942, ser. 15, carton 288, folder 7, Henry J. Kaiser Papers, Bancroft Library, University of California, Berkeley (hereafter cited as Kaiser Papers); "The Transportation and Housing Problem as it Affects Labor Turnover in the Richmond Shipyards," February 1943, ser. 15, carton 288, folder 6, Kaiser Papers.

14. "Testimony of L. E. Jones," *Congested Areas Hearings,* 871; "Richmond Took a Beating," 267; Brown, "The Impact of War Worker Migration," 156–57.

15. Brown, "The Impact of War Worker Migration," 156–59; "Richmond Took a Beating," 267.

16. "Richmond Took a Beating," 267; Brown, "The Impact of War Worker Migration," 157–58.

17. The first three quotations in the text paragraph are from "Richmond Took a Beating," 267; the last quotation is from Brown, "The Impact of War Worker Migration," 187 (and see pp. 157–58). See also "Testimony of L. E. Jones, Chief of Police of the City of Richmond," *Congested Areas Hearings,* 871–78; *Richmond Record Herald,* July 15, 1951; Reinhardt, "Richmond—Boom That Didn't Bust."

18. "Richmond Took a Beating," 267.

19. Ivy Reid Lewis, interview with author, July 29, 1987.

20. *Richmond Independent,* August 10, 1943; Brown, "The Impact of War Worker Migration," 185–86; *Richmond Independent,* May 17, 1944; *Richmond Independent,* January 22, 1945.

21. *Richmond Independent,* February 11, 1944; Robert Wenkert, John Magney, and Fred Templeton, *An Historical Digest of Negro-White Relations in Richmond, California* (Berkeley: Survey Research Center, University of California, Berkeley, February 1967, rev. September 1967), 27–30; William Martin Camp, *Skip to My Lou* (New York: Doubleday, Doran, and Company, 1945), 339–59; Reinhardt, "Richmond—Boom That Didn't Bust."

22. Walter Freeman Jr. and Joseph Griffin III, interview with author, November 28, 1987; Joseph Malbrough and Irene Malbrough Batchan, interview with author, August 18, 1985; "Richmond Took a Beating," 265–68; Brown, "The Impact of War Worker Migration," 313–14; Lewis, interview.

23. Brown, "The Impact of War Worker Migration," 169; *Richmond Independent,* June 24, 1943.

24. Brown, "The Impact of War Worker Migration," 172; "Richmond Took a Beating," 265; Sherrill David Luke, "The Problems of Annexing North Richmond to the City of Richmond" (master's thesis, University of California, Berkeley, 1954), 5.

25. "Richmond Took a Beating," 262, 264. The population of North Richmond in 1950 was 3,114 and by 1954 had risen to 3,500. See Luke, "The Problem of Annexing North Richmond," 3–5.

26. "Testimony of Ivan W. Hill," *Congested Areas Hearings,* 883; Brown, "The Impact of War Worker Migration," 187.

27. "Detour through Purgatory," *Fortune,* February 1945, 180; "Richmond Took a Beating," 265, 267.

28. "Detour through Purgatory," 180; Dorothea Lange Photographic Collection, Oakland Museum of California; "Richmond Took a Beating," 265.

29. The significance of Lange's Richmond photographs as they appeared in *Fortune* in February 1945 was first discussed by Hubert Owen Brown in his 1973 dissertation, "The Impact of War Worker Migration," 171–73. My analysis is indebted to his and expands the discussion to include Lange's photographs of Richmond published in other works as well. See Dorothea Lange Photographic Collection, Oakland Museum of California.

30. E. P. (Edwin P.) "Red" Stephenson, "Transition: White Man in a Black

Town, 1950–1967," an oral history conducted in 1975, in "Bay Area Foundations History: Oral History Transcripts/Interviews, 1971–75," vol. 5, Regional Oral History Office, Bancroft Library, University of California, Berkeley, 1971, 28. Angelo Herndon, *The Negro Quarterly*, special issue, 1944, 8, quoted in L. D. Reddick, "The New Race Relations Frontier," *The Journal of Educational Sociology* 19, no. 3 (November 1945): 142; Freeman and Griffin, interview; Brown, "The Impact of War Worker Migration," 187; Lewis, interview.

31. Douglas Henry Daniels, *Pioneer Urbanites: A Social and Cultural History of Black San Franciscans* (Berkeley: University of California Press, 1990), 171–72; Freeman and Griffin, interview; Lee Hildebrand, "North Richmond Blues," *East Bay Express: The East Bay's Free Weekly*, February 9, 1979, 1; Lewis, interview.

32. For an examination of eastern black community building, class structure, and responses to black newcomers, see Peter Gottlieb, *Making Their Own Way: Southern Blacks' Migration to Pittsburgh, 1916–1930* (Urbana: University of Illinois Press, 1987), esp. chap. 7, pp. 183–210; Joe William Trotter Jr., *Black Milwaukee: The Making of an Industrial Proletariat, 1915–1945* (Urbana: University of Illinois Press, 1985), 57–65; James Borchert, *Alley Life in Washington, D.C.: Family, Community, Religion, and Folklife in the City, 1850–1970* (Urbana: University of Illinois Press, 1980), xi. For a discussion of the black middle class in other Bay Area cities, see Daniels, *Pioneer Urbanites,* 164–65. For an examination of another small black community on the Pacific Coast, see Quintard Taylor, *The Forging of a Black Community: Seattle's Central District from 1870 through the Civil Rights Era* (Seattle: University of Washington Press, 1994). Unfortunately the censuses for 1940, 1950, and 1960 specify only "non-white" categories to enumerate occupations by race in Richmond. See U.S. Department of Commerce, Bureau of the Census, *Sixteenth Census of the United States: 1940,* vol. 2 (Washington, D.C.: GPO, 1943), 618, table 33; U.S. Department of Commerce, Bureau of the Census, *A Report of the Seventeenth Decennial Census of the United States: Census of the Population, 1950,* vol. 2 (Washington, D.C.: GPO, 1952), pt. 5, 102, table 34; U.S. Department of Commerce, Bureau of the Census, *The Eighteenth Decennial Census of the United States: Census of Population, 1960,* vol. 1 (Washington, D.C.: GPO, 1961), pt. 6, 375, table 78.

33. Charles Radcliffe Fulweiler, "A Preliminary Investigation of the Accommodation Mechanism as a Factor in the Clinical Study of the Negro Adolescent" (master's thesis, University of California, Berkeley, 1951), 24–25.

34. Wenkert, Magney, and Templeton, *An Historical Digest of Negro-White Relations,* 87; *San Francisco Chronicle,* May 3, 1949; Wilbur Wheat and Vesper Wheat, interview with author, January 24, 1987; William H. McKinney, interview with author, June 18, 1991; Lewis, interview; Stephenson, "Transition," 28.

35. Barbour, *An Exploratory Study of Socio-Economic Problems,* 6–9, 50; Wilbur Wheat, telephone conversation with author, January 26, 1987.

36. Cleophas Brown, telephone conversation with author, October 18, 1987; Thurston, interview; McKinney, interviews with author, June 18, 22, 1991.

37. Luke, "The Problem of Annexing North Richmond," 3; William Sokol, "From Workingman's Town to All American City: The Socio-Political Economy of Richmond, California, during World War II," June 1971, Richmond Col-

lection, Richmond Public Library, 34; "Testimony of J. A. McVittie," 836, and "Testimony of Harry A. Barbour, Executive Director of the Housing Authority of the City of Richmond, Calif.," 841–853, both in *Congested Areas Hearings;* Wenkert, Magney, and Templeton, *An Historical Digest of Negro-White Relations,* 21–22; Hamachi, "Postwar Housing," 26–27.

38. Wenkert, Magney, and Templeton, *An Historical Digest of Negro-White Relations,* 21; *Richmond Independent,* January 14, 1941.

39. Helen Smith Alancraig, "Cordonices Village: A Study of Non-segregated Public Housing in the San Francisco Bay Area" (master's thesis, University of California, Berkeley, 1953), 26–27; Mayor John Stewart quoted in Nash, *The American West Transformed,* 98; Wenkert, Magney, and Templeton, *An Historical Digest of Negro-White Relations,* 21.

40. Sokol, "From Workingman's Town to All American City," 21; "Testimony of J. A. McVittie," *Congested Areas Hearings,* 836; Donald Devine Woodington, "Federal Public War Housing in Relation to Certain Needs and the Financial Ability of the Richmond School District" (Ed.D. diss., University of California, Berkeley, 1954), 82–83, 85.

41. Wenkert, Magney, and Templeton, *An Historical Digest of Negro-White Relations,* 22; Hamachi, "Postwar Housing," 30–31.

42. Roy Hamachi reported that the Richmond Housing Authority was rife with patronage and was so controlled by local developers that when federal officials tried to "muscle in on local patronage" by "placing one of their boys" on the "top management job in the Housing Authority," they found no "accom[m]odation from the local power factions." The 98 units of Triangle Court were the first to be constructed by the Richmond Housing Authority; they were followed by 102 units of Nystrom Village. Atchison Village, comprising 450 units, was designated "permanent low-income, but was switched over to the defense housing program and was completed in 1942." See Hamachi, "Postwar Housing," 52. For a discussion of segregated housing patterns in Richmond during the war boom, also see Luke, "The Problem of Annexing North Richmond," 3; Sokol, "From Workingman's Town to All American City," 34; "Testimony of J. A. McVittie," 836, and "Testimony of Harry A. Barbour," 841–53, both in *Congested Areas Hearings;* Wenkert, Magney, and Templeton, *An Historical Digest of Negro-White Relations,* 21–22; Woodington, "Federal Public War Housing in Relation to Certain Needs," 82–83, 85; Edward E. France, "Some Aspects of the Migration of the Negro to the San Francisco Bay Area since 1940" (Ph.D. diss., University of California, Berkeley, 1962), 53; *Richmond Independent,* August 23, 1943; Wheat and Wheat, interview; Brown, "The Impact of War Worker Migration," 177–78.

43. Hamachi, "Postwar Housing"; Thurston, interview; *Richmond Independent,* February 14, 1944.

44. Minutes, Richmond City Council, September 11, 1944, vol. 21, p. 61.

45. Ursula Brown, interview with author, August 28, 1993; Cleophas Brown, telephone conversation; Records of the National Association for the Advancement of Colored People, West Coast Region, 1946–1970, carton 16, 4 folders, Bancroft Library, University of California, Berkeley (hereafter cited as NAACP Records), and see especially Margaret Starks to N. W. Griffin, May 4, 1945,

folder "O.A. Correspondence Branch, Richmond 1944–1945"; "Federal Housing Problems Aired at Meeting Here," n.d., newspaper clipping, and "Boilermakers' Union Refuses to Accept Negro Members," January 12, no year, newspaper clipping, carton 16, folder "Undated Correspondence, 1944–1945." See also Noah Griffin to Cleophas Brown, May 1, 1946, and October 17, 1946, both in carton 16, folder "O.A. Correspondence Branch, Richmond 1946–1947," NAACP Records.

46. "Resolution to the Richmond Housing Authority," n.d., carton 16, folder "O.A. Correspondence Branch, Richmond 1944–1945," NAACP Records.

47. Wenkert, Magney, and Templeton, *An Historical Digest of Negro-White Relations,* 39; "United Negroes Threaten Rent Strike in Richmond," newspaper clipping [probably *Richmond Independent*], n.d. [ca. January 1945], carton 16, folder "Undated Correspondence, 1944–1945," NAACP Records; "Federal Housing Problems Aired at Meeting Here," newspaper clipping [probably *Richmond Independent*], n.d. [ca. January 1945], carton 16, folder "Undated Correspondence, 1944–1945," NAACP Records; minutes, Richmond City Council, January 8, 1945, vol. 21, p. 146; resolution from the Richmond NAACP to the Richmond Housing Authority, n.d., carton 16, folder "O.A. Correspondence Branch, Richmond 1944–1945," NAACP Records; Reinhardt, "Richmond—Boom That Didn't Bust"; Richard Reinhardt, "Swollen City Bogged Down in Redevelopment Plans," *San Francisco Chronicle,* August 17, 1953.

48. Minutes, Richmond City Council, January 8, 1945, vol. 21, p. 146; resolution from the Richmond NAACP to the Richmond Housing Authority, n.d.; Reinhardt, "Richmond—Boom That Didn't Bust"; Reinhardt, "Swollen City Bogged Down."

49. *Richmond Independent,* January 8, 1945; Brown, "The Impact of War Worker Migration," 178; minutes, Richmond City Council, January 8, 1945, vol. 21, p. 146; Cleophas Brown, telephone conversation; resolution from the NAACP to the Richmond Housing Authority, n.d.; Reinhardt, "Richmond—Boom That Didn't Bust"; Reinhardt, "Swollen City Bogged Down."

50. U.S. Department of Commerce, Bureau of the Census, *Special Census of Richmond, California: September 1943,* ser. P-SC, no. 6 (Washington, D.C.: GPO, 1943); Borchert, *Alley Life in Washington,* 4; John M. Goering, "Neighborhood Tipping and Racial Transition: A Review of Social Science Evidence," *Journal of the American Institute of Planners* 44 (January 1978): 68–78; Hamachi, "Postwar Housing," 27–28, 33–37, 137–39, 152–55, 160–62; Lewis, interview.

51. Hamachi, "Postwar Housing," 26–27.

52. Sokol, "From Workingman's Town to All American City," 34; Hamachi, "Postwar Housing," 26–27; Douglas Maher, "The Pattern of a Generation: A History of Post-War Community Organization in North Richmond, California" (senior thesis, University of California, Berkeley, June 6, 1966), 2–5; Wenkert, Magney, and Templeton, *An Historical Digest of Negro-White Relations,* 21–22, 36–37; McVittie, *An Avalanche Hits Richmond,* 37; Brown, "The Impact of War Worker Migration," 177.

53. Sokol, "From Workingman's Town to All American City," 33–34; Brown, "The Impact of War Worker Migration," 121; Lewis, interview.

54. Barbour, *An Exploratory Study of Socio-Economic Problems,* 24; *Richmond Independent,* September 14, 1943; Hamachi, "Postwar Housing," 27–28; Stephenson, "Transition," 27–28; Luke, "The Problems of Annexing North Richmond," 3.

55. France, "Some Aspects of the Migration of the Negro," 53; a black female newcomer identified by Barbour as "a woman" quoted in Barbour, *An Exploratory Study of Socio-Economic Problems,* 7.

56. Cleophas Brown, telephone conversation; McKinney, interview, June 18, 1991; Thurston, interview; Margaret Starks, interview with author, April 2, 1988. For membership and membership figures, see "Election of Officers, January 13, 1946," n.d.; N. W. Griffin to Lucille Black, January 25, 1946; N. W. Griffin to Cleophas Brown, May 1, 1946; N. W. Griffin to Louis Richardson, September 12, 1946; and N. W. Griffin to Cleophas Brown, October 17, 1946, all in carton 16, folder "O.A. Correspondence Branch, Richmond 1946–1947," NAACP Records.

57. N. W. Griffin to Gloster B. Current, November 19, 1947, carton 16, folder "O.A. Correspondence Branch, Richmond 1946–1947," NAACP Records. For more identifying the radical faction, also see N. W. Griffin to Roy Wilkins, memorandum, August 7, 1947, carton 16, folder "O.A. Correspondence Branch, Richmond 1946–1947," NAACP Records. Also see "Mildred Bowen to Aid N.A.A.C.P. Here," *Independent,* February 3, 1949, and *People's Daily World,* June 7, 1949, both in carton 16, folder "O.A. Correspondence Branch, Richmond 1946–1947," NAACP Records.

58. Griffin to Current, November 19, 1947, NAACP Records; Margaret Starks, telephone conversation with author, June 29, 1988; Ursula Brown, interviews with author, August 28, 1993, and September 11, 1993; Cleophas Brown, telephone conversation.

59. Margaret Starks to N. W. Griffin, May 4, 1945, carton 16, folder "O.A. Correspondence Branch, Richmond 1944–1945," NAACP Records; unsigned memorandum to file, November 9, 1945, carton 16, NAACP Records. A memorandum to the file of the NAACP regional offices, "Election of Officers, January 13, 1946," indicates that Juanita Wheeler, Cleophas Brown's cousin, was by January 1946 secretary of the branch, and Benjamin Clark of Harbor Gate Court replaced V. E. Butler as treasurer. In May of 1945 Margaret Starks asked for a leave of absence, and she let her membership lapse in July 1945; but at the time of the 1946 election she was once again listed as a member. The 1947 election saw Louis Richardson, a member of the AFL Laundry Workers Union Local 2 and the first African American to run for Richmond City Council, gain the presidency. John Hughes was elected vice president, and Cleophas Brown became the second vice president in that election. See memorandum, "Election of Officers, January 13, 1946," n.d.; N. W. Griffin to president NAACP Richmond branch, memorandum, January 23, 1947; and unsigned memorandum to the file, November 9, 1945, all in carton 16, NAACP Records.

60. Griffin to Current, November 19, 1947; Griffin to Wilkins, memorandum, August 7, 1947; and N. W. Griffin to Bernard Evans, January 12, 1948, all in carton 16, NAACP Records; *Richmond Independent,* February 3, 1949; *People's Daily World,* June 7, 1949.

61. All quotations come from Griffin to Current, November 19, 1947,

NAACP Records. See also unsigned letter (probably written by Margaret Starks) from "The People of Richmond, California," to the NAACP Board of Directors, "Re: Infiltration, Misrepresentation of the Richmond Branch of the National Association for the Advancement of Colored People and the Denunciation of that Branch by the Ministers, Churches, Civic Organizations, and Business Establishments of the City of Richmond, Calif.," February 28, 1949, carton 16, folder "O.A. Correspondence Branch, Richmond 1946–1947," NAACP Records.

62. Bernard Evans to Gloster B. Current, December 18, 1947; Griffin to Current, November 19, 1947; and Gloster B. Current to Noah Griffin, December 19, 1947, all in carton 16, folder "O.A. Correspondence Branch, Richmond 1946–1947," NAACP Records.

63. Cleophas Brown, telephone conversation; Starks, telephone conversation; "Federal Housing Problems Aired at Meeting Here"; "Boilermakers' Union Refuses to Accept Negro Members"; and Noah Griffin to Cleophus [*sic*] Brown, May 1, 1946, and October 17, 1946, carton 16, NAACP Records.

Chapter 4. Demobilization, Rising Expectations, and Postwar Realities

1. Walter White to Noah W. Griffin, July 16, 1945, carton 16, folder "O.A. Correspondence Branch, Richmond 1946–1947," Records of the National Association for the Advancement of Colored People, West Coast Region, 1946–1970, Bancroft Library, University of California, Berkeley (hereafter cited as NAACP Records); Albert S. Broussard, *Black San Francisco: The Struggle for Racial Equality in the West, 1900–1954* (Lawrence: University Press of Kansas, 1993), 209.

2. White to Griffin, July 16, 1945, NAACP Records; Lawrence P. Crouchett, Lonnie G. Bunch III, and Martha Kendall Winnacker, *Visions toward Tomorrow: The History of the East Bay Afro-American Community, 1852–1977* (Oakland: Northern California Center for Afro-American History and Life, 1989), 53; Broussard, *Black San Francisco*, 209–26; Cy W. Record, "Characteristics of Some Unemployed Negro Shipyard Workers in Richmond, California" (Berkeley: Library of Economic Research, University of California, Berkeley, September 1947), 12, Intergovernmental Studies Library, University of California, Berkeley.

3. Charles Raudebauch, "Richmond: Town with a Purple Heart Looks toward the Future," *San Francisco Chronicle*, March 18, 1946, carton 16, folder "O.A. Correspondence Branch, Richmond 1946–1947," NAACP Records; "Unemployment 13,800," *Council on Civic Unity* 1, no. 1 (June 5, 1946): 3, pamphlet, carton 16, folder "O.A. Correspondence Branch, Richmond 1946–1947," NAACP Records; White to Griffin, July 16, 1945; William Hogan, "Hangover Town," *Salute*, June 1946, 40–41; Record, "Characteristics of Some Unemployed Negro Shipyard Workers," 14.

4. U.S. Department of Commerce, Bureau of the Census: *A Report of the Seventeenth Decennial Census of the United States: Census of the Population, 1950*

(hereafter cited as 1950 Census), vol. 2 (Washington, D.C.: GPO, 1952), pt. 5, 102; W. Miller Barbour, *An Exploratory Study of Socio-Economic Problems affecting the Negro-White Relationship in Richmond, California* (Pasadena, Calif.: United Community Defense Services, Inc., and the National Urban League, 1952), 11–13; Robert Wenkert, John Magney, and Fred Templeton, *An Historical Digest of Negro-White Relations in Richmond, California* (Berkeley: Survey Research Center, University of California, Berkeley, February 1967, rev. September 1967), 11–13, 76; Matt Crawford, telephone conversation with author, October 18, 1987; Roy M. Hamachi, "Postwar Housing in Richmond, California: A Case Study of Local Housing Development in the Postwar Period" (master's thesis, University of California, Berkeley, 1954), 68, carton 6, "Subject Files, California, Richmond," Catherine Bauer Wurster Papers, Bancroft Library, University of California, Berkeley.

5. Record, "Characteristics of Some Unemployed Negro Shipyard Workers," 14; Crawford, telephone conversation; Barbour, *An Exploratory Study of Socio-Economic Problems,* 11–13; Wenkert, Magney, and Templeton, *An Historical Digest of Negro-White Relations,* 11–13, 76; Hamachi, "Postwar Housing," 68.

6. Record, "Characteristics of Some Unemployed Negro Shipyard Workers," 20, 24–25, 48–56; Luke, "The Problem of Annexing North Richmond" (master's thesis, University of California, Berkeley, 1954), 7–8; Barbour, *An Exploratory Study of Socio-Economic Problems,* 13; Margaret Starks, telephone conversation with author, June 29, 1988; William H. McKinney, telephone conversation with author, June 22, 1991.

7. Record, "Characteristics of Some Unemployed Negro Shipyard Workers," 24–25; Luke, "The Problem of Annexing North Richmond," 7–8; McKinney, telephone conversation.

8. Hamachi, "Postwar Housing," 29–31, 55–56; Richmond City Planning Commission, *Residential Richmond: Part One,* 1958, 3–9, typeset manuscript, Richmond Collection, Richmond Public Library; Richmond City Planning Commission, *A Report on Housing and Redevelopment: An Element of the Richmond Master Plan* (Richmond: Richmond City Planning Commission, January 1950), 18–20, 49–51; Richmond Redevelopment Agency, *Application for Preliminary Advance* (Richmond: Richmond Redevelopment Agency, September 12, 1950), 59–60, Richmond Collection, Richmond Public Library; Department of City and Regional Planning, "A Master Plan for the North Richmond Neighborhood" (Berkeley: University of California, Berkeley, Department of City and Regional Planning, March 1949), 12, mimeograph, Intergovernmental Studies Library, University of California, Berkeley; Wenkert, Magney, and Templeton, *An Historical Digest of Negro-White Relations,* 21–22, 36–43; Marilynn S. Johnson, *The Second Gold Rush: Oakland and the East Bay in World War II* (Berkeley: University of California Press, 1993), 218–22.

9. Luke, "The Problem of Annexing North Richmond," 74; Richard Reinhardt, series of articles in the *San Francisco Chronicle,* August 16–21, 1953, including "Richmond—Boom That Didn't Bust," August 16, 1953, and "Swollen City Bogged Down in Redevelopment Plans," August 17, 1953; "Building Richmond through Redevelopment Today and Tomorrow," *Richmond Independent,* September 6, 1963; Raymond P. deRomanett, "Public Action and Community

Planning: A Study in the Redevelopment of Richmond, California" (master's thesis, University of California, Berkeley, 1956); minutes, Richmond City Council, January 7, 1946, vol. 22, p. 72.

10. Wenkert, Magney, and Templeton, *An Historical Digest of Negro-White Relations,* 38–39; "United Negroes Threaten Rent Strike in Richmond," and "Federal Housing Problems Aired at Meeting Here," undated newspaper clippings [probably *Richmond Independent*], n.d. [ca. January 1945], carton 16, NAACP Records; undated Resolution from the Richmond NAACP to the Richmond Housing Authority, memorandum to file, November 9, 1945, carton 16, folder "O.A. Correspondence Branch, Richmond, 1944–1945," NAACP Records; minutes, Richmond City Council, *Meetings,* October 23, 1944, vol. 21, p. 38; Richard Reinhardt, "Richmond—Boom That Didn't Bust," *San Francisco Chronicle,* August 16, 1953; Reinhardt, "Swollen City Bogged Down in Redevelopment Plans"; Reinhardt, "No Place to Live, Negroes Fear," *San Francisco Chronicle,* August 18, 1953; La Beaux quoted in "Richmond Council Calls Racial Problem Parley," *California Voice,* March 21, 1952.

11. Nystrom and Triangle Court, the two hundred units of permanent low-income housing controlled by the housing authority, were occupied by white tenants only. North Richmond, where blacks were concentrated, was already overcrowded, and dwellings were scheduled for demolition. Wenkert, Magney, and Templeton, *An Historical Digest of Negro-White Relations,* 39–41; "Richmond Council Calls Racial Problem Parley"; Hamachi, "Postwar Housing," 63; Reinhardt, "No Place to Live, Negroes Fear."

12. Hamachi, "Postwar Housing," 111–13, 118; Wenkert, Magney, and Templeton, *An Historical Digest of Negro-White Relations,* 39–41; Reinhardt, "No Place to Live, Negroes Fear"; Richard Reinhardt, "Where Can Displaced Tenants Find Homes?" *San Francisco Chronicle,* August 21, 1953; "Richmond Council Calls Racial Problem Parley"; Barbour, *An Exploratory Study of Socio-Economic Problems,,* 22–23.

13. Richard Reinhardt, "Secret Plans, Rumors Have Tenants Worried," *San Francisco Chronicle,* August 19, 1953; Hamachi, "Postwar Housing"; Richmond City Planning Commission, *A Report on Housing and Redevelopment,* 40–44.

14. Wenkert, Magney, and Templeton, *An Historical Digest of Negro-White Relations,* 39–41; Luke, "The Problem of Annexing North Richmond," 75–76; "Richmond Council Calls Racial Problem Parley"; Reinhardt, "No Place to Live, Negroes Fear"; Reinhardt, "Where Can Displaced Tenants Find Homes?"

15. James McVittie, "Condemnation of Private, Commercial, and Residential Buildings Permitted for Temporary Occupancy during the War," in *An Avalanche Hits Richmond* (Richmond: Office of the City Manager, 1944), 37.

16. McVittie, "Condemnation of Private, Commercial, and Residential Buildings," 37; "Hensley Industrial Park Will Be Source of Jobs and Taxes," *Richmond Independent,* October 3, 1955; Reinhardt, "Where Can Displaced Tenants Find Homes?"; Luke, "The Problem of Annexing North Richmond," 77–78; Wenkert, Magney, and Templeton, *An Historical Digest of Negro-White Relations,* 36–38.

17. McVittie, "Condemnation of Private, Commercial, and Residential Buildings," 37. In 1955 of the eighty-four families living in what would become the Hensley Industrial Park who were required to move, seventy-six were "non-

white." Wenkert, Magney, and Templeton, *An Historical Digest of Negro-White Relations,* 36–38; *Richmond Independent,* October 3, 1955; Luke, "Problem of Annexing North Richmond," 77–78; Hamachi, "Postwar Housing," 34–35; Starks, telephone conversation.

18. 1950 Census, vol. 2, pt. 5, 102; Davis McEntire, "Postwar Status of Negro Workers in the San Francisco Area," *Monthly Labor Review* 70 (June 1950): 614–17; Barbour, *An Exploratory Study of Socio-Economic Problems,* 3, 5, 13; Richmond Model Cities Program and City of Richmond Planning Department, Research and Evaluation Unit, "Richmond Facts" (Richmond, December 1, 1974), 2, table 1, Richmond Collection, Richmond Public Library; U.S. Department of Commerce, Bureau of the Census, *United States Census of Population and Housing: 1960,* Final Report PHC (1)-138 (Washington, D.C.: GPO, 1961), table P-1; Wenkert, Magney, and Templeton, *An Historical Digest of Negro-White Relations,* 34–35.

19. Gerald D. Nash, *The American West Transformed: The Impact of the Second World War* (Bloomington: Indiana University Press, 1985), 95–118, 128–52; Richard Pollenberg, *War and Society: The United States, 1941–1945* (Westport, Conn.: Greenwood Press Publishers, 1972), 125–30; Davis McEntire, *Police Training Bulletin: A Guide to Race Relations for Police Officers* (Sacramento: California Department of Justice, 1946), 8, Richmond Collection, Richmond Public Library.

20. Robert W. Kenny, "Police and Minority Groups—An Experiment, An Address," 1946, 1–2, typescript, Richmond Collection, Richmond Public Library; Robert W. Kenny to N. W. Griffin, October 22, 1945, carton 16, NAACP Records; Cleophas Brown, telephone conversation with author, October 18, 1987; Walter Freeman Jr. and Joseph Griffin III, interview with author, November 28, 1987; Starks, telephone conversation.

21. Harry Williams and Marguerite Williams, "Reflections of a Longtime Black Family in Richmond," an oral history conducted 1985 by Judith R. Dunning, Regional Oral History Office, Bancroft Library, University of California, Berkeley, 1990, 127–28; Hubert Owen Brown, "The Impact of War Worker Migration on the Public School System of Richmond, California, from 1940–1945" (Ph.D. diss., Stanford University, 1973), 319–23.

22. Wenkert, Magney, and Templeton, *An Historical Digest of Negro-White Relations,* 52–58; McVittie, *An Avalanche Hits Richmond,* 74–75; Richmond City Planning Commission, *A Report on Schools, Parks, and Playgrounds, Richmond, California,* typeset manuscript, January 1948, 1, Richmond Collection, Richmond Public Library; Chamber of Commerce, *Handbook of Richmond, California,* 1940, 1945, 1947, in James R. Orosco, "A Survey of Voting Behavior in the City of Richmond, California, 1936–1956," spring 1963, 30, manuscript, Richmond Collection, Richmond Public Library.

23. Wenkert, Magney, and Templeton, *An Historical Digest of Negro-White Relations,* 52.

24. Ibid., 53.

25. For "injured," see Brown, "The Impact of War Worker Migration," 315. For the other quotations in the text paragraph, see Noah Griffin to Walter White, October 3, 1945, carton 16, folder "O.A. Correspondence Branch, Richmond 1944–1945," NAACP Records.

26. Brown, "The Impact of War Worker Migration," 314–23; City Attorney Pierce called the school policy of integrated classes one of "utter stupidity" and described how his son quit the school orchestra in "anger and disgust" because "Negro boys" had been permitted to ask "white girls to dance with them." Pierce also criticized the school board for allowing "Negro and white children to attend the same social functions." He stated his opposition to blacks and whites "occupying the same classrooms at the same time." *Richmond Independent,* October 2, 1945; Freeman and Griffin, interview; Joseph Griffin III, telephone conversation with author, November 11, 1987; Griffin to White, October 3, 1945, Griffin to Robert W. Kenny, October 11, 1945, Kenny to Griffin, October 22, 1945, and "Memorandum to Files," n.d., entry dated October 5, 1945, all in carton 16, NAACP Records; Freeman and Griffin, interview.

27. Wenkert, Magney, and Templeton, *An Historical Digest of Negro-White Relations,* 53; Lillian B. Rubin, *Busing and Backlash: White against White in an Urban School District* (Berkeley: University of California Press, 1972); Robert Wenkert, John Magney, and Ann Neel, "Two Weeks of Racial Crisis in Richmond, California" (Berkeley: Survey Research Center, University of California, Berkeley, February 1967), 2, 120–21.

28. For an overview of the U.S. and African Americans in the Cold War era, see John Hope Franklin and Alfred A. Moss Jr., *From Slavery to Freedom: A History of African Americans,* 7th ed. (New York: McGraw Hill, 1994), 461–91; Robert Weisbrot, *Freedom Bound: A History of America's Civil Rights Movement* (New York: Plume Books, 1991), 10; William H. Chafe, *The Unfinished Journey: America since World War II,* 2d ed. (New York: Oxford University Press, 1991), 54–105, 148–176; Richard Kluger, *Simple Justice: The History of Brown v. Board of Education, and Black America's Struggle for Equality* (New York: Vintage Books, 1975), 509–10, 655–56; Broussard, *Black San Francisco,* 181–204; Philip S. Foner, *Organized Labor and the Black Worker, 1619–1981,* 2d ed. (New York: International Publishers, 1982), 275–92. For anti-Communist hysteria in the Richmond NAACP, see N. W. Griffin to Gloster B. Current, November 10, 1947, and Gloster B. Current to Noah Griffin, December 19, 1947, both in folder "O.A. Correspondence Branch, Richmond 1946–1947," carton 16, NAACP Records.

29. Laurence I. Hewes Jr., "Race Relations on the West Coast," *The Nation,* special western suppl., September 21, 1946, 26; letter to NAACP National Board of Directors, February 28, 1949, carton 16, NAACP Records; Ollie Freeman, conversation with author, September 14, 1985; Cleophas Brown, telephone conversation.

30. "Richmond Groups Fight Picket Ban," *San Francisco Reporter,* June 14, 1947, carton 16, NAACP Records; Broussard, *Black San Francisco,* 193–204; "Memorandum Concerning the Fight for Fair Employment, vs. The Monopoly Chain Store, Lucky Stores, Inc., John E. Hughes, Petitioner and Respondent," n.d., carton 16, NAACP Records; "Richmond Groups Fight Picket Ban"; "Richmond Branch NAACP Fights Grocery Store Picketing Ban," NAACP news release, June 27, 1947, carton 16, NAACP Records.

31. Wenkert, Magney, and Templeton, *An Historical Digest of Negro-White Relations,* 87; Starks, telephone conversation; Cleophas Brown, telephone con-

versation; Bill Thurston, interview with author, September 10, 1983; *San Francisco Chronicle*, May 3, 1949.

32. Cleophas Brown, telephone conversation; "The People of Richmond, California" to Board of Directors, N.A.A.C.P., February 28, 1949, carton 16, NAACP Records. The letter indicates that the signatures of the petitioners were enclosed; but unfortunately no document containing the signatures is attached, and it does not appear in any of the other files.

33. Broussard, *Black San Francisco*, 194, 197, 204.

34. The BACAD was based in San Francisco but also drew its leadership from East Bay cities, including Richmond. Broussard, *Black San Francisco*, 192–204.

35. *Council on Civic Unity*, pamphlet, NAACP Records.

36. *Labor Herald*, February 16, March 9, March 30, and April 20, 1945. Of the three officers in the Richmond Council on Civic Unity, two were Richmond residents who had formerly resided in Tennessee and Boston. The other officer was an Oakland resident. *Council on Civic Unity*, pamphlet, NAACP Records; Gerald N. Beallor to California Federation for Civic Unity, June 16, 1948, box 5, folder "Incoming Correspondence, Richmond Council on Intergroup Relations," California Federation for Civic Unity, Records, 1945–1956, Bancroft Library, University of California, Berkeley (hereafter cited as CFCU Papers); W. W. Prall, announcement of meeting scheduled for February 18, 1949, n.d., box 5, folder "Incoming Correspondence, Richmond Council on Intergroup Relations," CFCU Papers; Winifred Sneddon to Richard Dettering, February 13, 1949, box 5, folder "Incoming Correspondence, Sneddon, Winifred," CFCU Papers; Winifred Sneddon to Mrs. Ruth Kaiser, March 4, 1949, box 5, folder "Incoming Correspondence, Sneddon, Winifred," CFCU Papers; Clara-Rae Genser to Mr. [Richard] Dettering, January 31, 1950, box 5, folder "Incoming Correspondence, Richmond Council on Intergroup Relations," CFCU Papers. In September 1951 the RCIR listed William Kretzmer, a white businessman and Richmond resident, as president. Percy Baker, director of the North Richmond Neighborhood House, served as vice president. Among the three newly elected officers, two lived in Richmond. The board's three members-at-large consisted of two Richmond residents. See Winifred Sneddon to Ruth Kaiser, September 16, 1951, box 5, folder "Incoming Correspondence, Sneddon, Winifred," CFCU Papers.

37. Wenkert, Magney, and Templeton, *An Historical Digest of Negro-White Relations*, 71–73; Broussard, *Black San Francisco*, 184; "Richmond Ordinance, Number 1303, Passed May 16, 1949," and N. W. Griffin to Cleophas Brown, May 20, 1949, both in carton 16, NAACP Records; Mrs. Leisa Sturtevant to "Dear Friends," n.d., folder "Incoming Correspondence, Richmond Council on Intergroup Relations," CFCU Papers.

38. Richmond Council on Intergroup Relations, draft addendum to Ordinance Number 1303, box 5, CFCU Papers. On May 9, 1966, the Richmond City Council passed Ordinance 166 N.S., which mandated nondiscrimination clauses in city contracts and gave the city's human relations officer enforcement authority, subject to review by the city's Commission on Human Relations. Wenkert, Magney, and Templeton, *An Historical Digest of Negro-White Relations*, 72 n.138. Cleophas Brown, telephone conversation; Starks, telephone conversation.

39. Cleophas Brown, telephone conversation; Winifred Sneddon to Fred R. Ross, December 11, 1952, box 5, folder "Incoming Correspondence, Sneddon, Winifred," CFCU Papers.

40. Noah W. Griffin to Gloster B. Current, November 19, 1947, Gloster B. Current to N. W. Griffin, December 1, 1947, and Gloster B. Current to N. W. Griffin, December [14?], 1947, all in carton 16, NAACP Records; *West [Contra Costa] County Times,* January 12, 1967, and July 31, 1984; *San Francisco Chronicle,* December 12, 1956; James McMillan, conversation with author, September 27, 1987; *Richmond Independent,* February 2, 1966; Barbour, *An Exploratory Study of Socio-Economic Problems,* 54–55; Lofton L. Fowler and Hazel Hall to Mr. and Mrs. Cleophas Brown, October 22, 1954, carton 16, NAACP Records. Dr. Robinson ran for reelection as NAACP president pledging to increase membership, establish a credit union, secure more black police officers, and integrate housing. His bid for reelection was endorsed by 165 of the 400 members of the organization. The endorsement of Robinson was ambivalent: "Because of his frankness of speech when you first meet him, you may dislike him, but the more you see him work in any good cause, the better you like him. . . . We know that every person in the public eye has some faults, but Dr. Robinson's good qualities overwhelmingly out weigh his undesirable ones." See "Dr. P. T. Robinson's Campaign Statement, 1959," carton 16, NAACP Records; Cleophas Brown, telephone conversation.

41. Douglas Maher, "The Pattern of a Generation: A History of Post-War Community Organization in North Richmond, California" (senior thesis, University of California, Berkeley, June 6, 1966), 25, 35; North Richmond Neighborhood House, "Annual Report, 1968" (Richmond: n.p., 1968); North Richmond Neighborhood House, "North Richmond Neighborhood House, Inc., U.S.A." (Richmond: n.p., 1955), 1; North Richmond Neighborhood House, "Annual Report" (Richmond: n.p., 1965), all in Richmond Collection, Richmond Public Library.

42. E. P. (Edwin P.) "Red" Stephenson, "Transition: White Man in a Black Town, 1950–1967," an oral history conducted 1975, in "Bay Area Foundations History: Oral History Transcripts/Interviews, 1971–75," vol. 5, Regional Oral History Office, Bancroft Library, University of California, Berkeley, 1971, 23, 33a–34.

43. North Richmond Neighborhood House, "Annual Report, 1965"; Stephenson, "Transition," 23, 33a–34.

44. Lucretia Edwards, telephone conversation with author, October 15, 1987; Starks, telephone conversation; Cleophas Brown, telephone conversation.

45. Olivier Zunz, *The Changing Face of Inequality: Urbanization, Industrial Development, and Immigrants in Detroit, 1880–1920* (Chicago: University of Chicago Press, 1982), 3; Richmond City Planning Commission, *Residential Richmond: Part One,* 11–12; Richard Spencer, "Recalling Richmond's Milkshake Days," *Oakland Tribune,* March 5, 1986.

46. Edward E. France, "Some Aspects of the Migration of the Negro to the San Francisco Bay Area since 1940" (Ph.D. diss., University of California, 1962), 54; Rubin, *Busing and Backlash,* see particularly Rubin's map of the Black Crescent, which details schools located inside and outside the Black Crescent, 36;

Contra Costa County Planning Department, "North Richmond-San Pablo Bay Study," 1971, 7, photocopy, Richmond Collection, Richmond Public Library; Wenkert, Magney, and Templeton, *An Historical Digest of Negro-White Relations,* 43–44.

47. *Richmond Independent,* April 14, 1947; Louis Campbell, "Our Town," *California Voice,* April 13, 1951; *San Francisco Chronicle,* December 4, 1946; *Oakland Tribune,* December 2, 1946, December 5, 1946, and May 14, 1974; *Oakland Voters' Herald,* May 9, 1947, Oakland History Room, Election Files Collection, Oakland Public Library; *Labor Herald,* May 20, 1947, and July 8, 1947; Johnson, *The Second Gold Rush,* 202–8.

48. Walter Freeman Jr., telephone conversation with author, August 19, 1988; *Richmond Independent,* April 14, 1947.

49. Hamachi, "Postwar Housing," 38–53; Orosco, "A Survey of Voting Behavior," 16–17, 29; Walter Freeman, telephone conversation, August 19, 1988; "Labor Man Nominated in Richmond," *Labor Herald,* April 22, 1947, carton 16, NAACP Records; *Richmond Independent,* April 14, 1947.

50. Walter Freeman, telephone conversation, August 19, 1988; *Labor Herald,* April 22, 1947; *Richmond Independent,* April 14, 1947.

51. Hamachi, "Postwar Housing," 53–54; *Richmond Independent,* April 14, 1947; *Labor Herald,* April 22, 1947; Walter Freeman, telephone conversation, August 19, 1988.

52. The private papers of John and Gladys Jordan (hereafter cited as Jordon Papers), residents of Parchester Village since 1950, were vital resources for information about Parchester Village. Also see Gordon Raddue, "The Little Village That Could," *Richmond Independent and Gazette,* December 4, 1980, newspaper clipping, Jordon Papers; Carolyn Penn, "Parchester Village Honors Its Achievers," *Oakland Tribune,* n.d. [probably 1975], newspaper clipping, Jordan Papers.

53. Penn, "Parchester Village"; Raddue, "The Little Village That Could."

54. John Jordan and Gladys Jordan, interview with author, September 11, 1987; Hamachi, "Postwar Housing," 29, 36; Parchester Village, "Presenting a Home Community for All Americans," n.d. [ca. 1949], sales advertisement, Jordan Papers; Parchester Joins with Richmond," *Richmond Independent,* n.d., Jordan Papers; Starks, telephone conversation.

55. Mrs. James Bryant, "Poem," printed in Parchester Baptist Church Groundbreaking Ceremony Program, August 19, 1952, Jordon Papers; Penn "Parchester Village."

56. Jordan and Jordan, interview; Starks, telephone conversation; Penn, "Parchester Village."

57. Wenkert, Magney, and Templeton, *An Historical Digest of Negro-White Relations,* 53.

58. Jordan and Jordan, interview; Penn "Parchester Village"; Wenkert, Magney, and Templeton, *An Historical Digest of Negro-White Relations,* 52–53.

59. Penn, "Parchester Village"; Jordon and Jordan, interview; Cleophas Brown, telephone conversation.

60. Wilbur Wheat and Vesper Wheat, interview with author, January 24, 1987.

61. John and Gladys Jordan recalled that some African American residents did not try to pass for white but used white intermediaries to get around the restrictive covenants and discriminatory practices in some Bay Area housing developments. For example, Irene Slaughter, a white Oakland real estate agent and community activist, frequently acted as a "subterfuge" buyer for many of her black clients. Jordan and Jordan, interview. Hamachi, "Postwar Housing," 36; Barbour, *An Exploratory Study of Socio-Economic Problems,* 26–27; Joseph Pereira, "Equality in Richmond, a Long, Quiet Struggle," *West [Contra Costa] County Times,* January 20, 1986; "Richmond Man Defies Whites in Tract," *California Voice,* March 7, 1952 [date misprinted as March 7, 1951]; *San Francisco Chronicle,* March 6, 1952, and April 20, 1952; Franklin H. Williams to Walter White, March 19, 1952, and Douglas Stout to Franklin H. Williams, memorandum, March 21, 1952, both in carton 40, files, "Wilbur Gary," NAACP Records; Wenkert, Magney, and Templeton, *An Historical Digest of Negro-White Relations,* 44.

62. *California Voice,* March 7, 1952, and March 21, 1952; Wheat and Wheat, interview.

63. Pereira, "Equality in Richmond."

64. *California Voice,* March 7, 1952, and March 21, 1952; Lofton L. Fowler, Frank Trotter, and Lizzie M. Lincoln, "Annual Report of the Richmond Branch of the N.A.A.C.P.," see page with memo regarding Wilbur Gary entitled "Report Continue," January 4, 1953, carton 16, NAACP Records.

65. The quotations from the National Urban League study are from Barbour, *An Exploratory Study of Socio-Economic Problems,* 26. See also Cleophas Brown, telephone conversation; Starks, telephone conversation.

66. Barbour, *An Exploratory Study of Socio-Economic Problems,* 26; Cleophas Brown, telephone conversation; Lee Hildebrand, "North Richmond Blues," *East Bay Express: The East Bay's Free Weekly,* February 9, 1979, 5; Pereira, "Equality in Richmond"; *California Voice,* March 28, 1952; Weisbrot, *Freedom Bound,* 10; Fowler, Trotter, and Lincoln, "Annual Report of the Richmond Branch of the N.A.A.C.P.," see page with memorandum regarding Wilbur Gary; Department of Justice brief to the Supreme Court, quoted in Leon F. Litwack and Winthrop D. Jordan, *The United States: Becoming a World Power,* 7th ed. (Englewood Cliffs, N.J.: Prentice Hall, 1991), 2:770; Ollie Freeman, conversation; Starks, telephone conversation.

67. Jacqueline Jones, *Labor of Love, Labor of Sorrow: Black Women, Work, and the Family from Slavery to the Present* (New York: Basic Books, 1985), 6; Starks, telephone conversation.

68. Richmond Model Cities Program, "Richmond Facts," table 1; U.S. Department of Commerce, Bureau of the Census, *Eighteenth Census of the United States, 1960* (Washington, D.C.: GPO, 1961), vol. 21, pt. 6, p. 140, table 21.

69. George Livingston, interview with author, August 6, 1987; Knox and Brombacher quoted in Pereira, "Equality in Richmond."

70. Freeman and Griffin, interview.

71. Wenkert, Magney, and Templeton, *An Historical Digest of Negro-White Relations,* 68–69.

72. Joan Kelly, conversation with author, October 2, 1987; David Weinstein,

"Odis Cotright Richmond Pioneer Businessman Dies," *West [Contra Costa] County Times*, July 7, 1985.

73. Weinstein, "Odis Cotright Richmond Pioneer Businessman Dies."

74. Crawford, telephone conversation; McEntire, *Police Training Bulletin*, 2–3; Carl M. Willensky, *Post War Richmond: A Pictorial Summary of Post War Accomplishments, 1945–1949* (Richmond: Chamber of Commerce, 1949), 26; Wenkert, Magney, and Templeton, *An Historical Digest of Negro-White Relations*, 68–69.

75. Memorandum to the file, April 4, 1946, carton 16, folder "O.A. Correspondence Branch, Richmond 1946–1947," NAACP Records.

76. Memorandum to the file, April 4, 1946, NAACP Records; Contra Costa Black Chamber of Commerce, "Meet CCBCC Member Jim McMillan," *Newsletter*, July 1987; McMillan, conversation; Lawrence P. Crouchett, "Archons in the News, George Carroll Retires from California Judgeship," *The Boule Journal* (fall 1984): 36–37.

77. Jones, *Labor of Love, Labor of Sorrow*, 127, 268–73. See also Miriam Frank, Marilyn Ziebarth, and Connie Field, *The Life and Times of Rosie the Riveter: The Story of Three Million Working Women during World War II* (Emeryville, Calif.: Clarity Educational Productions, 1982), 94–102; Susan M. Hartmann, *The Home Front and Beyond: American Women in the 1940s* (Boston: Twayne Publishers, 1982), 209–16; Elaine Tyler May, *Homeward Bound: American Families in the Cold War Era* (New York: Basic Books, 1988), 58–207; Priscilla H. Douglas, "Black Working Women" (Ph.D. diss., Harvard University, 1981), 2–3 (see also 15, table 1.2); Chafe, *The Unfinished Journey*, 83–85.

78. Louis Campbell, "Look Before You Leap," *California Voice*, August 1, 1941; Jones, *Labor of Love, Labor of Sorrow*, 4; Starks, telephone conversation.

79. Starks, telephone conversation; Joseph Malbrough and Irene Malbrough Batchan, interview with author, August 18, 1985.

80. Starks, telephone conversation; Joseph Malbrough and Irene Malbrough Batchan, interview; Minnie Lue Nichols, interview with author, January 6, 1980.

81. Cleophas Brown, telephone conversation.

82. Ibid.; Rubin, *Busing and Backlash*, 113; Rufus P. Browning, Dale Rogers Marshall, and David H. Tabb, *Protest Is Not Enough: The Struggle of Blacks and Hispanics for Equality in Urban Politics* (Berkeley: University of California Press, 1984), 2, 4–5, 31, 38–45, 59; Orosco, "A Survey of Voting Behavior."

83. Margaret Starks, interview with author, April 2, 1988.

84. Pereira, "Equality in Richmond"; *Richmond Independent*, April 4, 1967, April 5, 1967, and May 2, 1967. In addition to George Livingston and George Carroll, other black city council members elected by the mid-1960s were the following: Bernard Evans, former shipyard worker and Ford employee, who was appointed to the council in 1965 to serve out George Carroll's term; Nathaniel Bates, Richmond native, who was elected in 1967; the Reverend Booker T. Anderson, a Texas native, who settled in Richmond in the 1950s and was elected in 1969.

85. Crouchett, "Archons in the News," 36–37.

86. *Oakland Tribune*, July 7, 1964; *West [Contra Costa] County Times*, April 15, 1985.

87. Starks, interview.

88. Cleophas Brown, telephone conversation; Wheat and Wheat, interview; Wenkert, Magney, and Neel, "Two Weeks of Racial Crisis," 159–82; Starks, interview.

89. *Oakland Tribune,* July 7, 1964; Wenkert, Magney, and Templeton, *An Historical Digest of Negro-White Relations,* 45–47.

90. Wenkert, Magney, and Templeton, *An Historical Digest of Negro-White Relations,* 45–47; *Oakland Tribune,* July 7, 1964.

91. Starks, telephone conversation; Cleophas Brown, telephone conversation; Kenneth G. Goode, *California's Black Pioneers: A Brief Historical Survey* (Santa Barbara, Calif.: McNally and Loftin Publishers, 1974), 147–49.

92. Weisbrot, *Freedom Bound,* 21, 28, 35, 96, 126, 169.

Chapter 5.   Traditions from Home

1. Gutman quoted in Ira Berlin, "Herbert Gutman and the American Working Class," in *Power and Culture: Essays on the American Working Class,* ed. Ira Berlin (New York: Pantheon Books, 1987), 36–37; Herbert G. Gutman, *Work, Culture, and Society in Industrializing America: Essays in American Working-Class and Social History* (1966; reprint, New York: Vintage Books, 1977), 1–260; George Lipsitz, *Time Passages: Collective Memory and American Popular Culture* (Minneapolis: University of Minnesota Press, 1994), 99–132; Olly Wilson, "The Significance of the Relationship between Afro-American Music and West African Music," *The Black Perspective in Music* 2, no. 1 (1974): 3–22; Olly Wilson, "Black Music as an Art Form," *Black Music Research Journal* 4, no. 1 (1983): 2–3; Leroi Jones [Amiri Baraka], *Blues People: The Negro Experience in White America and the Music That Developed from It* (New York: William Morrow and Company, 1963), 95–140. Black Richmondites' use of cultural resources during the World War II era further dispels the "breakdown" theory of African American migration. Other works challenging the spurious theory include Quintard Taylor, *The Forging of a Black Community: Seattle's Central District from 1870 through the Civil Rights Era* (Seattle: University of Washington Press, 1994); James Borchert, *Alley Life in Washington, D.C.: Family, Community, Religion, and Folklife in the City, 1850–1970* (Urbana: University of Illinois Press, 1980); Gretchen Lemke-Santangelo, *Abiding Courage: African American Migrant Women and the East Bay Community* (Chapel Hill: University of North Carolina Press, 1996); Peter Gottlieb, *Making Their Own Way: Southern Blacks' Migration to Pittsburgh, 1916–1930* (Urbana: University of Illinois Press, 1987); Joe William Trotter Jr., *Black Milwaukee: The Making of an Industrial Proletariat, 1915–1945* (Urbana: University of Illinois Press, 1985); Earl Lewis, "Afro-American Adaptive Strategies: The Visiting Habits of Kith and Kin among Black Norfolkians during the First Great Migration," *Journal of Family History* 12, no. 4 (1987): 407–20; Kenneth L. Kusmer, "The Black Urban Experience in American History," in *The State of Afro-American History: Past, Present, and Future,* ed. Darlene C. Hine (Baton Rouge: Louisiana State University Press, 1986), 91–122; Carol Stack *All Our Kin: Strategies for Survival in a Black Community* (New York: Harper and Row, 1974).

2. Beryl Reid quoted in Lee Hildebrand, "North Richmond Blues," *East Bay Express: The East Bay's Free Weekly,* February 9, 1979, 4; Wilbur Wheat and Vesper Wheat, interview with author, January 24, 1987; Margaret Starks, telephone conversation with author, June 29, 1988. Across the bay in San Francisco, African Americans enjoyed wider access to health-care facilities. Historian Albert S. Broussard reports that though black physicians were barred from practicing in San Francisco's hospitals and clinics, black patients were allowed to use those facilities "on an integrated basis." Broussard, *Black San Francisco: The Struggle for Racial Equality in the West, 1900–1954* (Lawrence: University Press of Kansas, 1993), 27–28.

3. Margaret Starks, interview with author, April 2, 1988. Rosa Lewis Wilson (my mother) and Maggie Lewis Atkins (my aunt), daughters of sharecropping parents from Beggs, Oklahoma, migrated to California during the war. They were raised on and employed an array of folk medical customs, which they shared with me. Other information about folk medicine was gathered from Mildred Slocum, interview with author, November 17, 1987; Walter Freeman Jr. and Joseph Griffin III, interview with author, November 28, 1987; Bill Thurston, interview with author, September 10, 1983.

4. James H. Jones, *Bad Blood: The Tuskegee Syphilis Experiment* (New York: Free Press, 1981), 64–65; Gutman, "The Black Family in Slavery and Freedom: A Revised Perspective," in *Power and Culture: Essays on the American Working Class,* ed. Ira Berlin (New York: Pantheon Books, 1987), 357–70; Slocum, interview; Freeman and Griffin, interview.

5. A modified version of my discussion of blues and blues clubs in Richmond appears in my essay "Traditions from Home: African Americans in Wartime Richmond, California," in *The War in American Culture: Society and Consciousness during World War II,* ed. Lewis A. Erenberg and Susan E. Hirsch (Chicago: University of Chicago Press, 1996), 263–83. See also William Barlow, *Looking up at Down: The Emergence of Blues Culture* (Philadelphia: Temple University Press, 1989), 7–55, 325–40; Leroi Jones, *Blues People,* 95–140; Burton W. Peretti, *The Creation of Jazz: Music, Race, and Culture in Urban America* (Urbana: University of Illinois Press, 1992), 16–17; Lipsitz, *Time Passages,* 116–18; Wilson, "The Significance of the Relationship," 3–22; Wilson, "Black Music as an Art Form," 2–3.

6. Eileen Southern, *The Music of Black Americans: A History* (New York: W.W. Norton and Company, 1971), 336–39; Jeff Todd Titon, *Downhome Blues Lyrics: An Anthology from the Post–World War II Era,* 2d ed. (Urbana: University of Illinois Press, 1990); 1–11; Paul Oliver, *The Story of the Blues* (Radnor, Penn.: Chilton Book Company, 1969), 30–34; C. Vann Woodward, *Origins of the New South, 1977–1913* (Baton Rouge: Louisiana State University Press, 1971), 205; Robert W. Stephen, "Soul: A Historical Reconstruction of Continuity and Change in Black Popular Music," *The Black Perspective in Music* 12, no. 1 (spring 1984): 22–23; Peretti, *The Creation of Jazz,* 11–21; Booker T. "Bukka" White, British Broadcasting Corporation interview, Memphis, 1976, quoted in Giles Oakley, *The Devil's Music* (New York: Harcourt, Brace, Jovanovich, 1976), 46; Stephen E. Henderson, "The Heavy Blues of Sterling Brown," in *More Than Dancing: Essays on Afro-American Music and Musicians,* ed. Irene V. Jackson (Westport: Conn.: Greenwood Press, 1985), 198–201; Robert Springer, "The

Regulatory Function of the Blues," *The Black Perspective in Music* 4, no. 3 (fall 1977): 279–80, 283; Margaret W. McCarthy, "The Afro-American Sermon and the Blues," *The Black Perspective in Music* 4, no. 3 (fall 1977): 269–77; Larry Neal, "Ethos of the Blues," *Black Scholar* 3 (summer 1972): 44–46; Tony Russell, *Blacks, Whites, and Blues* (London: Studio Vista, 1970), 59–65; Titon, *Downhome Blues Lyrics*, 2–9.

7. Houston A. Baker Jr., *Blues, Ideology, and Afro-American Literature: A Vernacular Theory* (Chicago: University of Chicago Press, 1984), 3–5; Stephen, "Soul," 21–43; George H. Lewis, "Social Protest and Self Awareness in Black Popular Music," *Popular Music and Society* 2, no. 4 (summer 1974): 327–33; Leroi Jones, *Blues People*, 95–140; Charlie Gillett, *The Sound of the City* (New York: Dell Publishing Company, 1970), 141, 152; Michael Haralambos, *Right On: From Blues to Soul in Black America* (New York: Drake Publishers, 1975), 26–32; Titon, *Downhome Blues Lyrics*, 7; Southern, *The Music of Black Americans*, 389–90.

8. Stephen, "Soul," 25; Virginia Rose, interview with author, January 2, 1984; Carol P. Chamberland, "The House That Bop Built," *California History: The Magazine of the California Historical Society* 75, no. 3 (fall 1996): 272–83; Lee Hildebrand, "Oakland Blues," 3, undated photocopy of an article in the personal collection of record producer and blues songwriter Bob Geddins, whom I interviewed at his home in Oakland, California, May 8, 1987. It should be noted that black wartime migrants to Richmond brought their musical traditions into a black community that had established a strong prewar musical tradition. Black instrumentalists, composers, and singers performed and taught virtually every genre from European classical music to spirituals, gospel, jazz, and popular music. Local black institutions often were the only places these artists could perform, and some won international acclaim. African American tenor Roland Hayes was discovered by the Fannie Jackson Coppin Club, an East Bay black women's organization, which had an active Richmond membership. Before becoming a popular stage and radio performer as the nationally renowned director of the WPA's Northern California "Colored Chorus," William Elmer Keeton did a booming business at his Oakland music studio, offering "instruction in piano, organ playing, courses in music, theory, harmony, counterpoint, forum, analysis, history, composition and instrumentation" to blacks in the Bay Area. Like Hayes, Keeton frequently performed in black churches in Richmond and throughout the Bay Area. See pamphlets 1–3, esp. "The House Committee of the Linden Street Y.M.C.A. Presents Roena Eloise Mucklely Soprano assisted by Eugene Anderson, Tenor, with Elmer Keeton Accompanist, June 24, 1926," program, Miscellaneous Publications, YMCA, Oakland, California, Linden Branch, Bancroft Library, University of California, Berkeley; Michael Fried, "W. Elmer Keeton and His WPA Chorus: Oakland's Musical Civil Rights Pioneers of the New Deal Era," *California History: The Magazine of the California Historical Society* 75, no. 3 (fall 1996): 236–49; "There Was Real Jazz at Tenth and MacDonald," *Richmond Terminal*, January 14, 1921.

9. Tilghman Press, *We Also Serve: Ten Percent of a Nation Working and Fighting for Victory* (Berkeley, Calif.: Tilghman Press, 1945), 59, 61, 66; Tilghman Press, *We Also Serve: Armed Forces Edition* (Berkeley, Calif.: Tilghman Press, 1945), 38; Joseph Malbrough and Irene Malbrough Batchan, interview with author, August 18, 1985.

10. Hildebrand, "Oakland Blues," 3, 4; "Vice Is Held Rampant in North Richmond Area," *Oakland Tribune,* October 12, 1949; Thurston, interview; Starks, interview; Ivy Reid Lewis, interview with author, July 29, 1987.

11. Moore, "Traditions from Home," 270–83; Hildebrand, "Oakland Blues," 3; Hildebrand, "North Richmond Blues," 1; Thurston, interview; Starks, telephone conversation; Lowell Fulson, telephone interview with author, January 21, 1993; Joseph Malbrough and Irene Malbrough Batchan, interview; Sheldon Harris, *Blues Who's Who: A Biographical Dictionary of Blues Singers* (New Rochelle, N.Y.: Da Capo Press, 1979), 188–90.

12. Jimmy McCracklin, composer and performer, "Club Savoy," Irma 107, lyric quoted courtesy of Jimmy McCracklin. I am indebted to Opal Nations for providing me with a copy of this recording from his personal collection.

13. Tilghman Press, *We Also Serve: Armed Forces Edition,* 38; Joseph Malbrough and Irene Malbrough Batchan, interview; Starks, interview.

14. Minnie Lue Nichols, interview with author, January 6, 1980; Minnie Lue Nichols, "An Interview with Minnie Lue," interview by Eldreadge Wright, March 24, 1972, unpublished ms. in the personal collection of the author.

15. Nichols, "An Interview with Minnie Lue"; Hildebrand, "North Richmond Blues," 1; Nichols, interview.

16. "Vice Is Held Rampant in North Richmond Area"; Thurston, interview; Lewis, interview; Starks, interview.

17. Katrina Hazzard-Gordon, *Jookin': The Rise of Social Dance Formations in African-American Culture* (Philadelphia: Temple University Press, 1990), 88–92. Nichols, interview; Joseph Malbrough and Irene Batchan, interview; Starks, interview; "WWI Last Man's Club Loses Its Last Man," *Oakland Tribune,* February 20, 1989.

18. Starks, interview.

19. Starks, telephone conversation. See also Madelon Mae Powers, "Faces along the Bar: Lore and Order in the Workingman's Saloon, 1870–1920" (Ph.D. diss., University of California, Berkeley, 1991), 23–36; Upton Sinclair, *The Jungle* (1906; reprint, New York: New American Library, 1980), 7–25; Nichols, "An Interview with Minnie Lue," 3–5. The *Richmond Guide* was a weekly publication and cost two dollars for a yearly subscription. It was distributed in the blues clubs and in the projects. The paper reported on civil rights issues and employment news and kept readers informed of community activities. See the *Richmond Guide,* December 30, 1946, Richmond Collection, Richmond Public Library (this appears to be the only existing edition of the *Richmond Guide*).

20. Margaret Starks to Noah W. Griffin, May 4, 1945; memorandum to file, November 9, 1945; Noah Griffin to Margaret Starks, April 13, 1945; Noah W. Griffin to Margaret Starks, April 14, 1945; Gloster B. Current to Noah Griffin, December 1, 1947; and Noah W. Griffin to Gloster B. Current, November 19, 1947, all in carton 16, Records of the National Association for the Advancement of Colored People, West Coast Region, 1946–1970, Bancroft Library, University of California, Berkeley (hereafter cited as NAACP Records); Cleophas Brown, telephone conversation with author, October 18, 1987; Ursula Brown, interview with author, September 11, 1993; Starks, telephone conversation.

21. Nichols, interview. Some white immigrant saloons allowed women to use the "ladies entrance" or side door if they wanted to enjoy a "free lunch,"

purchase a pail of beer to take home, or attend social functions that were often held in the saloon's back room. Notable exceptions to the male-owned white immigrant saloons in the United States were the Irish "shebeens," or small drinking establishments, run by women who brewed and sold beer. Shebeens flourished in the 1840s but went into decline around 1890, when large corporate monopolies took over the American liquor industry. I am indebted to Madelon Mae Powers for her discussion of shebeens and the role of working-class women in immigrant saloons. Powers, "Faces along the Bar," 23–36. See also Roy Rosenzweig, *Eight Hours for What We Will: Workers and Leisure in an Industrial City, 1870–1920* (Oxford: Cambridge University Press, 1983), 35–64; Perry R. Duis, *The Saloon: Public Drinking in Chicago and Boston, 1880–1920* (Urbana: University of Illinois Press, 1983).

22. Shirley Ann Wilson Moore, "Not in Somebody's Kitchen: African American Women Workers in Richmond, California, and the Impact of World War II," in *Writing the Range: Race, Class, and Culture in the Women's West,* ed. Elizabeth Jameson and Susan Armitage (Norman: University of Oklahoma Press, 1997), 517–32; Shirley Ann Moore, "Her Husband Didn't Have a Word to Say: Black Women and Blues Clubs in Richmond, California, during World War II," in *American Labor in the Era of World War II,* ed. Sally M. Miller and Daniel Cornford (Westport, Conn.: Praeger, 1995), 147–64; Nichols, interview; *Colored Directory of Leading Cities in Northern California, 1916–1917* (Oakland, Calif.: Tilghman Press, 1917); Tilghman Press, *We Also Serve,* 59, 61, 66; Tilghman Press, *We Also Serve: Armed Forces Edition,* 38; Starks, interview.

23. Fulson, telephone interview; Nichols, interview; Norman Colby, "The City Mourns Minnie Lue Nichols," *Contra Costa Times,* May 10, 1983; Starks, interview; Joseph Malbrough and Irene Malbrough Batchan, interview; William Malbrough and Irene Malbrough Batchan, interview with author, September 14, 1985.

24. Nichols, interview; Walter White to Noah W. Griffin, July 16, 1945, carton 16, NAACP Records; Joseph Malbrough and Irene Malbrough Batchan, interview; Starks, interview; Nichols, "An Interview with Minnie Lue," 3–5.

25. Starks, telephone conversation.

26. Ollie Freeman, conversation with author, September 14, 1985; Springer, "The Regulatory Function of the Blues," 278–87; William Ferris Jr., "Racial Repertoires among Blues Performers," *Ethnomusicology* 14 (1970): 439–49. The observation about blues music was made by my father, John Louis Wilson, who left his home state of Oklahoma to settle in California about 1940.

27. Starks, interview.

28. Hildebrand, "Oakland Blues," 3–4; Nichols, interview. Charles Keil, *Urban Blues* (Chicago: University of Chicago Press, 1969), 157–58. The guitar player quote is from a former Louisiana resident who wished to be identified only as "Lena," conversation with author, July 1980.

29. E. P. (Edwin P.) "Red" Stephenson, "Transition: White Man in a Black Town, 1950–1967," an oral history conducted 1975, in "Bay Area Foundations History: Oral History Transcripts/Interviews, 1971–75," vol. 5, Regional Oral History Office, Bancroft Library, University of California, Berkeley, 1971, 28; *Richmond Independent,* February 14, 1944, May 17, 1944, and August 10, 1943; Robert Wenkert, John Magney, and Fred Templeton, *An Historical Digest of*

Negro-White Relations in Richmond, California (Berkeley: Survey Research Center, University of California, Berkeley, February 1967, rev. September 1967), 27–30; Katherine Archibald, *Wartime Shipyard: A Study in Social Disunity* (Berkeley: University of California Press, 1947), 3–4; "Auxiliary Lodge Number 36 of the International Brotherhood of Boilermakers, Iron Shipbuilders and Helpers of America (Local A-36)," in Tilghman Press, *We Also Serve: Ten Percent of a Nation Working and Fighting for Victory* (Berkeley, Calif.: Tilghman Press, 1945), 25. See also Shirley Ann Moore, "Getting There, Being There: African-American Migration to Richmond, California, 1910–1945," in *The Great Migration in Historical Perspective: New Dimension of Race, Class, and Gender,* ed. Joe William Trotter Jr. (Bloomington: Indiana University Press, 1991), 106–26; Moore, "'Her Husband Didn't Have a Word to Say,'" 147–64.

30. "Club Savoy" lyrics describe the egalitarian etiquette of the blues clubs. Hildebrand, "North Richmond Blues," 5; Nichols, interview; Starks, telephone conversation.

31. Hildebrand, "Oakland Blues," 3–54; Keil, *Urban Blues,* 157–58; Lawrence W. Levine, *Black Culture and Black Consciousness: Afro-American Folk Thought from Slavery to Freedom* (New York: Oxford University Press, 1977), 344–58; Hazzard-Gordon, *Jookin',* 92; Starks, interview.

32. Moore, "Getting There, Being There," 119; Wenkert, Magney, and Templeton, *An Historical Digest of Negro White Relations,* 87; Sherrill David Luke, "The Problem of Annexing North Richmond to the City of Richmond (master's thesis, University of California, Berkeley, 1954), 4; Roy M. Hamachi, "Postwar Housing in Richmond, California: A Case Study of Local Housing Developments in the Postwar Period" (master's thesis, University of California, Berkeley, 1954), 27–28, carton 6, "Subject Files, California, Richmond," Catherine Bauer Wurster Papers, Bancroft Library, University of California, Berkeley; Starks, interview; Richmond Model Cities Program and City of Richmond Planning Department, Research and Evaluation Unit, "Richmond Facts" (Richmond, December 1, 1974), table 1, Richmond Collection, Richmond Public Library; Nichols, interview.

33. *Ebony,* February 1946; *Chicago Defender,* January 16, 1954, and January 2, 1955, 7; Southern, *The Music of Black Americans,* 497–98; Keil, *Urban Blues,* 154, 157; Arnold Shaw, *Honkers and Shouters: The Golden Years of Rhythm and Blues* (New York: Macmillan, 1978), 166–77; Jonathan Kamin, "Taking the Roll Out of Rock and Roll: Reverse Acculturation," *Popular Music and Society* 2, no. 1 (fall 1972): 3.

34. Harris, *Blues Who's Who,* 59–60, 525–28; Kamin, "Taking the Roll Out of Rock and Roll," 3; Shaw, *Honkers and Shouters,* 116–17; Keil, *Urban Blues,* 154; Starks, telephone conversation.

35. Stephen, "Soul," 31–37; James Stewart, "Relationships between Black Males and Females in Rhythm and Blues Music of the 1960s and 1970s," in *More Than Dancing: Essays on Afro-American Music and Musicians,* ed. Irene V. Jackson (Westport, Conn.: Greenwood Press, 1985), 169–85; Robert Weisbrot, *Freedom Bound: A History of America's Civil Rights Movement* (New York: Plume Books, 1991), 176–78, 196–234; William L. Van DeBurg, *New Day in Babylon: The Black Power Movement and African American Culture, 1965–1975* (Chicago: University of Chicago Press, 1992), 11–29, 112–91.

36. Freeman in Hildebrand, "North Richmond Blues," 5.

37. Ibid., 1, 4–5; Starks, telephone conversation; Stephen, "Soul," 29–31.

38. Levine, *Black Culture and Black Consciousness,* 174–89; Wheat and Wheat, interview.

39. Slocum, interview; Horace Boyer, "Contemporary Gospel Music," *Music Educators' Journal* 64 (May 1978): 37.

40. Slocum, interview; Boyer, "Contemporary Gospel Music," 37.

41. Starks, interview; Mellonee V. Burnim, "The Black Gospel Music Tradition: A Complex of Ideology, Aesthetic, and Behavior," in *More Than Dancing: Essays on Afro-American Music and Musicians,* ed. Irene V. Jackson (Westport, Conn.: Greenwood Press, 1985), 161; Thurston, interview; Freeman and Griffin, interview.

42. Southern, *The Music of Black Americans,* 402; Mellonee V. Burnim, "The Black Gospel Music Tradition: Symbol of Ethnicity" (Ph.D. diss., Indiana University, 1980), 2, 157; Mellonee V. Burnim, "The Black Gospel Music Tradition: A Complex of Ideology, Aesthetic, and Behavior," 161.

43. Slocum, interview; Geddins, interview.

44. Thurston, interview.

45. Ibid.

46. Southern, *The Music of Black Americans,* 404; Slocum, interview.

47. "Flamboyant King Narcisse Is Dead," *Oakland Tribune,* February 7, 1989.

48. Rose, interview; Thurston, interview; Nichols, interview; Starks, telephone conversation. When King Narcisse died in 1989, thousands of mourners lined San Pablo Avenue as his horse-drawn hearse carried him to his final resting place in the once segregated Rollingwood section of Richmond. See "Flamboyant King Narcisse Is Dead."

49. Thurston, interview.

50. Ibid.; Joseph Malbrough and Irene Malbrough Batchan, interview.

51. Thurston, interview; Joseph Malbrough and Irene Malbrough Batchan, interview.

52. Joseph Malbrough and Irene Malbrough Batchan, interview.

53. Rob Ruck, *Sandlot Seasons: Sport in Black Pittsburgh* (Urbana: University of Illinois Press, 1987), 3–7.

54. Hildebrand, "North Richmond Blues," 4; Freeman and Griffin, interview; Joseph Malbrough and Irene Malbrough Batchan, interview.

55. Lewis, interview.

56. Thurston, interview; Ruck, *Sandlot Seasons,* 3; Nichols, telephone conversation with author, January 6, 1980.

57. "Hangover Town," *Salute,* June 1946, 41; Joseph Malbrough and Irene Malbrough Batchan, interview; Thurston, interview.

Chapter 6.   Epilogue

1. Mildred Slocum, interview with author, November 17, 1987. For Richmond population figures, see "Richmond, Contra Costa County, Demographics and

Socio-economic Characteristics," in *California: Cities, Towns, and Counties: Basic Data Profiles for All Municipalities and Counties,* ed. Edith R. Hornor (Palo Alto, Calif.: Information Publications, 1995), 337; California Fair Employment and Housing Commission, "Report and Recommendations of the California Fair Employment and Housing Commission—Public Hearings on Racial, Ethnic, and Religious Conflicts and Violence in Contra Costa County, Held October 5–7, 1981, Richmond Memorial Auditorium," April 8, 1982, photocopy, Richmond Collection, Richmond Public Library.

2. I am indebted to Professor Earl Lewis for sharing with me his ideas on urban blacks and the "culture of expectation." See also Joe William Trotter Jr., *Black Milwaukee: The Making of an Industrial Proletariat, 1915–1945* (Urbana: University of Illinois Press, 1985), 226–27; Theodore Hershberg, *A Tale of Three Cities: Blacks and Immigrants in Philadelphia, 1850–1880, 1930, and 1970* (Philadelphia: Center for Philadelphia Studies, School of Public and Urban Policy, University of Pennsylvania, 1979), 461–91; Kenneth Kusmer, *A Ghetto Takes Shape: Black Cleveland, 1870–1930* (Urbana: University of Illinois Press, 1980), 190–205; Lance Burris, "Richmond, California: A Case Study in Economic Development," *Urban Land* 39 (May 1980): 9–10.

3. Lee Howard (speech delivered at the African American History Month Forum, Richmond Public Library, Richmond, Calif., February 12, 1989).

4. "Richmond: A City of High Hopes and Big Headaches," *Fortnight: The News Magazine of California* 3, no. 12 (December 19, 1947): 19; California Fair Employment and Housing Commission, "California Fair Employment and Housing Report," 19–24. In 1986 Elton Brombacher, a member of Richmond's police commission, noted: "Richmond has a bad image because of the complexion of many of its citizens. . . . As long as people are afraid to drive through a street that has a lot of black faces, Richmond will have a bad image. The problem is not with the city, it's with the people that look at the city." Also see "Richmond Moves to Enhance Its Image," *San Francisco Chronicle,* August 5, 1997. See Joseph Pereira, "Equality in Richmond a Long, Quiet Struggle," *West [Contra Costa] County Times,* January 20, 1986; "U.S. Seeks Parley for Sale of Shipyards, City Seeks Land for Industry to Use Unemployed," *Richmond Record Herald,* March 12, 1946, in ser. 2, carton 27, folder 26, Henry J. Kaiser Papers, Bancroft Library, University of California, Berkeley (hereafter cited as Kaiser Papers); Amos Hinkley and Wayne Carlson to President Harry Truman, telegram, August 16, 1946, ser. 2, carton 29, folder 29, Kaiser Papers; Oscar Cox, memorandum, August 12, 1946; L. H. Oppenheim to E. E. Trefethen Jr., telegram, March 11, 1947; Chad F. Calhoun to E. E. Trefethen, telegram, February 26, 1947; and William Marks to E. E. Trefethen Jr., telegram, February 26, 1947, all in ser. 8, carton 157, folder 12, Kaiser Papers; California Fair Employment and Housing Commission, "California Fair Employment and Housing Report," 102–11; Burris, "Richmond, California," 8–17. Burris estimated that in 1980 there was an 8.7 percent unemployment rate for the city of Richmond and that the black unemployment rate stood at almost 15 percent. For black youth between sixteen and twenty-two years of age unemployment hit 35 percent. He also concluded that Richmond's "image problem" stems from several factors, including the attitude of residents: "The aging white population looked

backward to the 'halcyon' days of World War II, while young blacks saw no future" (10). Richmond Chamber of Commerce, "Community Economic Profile," 1987, photocopy, Richmond Collection, Richmond Public Library.

5. Walter Freeman Jr. and Joseph Griffin III, interview with author, November 28, 1987; Slocum, interview; Harry Williams and Marguerite Williams, "Reflections of a Longtime Black Family in Richmond," an oral history conducted in 1985 by Judith R. Dunning, Regional Oral History Office, Bancroft Library, University of California, Berkeley, 1990, 26; Ivy Reid Lewis, interview with author, July 29, 1987; Slocum, interview.

6. Cleophas Brown, telephone conversation with author, October 18, 1987.

7. Peter J. Paris, *The Social Teaching of the Black Churches* (Philadelphia: Fortress Press, 1985), 1–25; Katrina Hazzard-Gordon, *Jookin': The Rise of Social Dance Formations in African-American Culture* (Philadelphia: Temple University Press, 1990), 121–71; Shirley Ann Wilson Moore, "Traditions from Home: African Americans in Wartime Richmond, California," in *The War in American Culture: Society and Consciousness during World War II,* ed. Lewis A. Erenberg and Susan E. Hirsch (Chicago: University of Chicago Press), 263–83.

8. Thomas Bender, *Community and Social Change in America* (Baltimore: Johns Hopkins University Press, 1982), 5, 7; Ferdinand Tonnies, *Fundamental Concepts of Sociology,* trans. Charles P. Loomis (New York: American Books, 1940), 37–41; Susan Lobo, "The Bay Area American Indian Community" (paper delivered at the conference of the American Society for Ethnohistory, Berkeley, Calif., November 6, 1987). I am indebted to Quintard Taylor's discussion of the black urban community "ethos" and its "guiding complex of beliefs." Quintard Taylor, *The Forging of a Black Community: Seattle's Central District from 1870 through the Civil Rights Era* (Seattle: University of Washington Press, 1994), 6, 135–56; Blaine A. Brownwell, *The Urban Ethos in the South, 1920– 1930* (Baton Rouge: Louisiana State University Press, 1975), xvi.

9. Margaret Starks, telephone conversation with author, June 29, 1988.

10. Unsigned memorandum to file, April 4, 1946, and "Richmond Branch NAACP Fights Grocery Store Picketing Bay," NAACP news release, June 27, 1947, both in carton 16, folder "O.A. Correspondence Branch, Richmond 1946–1947," Records of the National Association for the Advancement of Colored People, West Coast Region, 1946–1970, Bancroft Library, University of California, Berkeley (hereafter cited as NAACP Records); "Public Accommodations," West Coast Regional NAACP *Annual Report, 1956,* carton 26, "Annual Reports, 1952–58," NAACP Records; *Ebony,* August 1948; "Richmond Man Defies Whites in Tract," *California Voice,* March 7, 1952 [date is misprinted as March 7, 1951]; Robert Wenkert, John Magney, and Fred Templeton, *An Historical Digest of Negro-White Relations* (Berkeley: Survey Research Center, University of California, Berkeley, February 1967, rev. September 1967), 44; *California Voice,* March 21, 1952; Wilbur Wheat and Vesper Wheat, interview with author, January 24, 1987; Taylor, *The Forging of a Black Community,* 40–42, 79–105, 170–72, 181–89.

11. Cleophas Brown, telephone conversation; Lewis, interview; Stanley Nystrom, interview with author, July 31, 1986.

12. Wilbur Wheat, telephone conversation with author, January 26, 1987.

13. Wenkert, Magney, and Templeton, *An Historical Digest of Negro-White Relations,* 53; Lillian B. Rubin, *Busing and Backlash: White against White in an Urban School District* (Berkeley: University of California Press, 1972); California Fair Employment and Housing Commission, "California Fair Employment and Housing Report"; Burris, "Richmond, California," 8–17; Margaret Starks, interview with author, April 2, 1988.

14. Robert Wenkert, John Magney, and Ann Neel, "Two Weeks of Racial Crisis in Richmond, California" (Berkeley: Survey Research Center, University of California, Berkeley, February 1967), 2, 120–21, 159–82. The violence at the high school prompted a meeting of parents and students at the North Richmond Neighborhood House. The meeting resulted in a list of grievances presented to school officials. The petition called for a review of student tracking based on testing, the implementation of a schoolwide discipline review committee, employment of black school counselors, remedial education tutors, and the inclusion of African American history and films in the curriculum. Placed in a national context, the outbreak of fights at the high school and the incidents of vandalism, looting, and violence in the city were not as devastating as the black uprisings that swept through Watts, Detroit, and Newark, but they signaled a new black attitude.

Bibliography

Public Records: Census

U.S. Department of Commerce, Bureau of the Census. *Thirteenth Census of the United States, 1910*. Washington, D.C.: GPO, 1911.

————. *Thirteenth Census of the United States, 1910*. Vol. 19, township 15, enumeration district 177 (Washington, D.C.: National Archives Administration, n.d.).

————. *Fourteenth Census of the United States, 1920*. Washington, D.C.: GPO, 1921.

————. *Fifteenth Census of the United States, 1930*. Washington, D.C.: GPO, 1931.

————. *Sixteenth Census of the United States, 1940*. Washington, D.C.: GPO, 1943.

————. *Special Census of Richmond, California: September 1943*. Ser. P-SC., no. 6. Washington, D.C.: GPO, 1943.

————. *Special Census of Richmond, California, 1947*. Ser. P-28, no. 280. Washington, D.C.: GPO, 1947.

————. *A Report of the Seventeenth Decennial Census of the United States: Census of the Population, 1950*. Washington, D.C.: GPO, 1952.

————. "Population by Race, by States, 1930 to 1950." No. 45 in *Statistical Abstract of the United States*. Washington, D.C.: GPO, 1960.

————. *The Eighteenth Decennial Census of the United States: Census of the Population, 1960*. Washington, D.C.: GPO, 1961.

————. *United States Census of Population and Housing: 1960*. Final Report PHC (1)-138. Washington, D.C.: GPO, 1961.

Public Records: Miscellaneous Reports

Barbour, W. Miller. *An Exploratory Study of Socio-Economic Problems affecting the Negro-White Relationship in Richmond, California.* Pasadena, Calif.: United Community Defense Services, Inc., and the National Urban League, 1952.

California Fair Employment and Housing Commission. "Report and Recommendations of the California Fair Employment and Housing Commission—Public Hearings on Racial, Ethnic, and Religious Conflicts and Violence in Contra Costa County, Held October 5–7, 1981, Richmond Memorial Auditorium." April 8, 1982. Richmond Collection, Richmond Public Library. Photocopy.

Contra Costa County Planning Department. "North Richmond–San Pablo Bay Study." 1971. Richmond Collection, Richmond Public Library. Photocopy.

Department of City and Regional Planning. "A Master Plan for the North Richmond Neighborhood." Berkeley: University of California, Berkeley, Department of City and Regional Planning, March 1949. Intergovernmental Studies Library, University of California, Berkeley. Mimeograph.

Ramsey, Eleanor Mason. "Richmond, California, between 1850–1940: An Ethnohistorical Reconstruction." Draft submitted to California Archaeological Consultants, Inc., February 15, 1980. Photocopy in author's possession.

———. "Richmond, California, between 1850–1940." Chap. 5 in "Investigation of Cultural Resources within the Richmond Harbor Redevelopment Project 11-A, Richmond, Contra Costa County, California." Prepared by California Archaeological Consultants, Banks and Orlins, March 1981, San Francisco. Richmond Collection, Richmond Public Library. Bound typescript.

Richmond Chamber of Commerce. "Community Economic Profile." 1987. Richmond Collection, Richmond Public Library. Photocopy.

Richmond City Planning Commission. *A Report on Housing and Redevelopment: An Element of the Richmond Master Plan.* Richmond: Richmond City Planning Commission, January 1950.

———. *A Report on Schools, Parks, and Playgrounds, Richmond, California.* 1948. Richmond Collection, Richmond Public Library. Typeset manuscript.

———. *Residential Richmond: Part One.* 1958. Richmond Collection, Richmond Public Library. Typeset manuscript.

Richmond Department of Health. "Vital Statistics Report." January 2, 1945. Government Documents Library, University of California, Berkeley.

Richmond Model Cities Program and City of Richmond Planning Department, Research and Evaluation Unit. "Richmond Facts." Richmond, December 1, 1974. Richmond Collection, Richmond Public Library.

Richmond Redevelopment Agency. *Application for Preliminary Advance.* Richmond: Richmond Redevelopment Agency, September 12, 1950. Richmond Collection, Richmond Public Library.

"U.S. Committee on Fair Employment Practice, Miscellaneous Publications."
    N.d. Doe Library, University of California, Berkeley. Bound typescript.
Wenkert, Robert, John Magney, and Ann Neel. "Two Weeks of Racial Crisis
    in Richmond, California." Berkeley: Survey Research Center, University of
    California, February 1967.
Wenkert, Robert, John Magney, and Fred Templeton. *An Historical Digest
    of Negro-White Relations in Richmond, California.* Berkeley: Survey
    Research Center, University of California, Berkeley, February 1967, rev.
    September 1967.

Public Records: Minutes

Minutes, Richmond City Council, Richmond City Hall, Richmond, Calif.

Archival and Manuscript Collections

California Federation for Civic Unity Papers. Bancroft Library, University of
    California, Berkeley.
Dellums, Cotrell L. [C. L.], Papers. Bancroft Library, University of California,
    Berkeley.
Kaiser, Henry J., Papers. Bancroft Library, University of California, Berkeley.
Lange, Dorothea, Photographic Collection. Oakland Museum of California.
Pullman Company Papers. Newberry Library, Chicago, Illinois.
Records of the Committee on Fair Employment Practice. National Archives,
    Pacific Sierra Region (Region 12), San Bruno, California.
Records of the National Association for the Advancement of Colored People,
    West Coast Region, 1946–1970. Bancroft Library University of California,
    Berkeley.
U.S. Congress. House. Subcommittee of the Committee on Merchant
    Marines and Fisheries. *Hearings on Shipyard Profits,* 78th Cong., 2d sess.,
    1944.
U.S. Congress. House. Subcommittee of the Committee on Military Affairs.
    *Hearings on Labor Shortages in the Pacific Coast and Rocky Mountain
    States.* 78th Cong., 1st sess., 1943.
U.S. Congress. House. Subcommittee of the Committee on Naval Affairs In-
    vestigating Congested Areas. *Hearings before the United States House Com-
    mittee on Naval Affairs.* 78th Cong., 1st sess., 1943.
Wurster, Catherine Bauer, Papers. Bancroft Library, University of California,
    Berkeley.

Primary Sources: Published

Gondolfo v. Hartman, 49 Fed. 181 (C.C.S.C., California).
International Brotherhood of Boilermakers, Iron Shipbuilders, and Helpers of
    America, Local No. 513. *Arsenal of Democracy.* Berkeley, Calif.: Tam Gibbs,
    1947.

Janss Investment Co. v. Walden, 196 Cal. 653 (1925).

Los Angeles Inv. Co. v. Gary, 181 Cal. 680 (1919).

Permanente Metals Corporation. *A Booklet of Illustrated Facts about the Ship-yards at Richmond, California.* Oakland, Calif., Permanente Metals Corp., 1944.

Sanborn Insurance Company. *Sanborn Insurance Map.* Vol. 1. New York: Sanborn Insurance Company, 1930, amended 1957.

Tilghman Press. *Colored Directory of the Leading Cities of Northern California, 1916–1917.* Oakland, Calif.: Tilghman Press, 1917.

"Walls Addition to the City of Richmond Map." 1909. Richmond Pamphlets Collection, Bancroft Library, University of California, Berkeley. Pamphlet.

Wayt v. Patee, 205 Cal. 46 (1928).

Primary Sources: Unpublished

Ashler Lodge No. 35, "Centennial Yearbook of the Most Worshipful Prince Hall Grand Lodge Free Accepted Masons, California and Jurisdiction." Richmond, California, at the centennial communication of the Grand Lodge, San Francisco, July 17–21, 1955.

Benevolent and Protective Order of Elks, Richmond Lodge, Number 1251. "Golden Anniversary, 1911–1961." N.d. Richmond Museum Collection, Richmond, Calif. Commemorative booklet.

Burg Brothers Real Estate Company. "Burg Brothers Real Estate Company for the Pullman Townsite, Burg Brothers Exclusive Agents." 1910. Miscellaneous pamphlet collection, Richmond Museum, Richmond, Calif. Pamphlet.

First African Methodist Episcopal Church. "Sunday Bulletin, No. 3." Miscellaneous pamphlet collection, Bancroft Library, University of California, Berkeley.

"The House Committee of the Linden Street Y.M.C.A. Presents Roena Eloise Mucklely Soprano assisted by Eugene Anderson, Tenor, with Elmer Keeton Accompanist, June 24, 1926." Program in Miscellaneous Publications, YMCA, Oakland, California, Linden Branch, Bancroft Library, University of California, Berkeley.

Jordan, John, and Gladys Jordan. Private papers on Parchester Village.

Kenny, Robert W. "Police and Minority Groups—An Experiment, an Address." 1946. Richmond Collection, Richmond Public Library. Typescript.

McEntire, Davis. *Police Training Bulletin: A Guide to Race Relations for Police Officers.* Sacramento: California Department of Justice, 1946. Richmond Collection, Richmond Public Library.

North Richmond Missionary Baptist Church. "Sixtieth Anniversary Program," May 27, 1979. In the personal papers of Mildred Slocum.

North Richmond Neighborhood House. "Annual Report, 1965." Richmond: n.p., 1965. Richmond Collection, Richmond Public Library.

———. "Annual Report, 1968." Richmond: n.p., 1968. Richmond Collection, Richmond Public Library.

————. "North Richmond Neighborhood House, Inc., U.S.A." Richmond: n.p., 1955. Richmond Collection, Richmond Public Library.

Oral History Collections

Albrier, Frances Mary. "Determined Advocate for Racial Equality." An oral history conducted 1977–78 by Malca Chall. Regional Oral History Office, Bancroft Library, University of California, Berkeley, 1978.

Brown Cleophas. Interview conducted by Judith Dunning for "On the Waterfront: An Oral History of Richmond, California," March 1, 1985. Audiotapes in the collection of Mrs. Ursula Brown.

Nystrom, Stanley. "A Family's Roots in Richmond: Recollections of a Lifetime Resident." An oral history conducted in 1985 by Judith R. Dunning. Regional Oral History Office, Bancroft Library, University of California, Berkeley, 1990.

Stephenson, E. P. (Edwin P.) "Red." "Transition: White Man in a Black Town, 1950–1967." An oral history conducted in 1975. In "Bay Area Foundations History: Oral History Transcripts/Interviews, 1971–75," vol. 5. Regional Oral History Office, Bancroft Library, University of California, Berkeley, 1971.

Williams, Harry, and Marguerite Williams. "Reflections of a Longtime Black Family in Richmond." An oral history conducted in 1985 by Judith R. Dunning. Regional Oral History Office, Bancroft Library, University of California, Berkeley, 1990.

Interviews by Author

Blair, Claude A., and Bessie Clemons, July 29, 1980.

Brown, Cleophas, telephone conversation, October 18, 1987.

Brown, Ursula, August 28, 1993.

————, September, 11, 1993.

Clark, Emma, conversation, October 15, 1987.

Crawford, Matt, telephone conversation, October 18, 1987.

Crouchett, Lawrence, telephone conversation, October 6, 1987.

Edwards, Lucretia, telephone conversation, October 15, 1987.

Freeman, Ollie, conversation, September 14, 1985.

Freeman, Walter, Jr., telephone conversation, January 1, 1988.

————, telephone conversation, August 19, 1988.

————, telephone conversation, January 16, 1989.

Freeman, Walter, Jr., and Annie Mae Freeman, January 14, 1988.

Freeman, Walter, Jr., and Joseph Griffin III, November 28, 1987.

Fulson, Lowell, telephone interview, January 21, 1993.

Geddins, Bob, May 8, 1987.

Greene, Ernestine, August 18, 1985.

Griffin, Joseph, III, telephone conversation, November 11, 1987.

Japanese American residents of Richmond and Native American employees of
    Santa Fe Railroad yards, interviews by author and Eleanor Mason Ramsey,
    July–November 1980.
Johnson, George, August 13, 1985.
Jordan, John, and Gladys Jordan, September 11, 1987.
Kelly, Joan, conversation, October 2, 1987.
Lewis, Ivy Reid, July 29, 1987.
Livingston, George, August 6, 1987.
Malbrough, Joseph, telephone conversation, August 21, 1985.
Malbrough, Joseph, and Irene Malbrough Batchan, August 18, 1985.
Malbrough, William, and Irene Malbrough Batchan, September 14, 1985.
McKinney, William H., June 18, 1991.
———, June 22, 1991.
———, telephone conversation, June 22, 1991.
McMillan, James, conversation, September 27, 1987.
Nichols, Minnie Lue. January 6, 1980.
———, telephone conversation, January 6, 1980.
Nystrom, Stanley, July 31, 1986.
Rose, Virginia, January 2, 1984.
Slocum, Mildred, November 17, 1987.
Starks, Margaret, April 2, 1988.
———, telephone conversation, June 29, 1988.
Thurston, Bill, September 10, 1983.
Wilbur Wheat, telephone conversation, January 26, 1987.
Wheat, Wilbur, and Vesper Wheat, January 24, 1987.

Periodicals: Newspapers

California Eagle
California Voice
Chicago Defender
East Bay Express: The East Bay's Free Weekly
Labor Herald
Oakland Independent
Oakland Sunshine
Oakland Tribune
Oakland Voters' Herald
Pacific Coast Appeal
People's Daily World
People's World
Richmond Guide
Richmond Independent
Richmond Independent and Gazette
Richmond Independent, "Woman's Edition"
Richmond Record Herald
Richmond Terminal
San Francisco Chronicle

San Francisco Reporter
West [Contra Costa] County Times
Western American
Western Appeal
Western Outlook

Periodicals: Magazines

Colliers, July 21, 1945
Core, fall/winter 1973
Crisis, March 1944
Ebony, February 1946
Fortnight: The News Magazine of California, December 19, 1947
Fortune, February 1945
Frontier: The Voice of the New West, April 1960
Labor and Nation, May–June 1948
Living Blues Magazine, September–October 1977
Monthly Labor Review, June 1950
The Nation (special Western suppl.), September 21, 1946
Salute, June 1946

Journal Articles

Boyer, Horace. "Contemporary Gospel Music." Music Educators' Journal 64
    (May 1978): 37–41.
Burris, Lance. "Richmond, California: A Case Study in Economic Develop-
    ment." Urban Land 39 (May 1980): 8–17.
Chamberland, Carol P. "The House That Bop Built." California History: The
    Magazine of the California Historical Society 75, no. 3 (fall 1996): 272–83.
Crouchett, Lawrence P. "Archons in the News, George Carroll Retires from
    California Judgeship." The Boule Journal (fall 1984): 36–37.
Evans, Hiram. "Klan's Fight for Americanism." North American Review 123
    (March–May 1926): 33–63.
Ferris, William, Jr. "Racial Repertoires among Blues Performers." Ethnomusi-
    cology 14 (1970): 439–49.
Fried, Michael. "W. Elmer Keeton and His WPA Chorus: Oakland's Musical
    Civil Rights Pioneers of the New Deal Era." California History: The Maga-
    zine of the California Historical Society 75, no. 3 (fall 1996): 236–49.
Goering, John M. "Neighborhood Tipping and Racial Transition: A Review
    of Social Science Evidence." Journal of the American Institute of Planners 44
    (January 1978): 68–78.
Kamin, Jonathan. "Taking the Roll Out of Rock and Roll: Reverse Accultura-
    tion." Popular Music and Society 2, no. 1 (fall 1972): 3–11.
Lewis, Earl. "Afro-American Adaptive Strategies: The Visiting Habits of Kith
    and Kin among Black Norfolkians during the First Great Migration." Jour-
    nal of Family History 12, no. 4 (winter 1987): 407–20.
Lewis, George. "Social Protest and Self Awareness in Black Popular Music."
    Popular Music and Society 2, no. 4 (summer 1974): 327–33.

McCarthy, Margaret W. "The Afro-American Sermon and the Blues." *The Black Perspective in Music* 4, no. 3 (fall 1977): 269–77.

McEntire, Davis. "Postwar Status of Negro Workers in the San Francisco Area." *Monthly Labor Review* 70 (June 1950): 614–17.

Miller, Loren. "The Power of Restrictive Covenants." *Survey Graphic* 36, no. 1 (January 1947): 46.

Neal, Larry. "Ethos of the Blues." *Black Scholar* 3 (summer 1972): 44–46.

Nelson, Bruce. "Organized Labor and the Struggle for Black Equality in Mobile during World War II." *The Journal of American History* 80, no 3 (December 1993): 952–88.

Reddick, L. D. "The New Race Relations Frontier." *The Journal of Educational Sociology* 19, no. 3 (November 1945): 142–43.

Savage, W. Sherman. "The Negro in the Westward Movement." *Journal of Negro History* 25 (1940): 533–34.

Springer, Robert. "The Regulatory Function of the Blues." *The Black Perspective in Music* 4, no. 3 (fall 1977): 279–87.

Stephen, Robert W. "Soul: A Historical Reconstruction of Continuity and Change in Black Popular Music." *The Black Perspective in Music* 12, no. 1 (spring 1984): 21–43.

Wilson, Olly. "Black Music as an Art Form." *Black Music Research Journal* 4, no. 1 (1983): 1–22.

———. "The Significance of the Relationship between Afro-American Music and West African Music." *The Black Perspective in Music* 2, no. 1 (fall 1974): 3–22.

Dissertations and Theses

Alancraig, Helen Smith. "Cordonices Village: A Study of Non-segregated Public Housing in the San Francisco Bay Area." Master's thesis, University of California, Berkeley, 1953.

Brown, Hubert Owen. "The Impact of War Worker Migration on the Public School System of Richmond, California, from 1940–1945." Ph.D. diss., Stanford University, 1973.

Burnim, Mellonee V. "The Black Gospel Music Tradition: Symbol of Ethnicity." Ph.D. diss., Indiana University, 1980.

deRomanett, Raymond P. "Public Action and Community Planning: A Study in the Redevelopment of Richmond, California." Master's thesis, University of California, Berkeley, 1956.

Douglas, Priscilla H. "Black Working Women." Ph.D. diss, Harvard University, 1981.

France, Edward E. "Some Aspects of the Migration of the Negro to the San Francisco Bay Area since 1940." Ph.D. diss., University of California, 1962.

Fulweiler, Charles Radcliffe. "A Preliminary Investigation of the Accommodation Mechanism as a Factor in the Clinical Study of the Negro Adolescent." Master's thesis, University of California, Berkeley, 1951.

Hamachi, Roy M. "Postwar Housing in Richmond, California: A Case Study of Local Housing Developments in the Postwar Period." Master's thesis,

University of California, Berkeley, 1954. Carton 6, "Subject Files California, Richmond," Catherine Bauer Wurster Papers, Bancroft Library, University of California, Berkeley.

Luke, Sherrill David. "The Problem of Annexing North Richmond to the City of Richmond." Master's thesis, University of California, Berkeley, 1954.

Maher, Douglas. "The Pattern of a Generation: A History of Post-war Community Organization in North Richmond, California." Senior thesis, University of California, Berkeley, June 6, 1966.

Orosco, James R. "Survey of Voting Behavior in the City of Richmond, California, 1936–1956." Political Science 163 paper, University of California, Berkeley, spring 1963. Richmond Collection, Richmond Public Library.

Powers, Madelon Mae. "Faces along the Bar: Lore and Order in the Workingman's Saloon, 1870–1920." Ph.D. diss., University of California, Berkeley, 1991.

Ramsey, Eleanor. "Allensworth: A Study in Social Change." Ph.D. diss., University of California, Berkeley, 1977.

Woodington, Donald Devine. "Federal Public War Housing in Relation to Certain Needs and the Financial Ability of the Richmond School District." Ed.D. diss., University of California, Berkeley, 1954.

Other Sources

Addams, Jane. *The Spirit of Youth and the City Streets.* 1909. Reprint, Urbana: University of Illinois Press, 1972.

Archibald, Katherine. *Wartime Shipyard: A Study in Social Disunity.* Berkeley: University of California Press, 1947.

Baker, Houston, Jr. *Blues Ideology and Afro-American Literature: A Vernacular Theory.* Chicago: University of Chicago Press, 1984.

Barlow, William. *Looking up at Down: The Emergence of Blues Culture.* Philadelphia: Temple University Press, 1989.

Bell, Thomas. *Out of This Furnace.* Pittsburgh: University of Pittsburgh Press, 1976.

Bender, Thomas. *Community and Social Change in America.* Baltimore: Johns Hopkins University Press, 1982.

Berkeley Art Center. *Ethnic Notions: Black Images in the White Mind.* Berkeley, Calif.: Berkeley Art Center, 1982.

Berlin, Ira. "Herbert Gutman and the American Working Class." In *Power and Culture: Essays on the American Working Class,* ed. Ira Berlin. New York: Pantheon Books, 1987.

———, ed. *Power and Culture: Essays on the American Working Class.* New York: Pantheon Books, 1987.

Bodnar, John. *Immigration and Industrialization: Ethnicity in an American Mill Town, 1870–1940.* Pittsburgh: University of Pittsburgh Press, 1977.

Bodnar, John, Roger Simon, and Michael P. Weber. *Lives of Their Own: Blacks, Italians, and Poles in Pittsburgh, 1900–1960.* Urbana: University of Illinois Press, 1982.

Borchert, James. *Alley Life in Washington, D.C.: Family, Community, Religion, and Folklife in the City, 1850–1970*. Urbana: University of Illinois Press, 1980.

Broussard, Albert S. *Black San Francisco: The Struggle for Racial Equality in the West, 1900–1954*. Lawrence: University Press of Kansas, 1993.

Browning, Rufus P., Dale Rogers Marshall, and David H. Tabb. *Protest Is Not Enough: The Struggle of Blacks and Hispanics for Equality in Urban Politics*. Berkeley: University of California Press, 1984.

Brownwell, Blaine A. *The Urban Ethos in the South, 1920–1930*. Baton Rouge: Louisiana State University Press, 1975.

Burnim, Mellonee V. "The Black Gospel Music Tradition: A Complex of Ideology, Aesthetic, and Behavior." In *More Than Dancing: Essays on Afro-American Music and Musicians,* ed. Irene V. Jackson. Westport, Conn.: Greenwood Press, 1985.

Cameron-Stanford House. *Oakland's Sleeping Car Porters*. Oakland, Calif.: Cameron-Stanford House, 1979.

Camp, William Martin. *Skip to My Lou*. New York: Doubleday, Doran and Company, 1945.

Carr, Lowell Juilleard, and James Edson Stermer. *Willow Run*. New York: Harper, 1952. Reprint, New York: Arno Press, 1977.

Chafe, William. *The Unfinished Journey: America since World War II*. 2d ed. New York: Oxford University Press, 1991.

Chan, Sucheng, Douglas Henry Daniels, Mario T. Garcia, and Terry P. Wilson, eds. *Peoples of Color in the American West*. Lexington, Mass.: D.C. Heath and Company, 1994.

Clark, Tom C., and Philip B. Perlman. *Prejudice and Property: An Historic Brief against Racial Covenants submitted to the Supreme Court*. Washington, D.C.: Public Affairs Press, 1948.

Clark-Lewis, Elizabeth. *Living In, Living Out: African American Domestics in Washington, D.C., 1910–1940*. Washington, D.C.: The Smithsonian Institution, 1994.

Clawson, Augusta H. *Shipyard Diary of a Woman Welder*. New York: Penguin Books, 1944.

Cocoltchos, Christopher N. "The Invisible Empire and the Search for the Orderly Community: The Ku Klux Klan in Anaheim, California." In *The Invisible Empire in the West: Toward a New Historical Appraisal of the Ku Klux Klan of the 1920s,* ed. Shawn Lay. Urbana: University of Illinois Press, 1992.

Cohen, Lizabeth. *Making a New Deal: Industrial Workers in Chicago, 1919–1930*. New York: Cambridge University Press, 1990.

Cole, Susan D. *Richmond: Windows to the Past*. Richmond: Wild Cat Canyon Books, 1980.

Collins, Keith E. *Black Los Angeles: The Maturing of the Ghetto, 1940–1950*. Saratoga, Calif.: Century Twenty-One Publishing, 1980.

Cooper, Patricia. *Once a Cigar Maker: Men, Women, and Work Culture in American Cigar Factories, 1900–1919*. Urbana: University of Illinois Press, 1987.

Crouchett, Lawrence P., Lonnie G. Bunch III, and Martha Kendall Winnacker. *Visions toward Tomorrow: The History of the East Bay Afro-American Com-*

munity, 1852–1977. Oakland: Northern California Center for Afro-American History and Life, 1989.

Daniels, Douglas Henry. *Pioneer Urbanites: A Social and Cultural History of Black San Franciscans.* Berkeley: University of California Press, 1990.

DuBois, W. E. Burghardt. "The Function of the Negro Church." In *The Black Church in America,* ed. Hart M. Nelsen, Raytha L. Yokley, and Anne K. Nelsen. New York: Basic Books, 1971.

———. *The Souls of Black Folk: Essays and Sketches.* 1903. Reprint, Greenwich, Conn.: A Fawcett Premier Book, 1961.

Duis, Perry. *The Saloon: Public Drinking in Chicago and Boston, 1880–1920.* Urbana: University of Illinois Press, 1983.

Erenberg, Lewis A., and Susan E. Hirsch, eds. *The War in American Culture: Society and Consciousness during World War II.* Chicago: University of Chicago Press, 1996.

Ervin, J. McFarline. *The Participation of the Negro in the Community Life of Los Angeles.* 1930. Reprint, Los Angeles: R & E Research Associates, 1973.

Fabry, Joseph. *Swingshift: Building the Liberty Ships.* San Francisco: Strawberry Hill Press, 1982.

Foner, Philip S. *Organized Labor and the Black Worker, 1619–1981.* 2d ed. New York: International Publishers, 1982.

Foster, Mark S. *Henry J. Kaiser: Builder in the Modern American West.* Austin: University of Texas Press, 1989.

Frank, Miriam, Marilyn Ziebarth, and Connie Field. *The Life and Times of Rosie the Riveter: The Story of the Three Million Working Women during World War II.* Emeryville, Calif.: Clarity Educational Productions, 1982.

Franklin, John Hope, and Alfred A. Moss Jr. *From Slavery to Freedom: A History of African Americans.* 7th ed. New York: McGraw Hill, 1994.

Frazier, E. Franklin. *The Negro Church in America.* New York: Schocken Books, 1964.

———. *The Negro in the United States.* New York: Macmillan, 1957.

Giddings, Paula. *When and Where I Enter: The Impact of Black Women on Race and Sex in America.* New York: Bantam Books, 1984.

Gillett, Charlie. *The Sound of the City.* New York: Dell Publishing Company, 1970.

Goode, Kenneth G. *California's Black Pioneers: A Brief Historical Survey.* Santa Barbara, Calif.: McNally and Loftin, 1974.

Gottlieb, Peter. *Making Their Own Way: Southern Blacks' Migration to Pittsburgh, 1916–1930.* Urbana: University of Illinois Press, 1987.

Gregory, James Nobel. *American Exodus: The Dust Bowl Migration and Okie Culture.* New York: Oxford University Press, 1989.

Griffins, Evan. "Early History of Richmond, Contra Costa County, California," December 1938, suppl., December 1939. Richmond Museum, Richmond, Calif.

Grossman, James R. *Land of Hope: Chicago, Black Southerners, and the Great Migration.* Chicago: University of Chicago Press, 1991.

Gutman, Hubert G. "The Black Family in Slavery and Freedom: A Revised Perspective." In *Power and Culture: Essays on the American Working Class,* ed. Ira Berlin. New York: Pantheon Books, 1987.

————. *Work, Culture, and Society in Industrializing America: Essays in American Working-Class and Social History.* 1966. Reprint, New York: Vintage Books, 1977.

Haralambos, Michael. *Right On: From Blues to Soul in Black America.* New York: Drake Publishers, 1975.

Harris, Sheldon. *Blues Who's Who: A Biographical Dictionary of Blues Singers.* New Rochelle, N.Y.: Da Capo Press, 1979.

Hartmann, Susan M. *The Home Front and Beyond: American Women in the 1940s.* Boston: Twayne Publishers, 1982.

Hausler, Donald. "Blacks in Oakland." 1987. Oakland Public Library History Room, Oakland, Calif. Monograph.

Havighurst, Robert J., and H. Gerthon Morgan. *The Social History of a War Boom Community.* New York: Longmans Greene, 1951.

Hazzard-Gordon, Katrina. *Jookin': The Rise of Social Dance Formations in African American Culture.* Philadelphia: Temple University Press, 1990.

Heizer, Robert F, and Alan F. Almquist. *The Other Californians: Prejudice and Discrimination under Spain, Mexico, and the United States to 1920.* Berkeley: University of California Press, 1977.

Henderson, Stephen E. "The Heavy Blues of Sterling Brown." In *More Than Dancing: Essays on Afro-American Music and Musicians,* ed. Irene V. Jackson. Westport: Conn.: Greenwood Press, 1985.

Henri, Florette. *Black Migration: Movement North, 1900–1920.* Garden City, N.Y.: Anchor Books, 1976.

Hershberg, Theodore. *A Tale of Three Cities: Blacks and Immigrants in Philadelphia, 1850–1880, 1930, and 1970.* Philadelphia: Center for Philadelphia Studies, School of Public and Urban Policy, University of Pennsylvania, 1979.

Hine, Darlene Clark. "Black Migration to the Urban Midwest: The Gender Dimension, 1915–1945." In *The Great Migration in Historical Perspective: New Dimensions of Race, Class, and Gender,* ed. Joe William Trotter Jr. Bloomington: Indiana University Press, 1991.

————. *The State of Afro-American History: Past, Present, and Future.* Baton Rouge: Louisiana State University Press, 1986.

————, ed. *Black Women in America: An Historical Encyclopedia.* New York: Carlson Publishing, 1993.

Hirsch, Susan E. "No Victory in the Workplace: Women and Minorities at Pullman during World War II." In *The War in American Culture: Society and Consciousness during World War II,* ed. Lewis A. Erenberg and Susan E. Hirsch. Chicago: University of Chicago Press, 1996.

Hornor, Edith R., ed. *California: Cities, Towns, and Counties: Basic Data Profiles for All Municipalities and Counties.* Palo Alto, Calif.: Information Publications, 1995.

Hornsby, Alton, Jr. *The Black Almanac.* New York: Barrons Educational Services, 1975.

Hulaniski, F. J., ed. *History of Contra Costa County, California.* Berkeley, Calif.: Elms Publishing Company, 1917.

Hurston, Zora Neal. *The Sanctified Church.* Berkeley, Calif.: Turtle Island, 1983.

Jackson, Irene V., ed. *More Than Dancing: Essays on Afro-American Music and Musicians.* Westport, Conn.: Greenwood Press, 1985.

Jameson, Elizabeth, and Susan Armitage. *Writing the Range: Race, Class, and Culture in the Women's West.* Norman: University of Oklahoma Press, 1997.

Johnson, Charles S. *The Negro War Worker in San Francisco.* San Francisco: n.p., 1944.

Johnson, Marilynn S. *The Second Gold Rush: Oakland and the East Bay in World War II.* Berkeley: University of California Press, 1993.

Jones, Jacqueline. *Labor of Love, Labor of Sorrow: Black Women, Work, and the Family from Slavery to the Present.* New York: Basic Books, 1985.

Jones, James H. *Bad Blood: The Tuskegee Syphilis Experiment.* New York: Free Press, 1981.

Jones, Leroi [Amiri Baraka]. *Blues People: The Negro Experience in White America and the Music That Developed from It.* New York: William Morrow and Company, 1963.

Katzman, David. *Seven Days a Week: Women and Domestic Service in Industrializing America.* Urbana: University of Illinois Press, 1981.

Keil, Charles. *Urban Blues.* Chicago: University of Chicago Press, 1969.

Kiser, Clyde. *Sea Island to City: A Study of St. Helena Islanders in New York City.* 1932. Reprint, New York: AMS Press, 1969.

Kluger, Richard. *Simple Justice: The History of Brown v. Board of Education and Black America's Struggle for Equality.* New York: Vintage Books, 1975.

Kusmer, Kenneth L. "The Black Urban Experience in American History." In *The State of Afro-American History: Past, Present, and Future,* ed. Darlene C. Hine. Baton Rouge: Louisiana State University Press, 1986.

———. *A Ghetto Takes Shape: Black Cleveland, 1870-1930.* Urbana: University of Illinois Press, 1980.

Lay, Shawn, ed. *The Invisible Empire in the West: Toward a New Historical Appraisal of the Ku Klux Klan of the 1920s.* Urbana: University of Illinois Press, 1992.

Lemann, Nicholas. *The Promised Land: The Great Black Migration and How It Changed America.* New York: Alfred A. Knopf, 1991.

Lemke-Santangelo, Gretchen. *Abiding Courage: African American Migrant Women and the East Bay Community.* Chapel Hill: University of North Carolina Press, 1996.

Levine, Lawrence. *Black Culture and Black Consciousness: Afro-American Folk Thought from Slavery to Freedom.* New York: Oxford University Press, 1977.

Lewis, Earl. "Expectations, Economic Opportunities, and Life in the Industrial Age: Black Migration to Norfolk, Virginia, 1910–1945." In *The Great Migration in Historical Perspective: New Dimensions of Race, Class, and Gender,* ed. Joe William Trotter Jr. Bloomington: Indiana University Press, 1991.

Lipsitz, George. *Time Passages: Collective Memory and American Popular Culture.* Minneapolis: University of Minnesota Press, 1994.

Litwack, Leon. *Been in the Storm So Long: The Aftermath of Slavery.* New York: Vintage Books, 1980.

———. "The Blues Keep Falling." In Berkeley Art Center, *Ethnic Notions: Black Images in the White Mind.* Berkeley, Calif.: Berkeley Art Center, 1982.

Litwack, Leon, Winthrop D. Jordan, Richard Hofstadter, William Miller, and

Daniel Aaron. *The United States: Becoming a World Power.* 7th ed., vol. 2. Englewood Cliffs, N.J.: Prentice-Hall, 1991.

Lobo, Susan. "The Bay Area American Indian Community." Paper delivered at the conference of the American Society for Ethnohistory, Berkeley, Calif., November 6, 1987.

Lowe, W. A., and V. A. Clift, eds. *Encyclopedia of Black America.* New York: McGraw Hill, 1981.

Marks, Carole. *Farewell—We're Good and Gone: The Great Black Migration.* Bloomington: Indiana University Press, 1989.

May, Elaine Tyler. *Homeward Bound: American Families in the Cold War Era.* New York: Basic Books, 1988.

McBroome, Delores Nason. *Parallel Communities: African Americans in California's East Bay, 1850–1963.* New York: Garland Publishing, 1993.

McVittie, James A. *An Avalanche Hits Richmond.* Richmond: Office of the City Manager, 1944.

Miller, Sally M., and Daniel Cornford, eds. *American Labor in the Era of World War II.* Westport, Conn.: Praeger, 1995.

Meier, August. *Negro Thought in America, 1880–1915: Racial Ideologies in the Age of Booker T. Washington.* Ann Arbor: University of Michigan Press, 1988.

Meier, August, and Elliott M. Rudwick. *From Plantation to Ghetto: An Interpretive History of American Negroes.* New York: Hill and Wang, 1966.

Moore, Shirley Ann. "Getting There, Being There: African American Migration to Richmond, California, 1910–1945." In *The Great Migration in Historical Perspective: New Dimensions of Race, Class, and Gender,* ed. Joe William Trotter Jr. Bloomington: Indiana University Press, 1991.

———. "Her Husband Didn't Have a Word to Say: Black Women and Blues Clubs in Richmond, California, during World War II." In *American Labor in the Era of World War II,* ed. Sally M. Miller and Daniel Cornford. Westport, Conn.: Praeger, 1995.

Moore, Shirley Ann Wilson. "Not in Somebody's Kitchen: African American Women Workers in Richmond, California, and the Impact of World War II." In *Writing the Range: Race, Class, and Culture in the Women's West,* ed. Elizabeth Jameson and Susan Armitage. Norman: University of Oklahoma Press, 1997.

———. "Traditions from Home: African Americans in Wartime Richmond, California." In *The War in American Culture: Society and Consciousness during World War II,* ed. Lewis A. Erenberg and Susan E. Hirsch. Chicago: University of Chicago Press, 1996.

———. "Your Life Is Really Not Just Your Own: African American Women in Twentieth Century California," 1997. Unpublished manuscript.

Nash, Gerald D. *The American West Transformed: The Impact of the Second World War.* Bloomington: Indiana University Press, 1985.

Nelsen, Hart M., Raytha L. Yokley, and Anne K. Nelsen, eds. *The Black Church in America.* New York: Basic Books 1971.

Nichols, Minnie Lue. "An Interview with Minnie Lue," by Eldreadge Wright. March 24, 1972. Unpublished manuscript.

Nottage, Margaret Marlowe, ed. *Women's Journal: California Association of Colored Women's Clubs.* N.p., 1945.

Oakley, Giles. *The Devil's Music.* New York: Harcourt, Brace, Jovanovich, 1976.

Oliver, Paul. *The Story of the Blues.* Radnor, Penn.: Chilton Book Company, 1969.

Osofsky, Gilbert. *Harlem: The Making of a Ghetto, Negro New York, 1880–1930.* New York: Harper and Row, 1971.

Paris, Peter J. *The Social Teaching of the Black Churches.* Philadelphia: Fortress Press, 1985.

Peretti, Burton. *The Creation of Jazz: Music, Race, and Culture in Urban America.* Urbana: University of Illinois Press, 1992.

Peyton, Thomas Roy. *Quest for Dignity: An Autobiography of a Negro Doctor.* Los Angeles: Warren F. Lewis Publishing, 1950.

Pollenberg, Richard. *War and Society: The United States, 1941–1945.* Westport, Conn.: Greenwood Press, 1972.

Raboteau, Albert J. *Slave Religion: The Invisible Institution in the Antebellum South.* New York: Oxford University Press, 1980.

Record, Cy W. "Characteristics of Some Unemployed Negro Shipyard Workers in Richmond California." Library of Economic Research, University of California, Berkeley, September 1947. Intergovernmental Studies Library, University of California, Berkeley.

Rosenzweig, Roy. *Eight Hours for What We Will: Workers and Leisure in an Industrial City, 1870–1920.* Oxford: Cambridge University Press, 1983.

Rubin, Lillian B. *Busing and Backlash: White against White in an Urban School District.* Berkeley: University of California Press, 1972.

Ruck, Rob. *Sandlot Seasons: Sport in Black Pittsburgh.* Urbana: University of Illinois Press, 1987.

Russell, Tony. *Blacks, Whites, and Blues.* London: Studio Vista, 1970.

Shaw, Arnold. *Honkers and Shouters: The Golden Years of Rhythm and Blues.* New York: Macmillan, 1978.

Sinclair, Upton. *The Jungle.* 1906. Reprint, New York: New American Library, 1980.

Slayton, Robert A. *Back of the Yards: The Making of Local Democracy.* Chicago: University of Chicago Press, 1986.

Sokol, William. "From Workingman's Town to All American City: The Socio-Political Economy of Richmond, California, during World War II." June 1971. Richmond Collection, Richmond Public Library.

Southern, Eileen. *The Music of Black Americans: A History.* New York: W.W. Norton and Company, 1971.

Spear, Allen. *Black Chicago: The Making of a Negro Ghetto.* Chicago: University of Chicago Press, 1967.

Stack, Carol. *All Our Kin: Strategies for Survival in a Black Community.* New York: Harper and Row, 1974.

Stewart, James. "Relationships between Black Males and Females in Rhythm and Blues Music of the 1960s and 1970s." In *More Than Dancing: Essays on Afro-American Music and Musicians,* ed. Irene V. Jackson. Westport, Conn.: Greenwood Press, 1985.

Taylor, Quintard. *The Forging of a Black Community: Seattle's Central District from 1870 through the Civil Rights Era.* Seattle: University of Washington Press, 1994.

Terkel, Studs. *Hard Times: An Oral History of the Great Depression.* New York: Pocket Books, 1970.

Tilghman Press. *We Also Serve: Armed Forces Edition.* Berkeley, Calif.: Tilghman Press, 1945.

———. *We Also Serve: Ten Percent of a Nation Working and Fighting for Victory.* Berkeley, Calif.: Tilghman Press, 1945.

Titon, Jeff Todd. *Downhome Blues Lyrics: An Anthology from the Post–World War II Era.* 2d. ed. Urbana: University of Illinois Press, 1990.

Tonnies, Ferdinand. *Fundamental Concepts of Sociology.* Translated by Charles P. Loomis. New York: American Books, 1940.

Trachtenberg, Alan. *The Incorporation of America: Culture and Society in the Gilded Age.* New York: Hill and Wang, 1982.

Trotter, Joe William, Jr. "Black Migration in Historical Perspective: A Review of the Literature." In *The Great Migration in Historical Perspective: New Dimensions of Race, Class, and Gender,* ed. Joe William Trotter Jr. Bloomington: Indiana University Press, 1991.

———. *Black Milwaukee: The Making of an Industrial Proletariat, 1915–1945.* Urbana: University of Illinois Press, 1985.

———, ed. *The Great Migration in Historical Perspective: New Dimension of Race, Class, and Gender.* Bloomington: Indiana University Press, 1991.

Van DeBurg, William L. *New Day in Babylon: The Black Power Movement and African American Culture, 1965–1975.* Chicago: University of Chicago Press, 1992.

Weisbrot, Robert. *Freedom Bound: A History of America's Civil Rights Movement.* New York: Plume Books, 1991.

Whitnah, Joseph C. *A History of Richmond, California: The City That Grew from a Rancho.* Richmond: Chamber of Commerce, 1944.

Willensky, Carl M. *Post War Richmond: A Pictorial Summary of Post War Accomplishments, 1945–1949.* Richmond: Chamber of Commerce, 1949.

Wiltz, John E. *From Isolation to War, 1931–1941.* New York: Thomas Y. Crowell Company, 1968.

Wollenberg, Charles. *Golden Gate Metropolis: Perspectives on Bay Area History.* Berkeley, Calif.: Institute of Governmental Studies, 1985.

———. *Marinship at War: Shipbuilding and Social Changes in Wartime Sausalito.* Berkeley, Calif.: Western Heritage Press, 1990.

Woodson, Carter G. *A Century of Negro Migration.* 1918. New York: Russell and Russell, 1969.

Woodward, C. Vann. *Origins of the New South, 1977–1913.* Baton Rouge: Louisiana State University Press, 1971.

———. *The Strange Career of Jim Crow.* New York: Oxford Press, 1955.

Zunz, Olivier. *The Changing Face of Inequality: Urbanization, Industrial Development, and Immigrants in Detroit, 1880–1920.* Chicago: University of Chicago Press, 1982.

Index

Note: Page numbers in italics refer to tables and maps.

Abbott, Robert S., 65
absenteeism, in shipyards, 64, 67–69
accommodation, appearance of, 25, 82
AFL (American Federation of Labor), 53, 58
African Americans: determination of, 89; expectations of, 4, 65, 70, 97, 147–48; legitimization for, 90; longtimers vs. newcomers, 80–83, 93, 101, 112–13, 118, 125, 138, 142; negative images of, 80; skills of, 54–56; status of, 16, 33–34, 71, 148; stigmatization of, 1–2, 39, 77–80. *See also* discrimination; employment; gender; housing; leisure activities; race; schools; segregation; socioeconomic class; workers
AFSC (American Friends Service Committee), 110
after hours clubs, 4, 32–33, 134. *See also* blues clubs; taverns
age, of migrants, 51
agency: components of, 118–19; role of, 2, 149–50. *See also* culture; political action; voluntary racial congregation
agriculture: advice on, 47; blacks in, 21–22, 38; greenhouse type of, 16; mechanization in, 49
aircraft industry, 40, 73
Ake, Elmira, 58
Alabama: migration from, 51–52; racial violence in, 49
Alameda (city), blacks in, 16

Alameda (county), blacks in, 82
Albany, farm products for, 22
Albrier, Frances Mary, 58–59, 64
alumni clubs, 143
American Council on Race Relations, 101–2
American Federation of Labor (AFL), 53, 58
American Friends Service Committee (AFSC), 110
American Legion Baseball, 145
American Standard Company, 25, 154n12
American Standard Porcelain Works, 14
Anderson, Booker T., 191n84
annexation, motivation for, 100, 115
antilynching legislation, 31
Archibald, Katherine, 63
Arkansas: migration from, 3, 16, 53, 63, 77, 135; shipyard recruitment in, 45, 47; state club for migrants from, 144
Ashler Masonic Lodge, 31–32, 38–39, 162n102
Asians: discrimination against, 57; employment for, 15, 16; leisure activities of, 33
Atchison Village (housing), 85, 99, 179n42
Atkins, Maggie Lewis, 193n3
Austria, immigrants from, 12
automobiles, ownership of, fig. 4, 22

BACD (Bay Area Council against Discrimination), 55, 106, 187n34
Baker, Percy, 110, 187n36

Bally, George, 132
B and L Club, 135–36
Baptist Union, 125
Barbour, Harry, 86
Barbour, W. Miller, 53
Barrett Avenue: businesses on, 120; origin of, 153–54n7
baseball, as cultural channel, 144–46
Batchan, Irene Malbrough: on church and culture, 29; on cultural differences, 146; on employment, 19, 20, 37; occupation of, 21; on recreation center, 32; on state clubs, 144
Bates, George, 71, 72, 73
Bates, Nathaniel, 191n84
Bay Area Council against Discrimination (BACD), 55, 106, 187n34
Bayview Elementary School, 115
Bean, Albert, 18
Bell, Thomas, 168n28
Benicia Arsenal, 95
Beratta, Vera, 123
Berkeley: blacks in, 16, 39, 82, 119; churches in, 26; farm products for, 22; housing in, 84; integration in, 85
Berkeley Powder Plant, 72
Beth Eden Baptist Church (Oakland), 142
Big Town Records, 69
"Black Crescent" area, 111, 112
Black Draught (medicine), 129
blackface minstrel shows, 25
Black Panthers, 133
black power movement, 133–34, 139
Blair, Claude, 157n50
Bland, Bobby "Blue," 133
Blue Haven Cafe, 134
blues: cultural role of, 137–38; decline of, 138–40; development of, 130–32
blues clubs: blacks and whites in, 131, 133–34; booking agents for, 50; closure of, 139–40, 148; control of, 133–34; description of, 131–33; etiquette of, 137–38; newcomers and, 134–35; photos of, figs. 22–24; women in, 4, 135–37. See also after hours clubs; taverns
Boilermakers Union (Local A-36): ship sponsored by, 65–66; significance of, 59–62
Boilermakers Union (Local 513): challenges to, 59, 60–62; migrants derided by, 53; power of, 54; racial and gender discrimination by, 56–59; women barred from, 58

Bonaparte, Georgie Wheat, 48, 128, 140
Bonaparte, Louis, fig. 12, 48, 140
Bonaparte, Louis, Sr., 17
boomtown: crime rate in, 75–78, 76; cutbacks and, 94–95; development of, 72; drinking establishments in, 74–75; housing problems in, fig. 19, 75, 84–87; interracial conflict in, 77–80; intraracial conflict and, 80–83; organizations in, 71; political action and, 83–93; school problems in, 73–74, 78–79, 83. See also demobilization
Bost, William, 18
Bowen, Mildred, 90, 92
Boy Scouts, segregation in, 85
Bradford, Moses, 114
British Isles, immigrants from, 12
Brombacher, Elton, 117, 119, 199–200n4
Brooks, Isaiah, 57
Brookside Hospital, 121, 123
Broussard, Albert, 106, 193n2
Brown, Charles, 132, 133
Brown, Cleophas: background of, 163n131; on Brown v. Board of Education, 123; on fair employment ordinance, 109; on housing, 86–87, 116, 118; on labor unions, 61; on leadership, 111; NAACP and, 62, 86, 90, 92, 109; as political radical, 90, 91; on racial solidarity, 102, 126
Brown, Hubert Owen, 177n29
Brown, James, 133
Brown, Paul L., 91
Brown, Ursula, 109
Brown, William R., 58, 86–87
Brown Derby (club), 131
Brown v. Board of Education, 123, 138, 149
bullfights, 33
Burris, Lance, 199–200n4
Busher, Fred, 117
businesses: black-owned, 22–23, 120–21, 123; climate for, 41, 163n128; discrimination by, 82–83, 105; incentives for, 9; labor unions opposed by, 37–38; restrictive covenants and, 158n63. See also blues clubs; real estate development
Butler, V. E., 91

"Cabbage Patch," 21–22
California: allure of, 3, 36, 46, 47, 127–28, 146, 148, 149–50; defense industry investment in, 40–41; legislature in, 153–54n7. See also population; specific cities

California Association of Colored Women, 30
California Camergic Corporation, 72
California Council on Civic Unity (CCCU), 106
California Federation for Civic Unity, 107
California Missionary Baptist Convention, 160n82
California Supreme Court, 23
California Voice (newspaper): on boomtown, 71; on employment, 42; on political action, 111
California Wine Association Plant, 14
Camp, William Martin, 53, 78
Campbell, Louis, 42, 111
Canal housing project, 98, 99
Canal Queens (baseball team), 145
canning industry: antipollution suits against, 163n128; bus service of, 44; discrimination in, 34; employees in, 21, 96, 123, 157n50
Carlson, T. M., 169n35
Carroll, George, 124–26
cars, ownership of, fig. 4, 22
Carver, George Washington, fig. 14, 65
CCCU (California Council on Civic Unity), 106
CCU (Council for Civic Unity), 106–7, 121
Central Trade School (Oakland), 58–59
Certainteed Manufacturing Company, 18–19, 31, 35
Chamber of Commerce: job recruitment and, 45–46; members of, 154n12; public housing and, 84; urban renewal and, 99–100
Chamber of Commerce (black), 120
Chandler, Mattie, 79
Charles, Ray, 133
Chesley Street: club on, 131, 132; farming along, 22; newspaper on, 134
Chevron Oil Refinery, 148
Chicago (Ill.), migrants from, 36
Chicago Bridge and Iron Corporation, 73
Chicago Defender (newspaper), publisher of, 65
childbearing, 128–29
children: child care for, 65, 68–69; differing skill levels among, 74; health care for, fig. 21, 128–29; racial boundaries and, 24–25. *See also* schools
Childs, Lyn, 50
Chinese: discrimination against, 57; employment for, 15, 16
Chlora Hayes Sledge Club, 30, 124
churches: activities of, 38, 110, 142–43; characteristics of, 28–29; derision of, 27–28; establishment of, 27, 113, 140; music in, 140–42, 194n8; photos of, fig. 6, fig. 8; political action and, 106, 125; role of, 26, 29–30, 47–48, 116, 148; Sanctified type of, 140–43
Church of God in Christ (COGIC, North Richmond), 27, 140. *See also* McGlothen Temple
CIO (Congress of Industrial Organizations), 37
city hall, location of, 9
City-Wide Mission, 110
civic life: interracial coalitions on, 106–8; KKK's participation in, 25; leadership for, 13. *See also* community development; political action; voluntary organizations
Civil Rights Congress, 117
civil rights movement: changes in, 139; political action in, 123–26; voluntary organizations for, 34
Clark, Benjamin, 181n59
Clark, Emma, 160n77
Clemons, Bessie, 157n50
Cold War, rhetoric of, 104–5, 118
Coleman, G. C., 27
Colored Chorus, 194n8
Colored Directory of the Leading Cities of Northern California, 1916–1917, 23
Colored Methodist Episcopal Church (North Richmond), 27
Committee on Housing and Municipal Problems, 98–99
Communist Party: NAACP and, 90–93, 104–5, 106; unemployment and, 37–38
community development: auxiliary union's role in, 60; control of, 13, 15; control of wartime, 72–73; cultural transplantation in, 2–3, 127–28, 146, 148; in eastern vs. western areas, 2–5; experiential dimension of, 148–49; vs. industrial development, 41–42; men's roles in, 31–32; positive view of, 39; social continuity in, 1–2, 8, 81–82; war boom's impact on, 73–74; women's roles in, 30–31. *See also* churches; family; home ownership; voluntary organizations

Congress of Industrial Organizations (CIO), 37

Congress of Racial Equality (CORE), 123

Contra Costa County: churches in, 27; gold rush in, 8; housing in, 97; location of, 7. *See also* North Richmond; Richmond

Cordonices Village (Berkeley), 84

CORE (Congress of Racial Equality), 123

Cotright, Odis, 120

Cotright, Willie Mae, 120

Council for Civic Unity (CCU), 106–7, 121

courtship, churches and, 30

Cramer, Lawrence W., 170n43

Crawford, Matt, 120–21

Creeger, Henry, 154n12

crime, wartime boom in, 75–78, 76

Crowe, Thomas, 56–57

Cuba, Austin, 97

culture: baseball in, 144–46; folk healing practices in, 128–29; generational differences and, 29; men and women as bearers of, 130–31, 152n4; power linked to, 137–38; of shipyard workers, 66–70; state clubs' function in, 143–44; transformation of, 2–3, 127–28, 146, 148; work patterns linked to, 66–70, 174n89. *See also* churches; family; music; voluntary organizations

"culture of expectation," 4

Current, Gloster B., 92

Cutting Boulevard: businesses on, 105; churches on, 140; housing projects on, 85; industrial development on, 14

"Dateline Freedom" (radio program), 106

Debney, Henry, 146

defense industries: demobilization of, 94–95, 170n43; discrimination in, 45, 46; federal spending on, 36–37, 40–41; housing for workers in, fig. 19, 84; investment in, 40–41; migration and, 48; profits from, 72–73. *See also* aircraft industry; boomtown; shipyards

Dellums, C. L., 61, 66

Del Monte canneries, 21

demobilization: backlash against blacks in, 101–2; family problems in, 96–97; layoffs in, 94–96; racial motives in, 97; workers' hopes in, 100–101. *See also* urban renewal

Democratic Party, coalition in, 125

Denver Club, 74

DeSanto, Sugar Pie, 133

Detroit (Mich.), as boomtown, 73

Dew Drop Inn, 131

Diddley, Bo, 139

Diggens, S. E., 91

discrimination: acceptance of, 89–90; by businesses, 82–83, 105; in canning industry, 34; in defense industries, 45, 46, 170n43; in employment, 15–16, 45, 46, 100, 122, 149; government and, 45, 53, 54–58; by hospitals, 128; increase in, 71, 83, 96; in labor unions, 46, 47, 52–60, 135, 172n61; ordinance against, 107–9, 187n38; organizing against, 60–62, 65, 86–87, 105, 149; in shipyards, 52–58, 67; in South, 3, 82–83; in wages, 19–20, 52, 56

Dixon, W., 91

doctors, blacks as, 121, 128–29

domestic work: alternatives to, 44–45, 50–51, 135–36; steadiness of, 20–21; unemployment vs., 123

Down Beat (club), 131

Downer, Edward, 154n12

DuBois, W. E. B., 26, 51, 62

Durant cars, fig. 4, 22

East Bay area: as center of black life, 16; domestics in, 21; Garveyism in, 34

education: diverse needs in, 74, 82; political action and, 102–4; scholarships for, 31. *See also* schools

Edwards, Lucretia, 110–11

elections: black candidates in, 111–13, 114, 124–25, 181n59, 191n84; issues in, 112; for mayor, 119, 126; participation in, 13, 113

electricity, limitations on, 162n108

electric trolley, 14

Elks club, 25, 32, 124, 154n12

Ellison, Douglas, 121

Ellison family, housing for, 23

El Sobrante (suburb), integration of, 116

Emeryville, canneries in, 21

employment: city ordinances on, 107–9, 187n38; competition in, 20; discrimination in, 15–16, 45, 46, 100, 122, 149; equity demanded in, 104–5; hiring practices and, 54–55; in job work, 18; migration linked to, 8, 17, 45–47; opportunities for blacks in, 18–21, 40–44; professional base expanded in, 119; racial solidarity and, 83–84; stability of eastern vs. western, 4–5; women as ambassadors for, 21; women as referral agents for, 136. *See also* unemployment; women workers; workers

entrepreneurial class: emergence of, 120; women in, 123, 132–33, 135–37

Episcopal Church (Oakland), 26

Evans, Bernard, 92, 191n84

Evans, Hiram, 25

Everett, Ebb, 91

Executive Order 8802, 40–41, 53

Fabry, Joseph, 53

Fair Employment Practices Commission (FEPC): creation of, 40–41; on discrimination, 45, 53, 54–58; *Life* article on, 63

Fall Avenue, housing on, 99

family: as child care givers, 68; demobilization's impact on, 96–97; generational conflict and, 29; as migration factor, 17–18, 47–49. *See also* churches

Fannie Jackson Coppin Club, 194n8

Fanny Wall Home for Colored Orphans (Oakland), 30

Federal Labor Stabilization Program, 67

Federal Public Housing Administration, 43, 84, 86, 99

femininity, minimized in shipyards, 69

Fenell, Myrtle, 91

Fern Leaf (club), 74

Fifth Street: businesses on, 83, 120; Masonic Lodge on, 162n102

Filice and Perrelli Cannery, 96, 157n50

Filipinos: discrimination against, 57; occupations of, 21

First Christian Church (Richmond), 26

First Street, farming along, 22

fishing industry: camp for, 38, 155n30; control of, 16; women workers in, 21. *See also* canning industry

Fisk University, ship named for, 65

folk healing practices, 128–29, 193n3

Fong Wong Shrimp camp, 38, 155n30

food services, 64

Ford Motor Company: employment at, 36, 48, 96; wages at, 55; wartime production of, 72, 73

Fortune (periodical): on labor, 53; Lange photos in, 80

foundries, employees of, 19

Fountain, Oliver, 34–35

Fowler, Lofton L., 90, 109

France, Edward, 89

Fraser, Irene, 23

Frazier, E. Franklin, 26

Freeman, Jessie: home ownership of, fig. 9, 34–35; migration of, fig. 1, 17; occupation of, fig. 3, 20, 21; quilts of, fig. 9

Freeman, Liddy, 21

Freeman, Ollie, 104, 140

Freeman, Regina Hinkle, 30

Freeman, Walter, Jr.: on churches, 27, 28; council candidacy of, 111–13; on diversity, 33; on health care, 129; home ownership of, 35; on hunting, 38; on KKK, 25; on leisure activities, 33, 145, 162n102; marriage of, 30; on newcomers, 81; occupation of, fig. 3, 18–19, 22; on racial boundaries, 24–25; in shop class, fig. 5; on UNIA, 34

Freeman, Walter, Sr.: home ownership of, fig. 9, 34–35; as Mason, 31; migration of, fig. 1, 17; occupation of, 18, 22

friendships: child care and, 68; as migration factor, 17–18, 48–49

Fulson, Lowell, 131–32

Galvin, John, 154n12

gambling, 33, 139–40. *See also* blues clubs

Garcia, Father John, 100

Garvey, Marcus, 34, 120

Gary, Wilbur, 116–18

Geddins, Bob, 69, 141

gender: cultural preservation and, 2; discrimination based on, 4, 57–59, 122; divisions based in, 4; migration and, 50–51; statistics on, 12, *12, 101;* unemployment and, 95, *96;* wages and, 57; work culture and, 67–70. *See also* femininity; men; women

Georgia, migration from, 135

Germany, immigrants from, 12

Girl Scouts, segregation in, 85

Golden Gate Bridge, workers on, 18

Golden Gaters (group), 141

gold rush, impact of, 8

Gordon, Walter A., 66, 106

gospel music, 140–42

Gottlieb, Peter, 159–60n76

Graves, Sammy, 19, 23

Great Depression, 36–39

Greater Richmond Interfaith Program, 125

Great Migration (first): factors in, 47, 48; origins of, 16–17; transformation in, 130

Great Migration (second): extent of, 40–41; factors in, 47–48; origins of, 3, 29

greenhouse agriculture, 16

Griffin, Betty, 22–23

Griffin, Hattie. *See* Vaughn, Hattie Griffin

Griffin, Joseph: business of, 22–23; churches and, 27, 141; migration of, 17–18; on military, 119; on racial conflicts, 104; on schools, 120

Griffin, Noah, Sr.: on fair employment ordinance, 108; on ideological divisions, 90–92; as NAACP leader, 86; on school conflicts, 103; shipyard layoffs and, 94–95

Griffin family: car of, fig. 4; recreation center and, 32; saloon owned by, 33

Grove Street, Masonic Lodge on, 31–32

Gutman, Herbert G., 128

Hall, Arthur A., 46, 72

Hall, Hazel, 109

Hamachi, Roy, 179n42

Harbor Gate Court (housing): condition of, 116; demolition of, 99; meetings in, 86; residents of, 48, 85, 181n59

Harbor Gate School, 74

Harry Ells High School, 103

Hatter, Terry, 121

Hayes, Roland, 194n8

health care: clinic for, fig. 21, 129; folk practices of, 128–29, 193n3; for shipyard workers, 65. *See also* hospitals

Hensley Industrial Park, 184–85n17

Hercules Powder Plant, 72

Hill, Ivan H., 79

Hilliard, Flora M., 57–58

Hinkle, Regina. *See* Freeman, Regina Hinkle

Hinkley, Amos, 114

Hirsch, Susan E., 157n43

Holmes (minister), 27–28, 160n82

home ownership: attitudes toward, 115; importance of, 34–35, 89, 100–101; postwar construction and, 113–15; unemployment and, 37; white intermediaries and, 190n61. *See also* family; housing; Parchester Village

Hope, John, 65

Hornsby, Henry, 115

hospitals: access to, 193n2; discrimination by, 128; staff of, 121, 123. *See also* health care

House Un-American Activities Committee, 163n131

Housewives Market (Oakland), 22

housing: cost of, 85, 89; crime linked to, 78; demand for equity in, 85–86; description of, 34–36, fires in, 85; integration of, 116–18; postwar construction of, 113–15; postwar future of, 72; private market in, 87–89, 99; public projects for, fig. 19, 84–87, 97–100; racial solidarity and, 83–84; restrictive covenants in, 23–24, 88, 115; segregation in, 18, 23–24, 83–87, 99–101, 111, 130–31, 149; for shipyard workers, 43, 46, 48, 56, 73, 75; urban renewal and, 97; wartime boom and, 75, 84–87. *See also* home ownership; urban renewal

Housing Acts (1949 and 1950), 97

Howard, Lee, 148

Howden, Edward, 106

Hudson, Girtha, Jr., 17–18

Hudson, Girtha, Sr., 18, 35, 52

Hudson, Lilly, 18

Hudson, Mattie, 18, 20

Hudson, Mildred. *See* Slocum, Mildred Hudson

Hudson, Samuel D., 54

Hughes, John, 90, 91, 181n59

Huichin (Indians), settlement by, 8

Hunter, Ivory Joe, 132

Hunters Point, 95

hunting, as survival tool, 38

Hurston, Zora Neale, 32–33

immigration: fictional account of, 168n28; origins of, 12–13. *See also* migration

industrial development: beginnings of, 7–9, 13–14; control of wartime, 72–73; employment opportunities and, 16, 19; federal spending's effect on, 36–37, 40–41; negative impact of, 14–15, 41–42; neighborhoods impacted by, 9, 12; urban renewal linked to, 97–98, 100. *See also* aircraft industry; canning industry; defense industries; fishing industry; Richmond Industrial Commission; shipyards

Interdenominational Ministerial Alliance, 87, 113–14, 123, 125, 135

International Boilermakers Union, 56. *See also* Boilermakers Union (Local 513)

intraracial conflict: blues club etiquette and, 138; deemphasis of, 83, 93, 118, 124, 144; in migration process, 80–83; in NAACP, 72, 90–93, 104; overcoming, 125; role of, 3–4
Iowa, migration from, 80
Italians: immigration of, 12; leisure activities of, 33; occupations of, 21, 22
Iverson, Todd, 82

Jackson, Mahalia, 141
Jackson [Mississippi] State College Alumni Club, 143
James, Joseph, 61–62
James v. Marinship, 61–62
Japanese: discrimination against, 57; employment for, 15, 16
Jarret, Emma, 129
Jazzland Records, 140
Jenkins, Slim, 131
Johnson, Deacon, 136
Johnson, George, fig. 11, 21, 35–36, 157n48
Johnson, Ida, fig. 11, 21, 35–36, 157n48
Johnson, Wilbur, 124
Johnson, Willie Mae "Granny," 132, 136
Jones, Jacqueline, 122
Jordan, Gladys, 114–15, 189n52, 190n61
Jordan, John, 114–15, 189n52, 190n61
judges, blacks as, 126

Kaiser, Henry J., 1, 41, 43, 45. *See also* shipyards
Kaiser Shipbuilding Corporation: closed-shop contracts with, 54; discrimination in, 54; layoffs at, 94–97; number of employees of, 52, 169n35; racial conflict in, 63–64; recruitment by, 45–47; women workers in, fig. 13, 57–58; worker services in, 64–65. *See also* shipyards
Keeton, William Elmer, 194n8
Kenny, James, 113
Kenny, Robert W., 102, 117
Kentucky, migration from, 17
King, B. B., 132, 133
King, Martin Luther, Jr., 124, 126
Kingman, Harry, 63
Kiser, Clyde, 51
Knox, John, 119
Knox, Marcellus, 54
Kramer, Alyce Mano, 165n9
Kretzmer, William, 187n36
Ku Klux Klan, 25

La Beaux, W. Lee, 98, 99
labor unions: challenges to, 59, 60–62; classification by, 56; closed-shop contracts with, 54; discrimination in, 46, 47, 52–60, 135, 172n61; dues and benefits of, 172n61; lock outs of, 19–20; racial integration in, 37–38, 124; women barred from, 57–59. *See also specific unions*
Lake Elementary School, 115
Lange, Dorothea, 80
language: learning second, 33; of long-timers vs. newcomers, 81
Lanham Act (1940), 73
Las Deltas housing project, 111
Last Man's Club, 134
Laundry Workers Union (Local 2), 181n59
leisure activities: establishments for, 32–33; limitations of, 119; preferences in, 64, 68; segregation in, 85, 186n26; in wartime boom, 74–75. *See also* blues clubs; churches; music; sports teams; voluntary organizations
Lemke-Santangelo, Gretchen, 152n4
Lewis, Earl, 4
Lewis, Ivy Reid: on crime and race, 78; on hunting, 38; on leisure activities, 33, 131, 145; on Richmond as choice, 39; on schools, 24, 83; on segregation, 24, 88
Lewis, John L., 37
Life (periodical), shipyard article by, 63
Lincoln Street, housing on, 24
Livingston, George, 119, 124
loafing, definition of and response to, 67
Los Angeles: black-owned businesses in, 22–23; as boomtown, 73; riots in, 126
Louisiana: migration from, 3, 17–18, 22, 51, 120; shipyard recruitment in, 45
Lucky supermarket chain, boycott of, 105

Macdonald, Alfred Sylvester, 8–9
Macdonald Avenue: businesses on, 83, 97, 105; development on, 9; disturbances on, 77; housing on, 16
Malbrough, Irene. *See* Batchan, Irene Malbrough
Malbrough, Joseph: on cultural differences, 146; on leisure activities, 32, 144, 145; occupation of, 20; photo of, fig. 10; on prostitution, 69–70; on transportation, 19
Malbrough, Matthew, 17, 18, 35, 39, 52

Malbrough, Pearl, 21
Malbrough, William, 17, 18, 20, 35
Mare Island Naval Yard, 36, 95
Marinship yards, 61–62
marital status: demobilization and, 97; of
    migrants, 51; working women and, 122
Maslow, Will, 169n135
Masonic Lodge, Ashler, 31–32, 38–39,
    162n102
Maynard, John, 19
mayor, African Americans as, 119, 126
McCarthy era, 91–92, 109
McCracklin, Jimmy, 127, 132, 133
McGlothen Temple, 27, 28–29, 140, 141
McKinney, William H.: on auxiliary union,
    60; on demobilization, 97; on discrimi-
    nation, 82–83; NAACP and, 86; occu-
    pations of, 47, 52; on racism, 53–54; on
    urban renewal, 98
McMillan, James, 120, 121
McVittie, James, 76–77, 99–100
Mechanics Bank (Richmond), 154n12
men: as culture bearers, 130–31, 152n4;
    organizations of, 31–32; on working
    women, 122. See also workers
Mexican Americans: employment and, 15–
    16, 21, 36–37; housing for, 16; leisure
    activities of, 33
Mexicans: defense industry jobs for, 45;
    settlement by, 8
Mexico, bracero treaty with, 45
Mickens, Isaac (I. C.), 90, 91, 92
middle class, emergence of, 120–22
midwives, status of, 128–29
migration: conditions accepted in, 89–90;
    employment linked to, 8, 17, 45–47; ex-
    periential dimension of, 148–49; factors
    in, 17–18, 40–41, 47–49; gender and,
    50–51; hopes in, 3, 4, 36, 49–50, 52,
    127–28; interviews on, 156n33; intra-
    racial conflict in, 80–83; origins of, 3,
    16–17; patterns of, 51–52; racial tensions
    heightened by, 49, 63–64; resentment
    toward, 53, 73, 81; social continuity and,
    1–2, 8, 81–82; workers' skills and, 54–
    56. See also community development
Miles, Willie, 27
military, as opportunity, 119
Miller, George P., 86
Miller, John, 75
Minnesota, shipyard recruitment in, 45
Minnie Lue's (club): changing character
    of, 139–40; description of, 131, 132–33;

opening night at, fig. 23; ownership of,
    135, 136; success of, 123
Mississippi: migration from, 3, 16, 48, 51,
    54; shipyard recruitment in, 45; state
    club for migrants from, 143
Missouri Pacific Railroad, 17
Monroe Street, housing on, 34–35
Moore Dry Dock Company (Oakland),
    56–57, 59, 63, 64
Mt. Carmel Missionary Baptist Church,
    113
Mt. Zion Spiritual Temple, 142–43
movie theaters, in wartime, 75
music: African influence on, 129–30; in
    churches, 140–42, 194n8; commercial-
    ization of, 141; as cultural resource,
    129–30, 140; development of R&B,
    138–39; development of soul, 139–40;
    longtimers' and newcomers' traditions
    of, 194n8; race riot and, 78; record
    companies and, 69, 139; at shipyards,
    66. See also blues; blues clubs
mutual aid associations, 31–32

NAACP (national), 106, 123
NAACP (Richmond branch): alliances of,
    105, 107–8; conflicts within, 72, 90–93,
    104; criticism of, 106; fair employment
    practices and, 104–5, 107–9; formation
    of, 4, 86; housing and, 86–87, 117–18;
    in McCarthy era, 91–92; officers of, 50,
    91, 121, 135, 181n59; origins of, 60, 62, 71,
    82, 90; radicals purged in, 92–93, 109;
    school conflicts and, 103–4
NAACP (West Coast Regional Office), 86.
    See also Griffin, Noah, Sr.
Narcisse, Louis H., 142–43, 198n48
National Association of Colored Women
    (NACW), 31
National Council of Christians and Jews,
    117
National Ice Company, 18
National Negro Congress (Oakland), 91
National Unemployed Councils, 163n130
National Urban League: assistance from,
    82; on employment, 108–9; on hous-
    ing, 118; population count by, 8; on
    Richmond NAACP, 109
National Youth Administration (NYA), 36
Nations, Opal, 195n12
Native Americans, employment and, 16,
    36–37
nativity, statistics on, 7, 8, 9, 12, 12–13

Negro Baptist Missionary Associates, 28
Negro Protective League, 34
neighborhoods: industrialization's impact
    on, 9, 12; postwar future of, 72; racial
    change in, 87–88; segregation of, 85; for
    specialized workers, 13; wartime's im-
    pact on, 74–75. *See also* housing
newspapers: on crime and race, 77–78;
    migration advice in, 47; publisher of,
    50. *See also specific newspapers*
Nicholl, John, 9
Nichols, Minnie Lue: on baseball, 146; on
    blues, 137; business of, figs. 23–24, 123,
    131, 132–33, 135, 136, 139–40
nightclubs. *See* after hours clubs; blues
    clubs; taverns
North Carolina, migration from, 16
North Oakland Baptist Church, 27
North Richmond: annexation and, 100;
    black-owned businesses in, 22; descrip-
    tion of, 23–24, 39, 88; diversity in, 33;
    housing in, 88–89; infrastructure of, 88;
    as segregated area, 23–24, 88; stigmati-
    zation of, 79–80; unemployment in, 95,
    96; urban renewal plans for, 97, 99–100.
    See also boomtown; "Cabbage Patch";
    churches; demobilization; employment;
    housing; schools; shipyards
North Richmond Improvement Club
    (NRIC), 34
North Richmond Missionary Baptist
    Church (NRMBC): aid from, 38; char-
    acter of, 28–29, 142; establishment of,
    27–28; photo of, fig. 6; picnics of, 30
North Richmond Neighborhood House,
    81, 110–11, 201n14
North Richmond Spiders (baseball team),
    145
NRIC (North Richmond Improvement
    Club), 34
NRMBC. *See* North Richmond Mission-
    ary Baptist Church (NRMBC)
Nut Club, 74
NYA (National Youth Administration), 36
Nystrom, Stanley, 24
Nystrom Elementary School, 103
Nystrom Village (housing), 85, 179n42,
    184n11

Oakland: black-owned businesses in, 22–
    23; blacks in, 16, 39, 82, 119; canneries
    in, 21; churches in, 26, 27, 142; com-
    muters from, 75; domestics in, 20, 21;

Garveyism in, 34; nightclubs in, 131;
    race riot in, 78; schools in, 58–59
Ohio, migration from, 22
Ohio Street, housing on, 23
Ohlone Indians, settlement by, 8
Oklahoma: migration from, 53, 63, 77, 119,
    196n26; shipyard recruitment in, 45
Oliphant, E. H., 22
oral history, importance of, 5–6
ordinances (Richmond), on fair employ-
    ment practices, 107–9, 187n38
Orinda, domestics in, 21
Out of This Furnace (Bell), 168n28

Panama Pacific International Exposition,
    34
Parchester Baptist Church, 116
Parchester Hall of Fame, 115–16
Parchester Veterans' Wives Club, 115–16
Parchester Village: community programs
    in, 115–16; politics of, 113–14; residents
    of, 114–15
Parchester Village Improvement Associa-
    tion, fig. 20, 115
Parr, Fred, 114–15
Parr-Richmond Terminal Corporation,
    41, 163n128
PCA (Progressive Citizens of America),
    105
Pennsylvania, migration from, 16, 168n28
People of Richmond, California (group),
    105–6
Peres Elementary School (North Rich-
    mond), 24–25, 78–79
Petgrave, Lily, 23
pharmacists, blacks as, 121
Pierce, John, 103, 186n26
Pierce Colored Giants (baseball team), 145
Pink Kitchen (club), 33, 123, 131
Pittsburgh (Pa.): baseball teams in, 144–
    45; churches in, 159–60n76
"Pittsburgh of the West," Richmond as,
    7, 14
Point Pinole, housing near, 114
Point Richmond: development in, 8–9;
    name of, 153–54n7; neighborhoods in,
    13
police: blacks hired as, 121; brutality of,
    149; housing integration and, 117–18;
    raids by, 15, 139–40; wartime increase
    of, 75–78
political action: on civil rights, 123–26;
    conservatives vs. radicals on, 90–91;

political action (*continued*)
    against discrimination, 60–62, 65, 86–87, 105, 149; on education issues, 102–4; in elections, 111–13, 114; experiential dimension of, 148–49; on housing issues, 83–84, 111, 114–18; impetus for, 70, 71–72, 118–19, 126; timing of, 133–34; against urban renewal strategies, 98–100; in wartime boom, 83–93; on workplace equity, 104–5. *See also* agency; *specific organizations*
politics: blacks' influence on, 124; divisions based in, 4; leadership for, 13. *See also* elections; labor unions; political action
polka dances, 33
population: business success and, 22–23; comparison of cities, 16–17; of Richmond, 7, 8, 9, *12,* 12–13, 24, 36, 41, 52, 101, 138, 147, 151n1; war boom's explosion of, 73–74
Port Chicago, employees of, 95
Portuguese: housing and, 88; leisure activities of, 33; occupations of, 21–22
Powers, Madelon Mae, 195–96n21
produce canneries. *See* canning industry
professional class: absence of, 119; emergence of, 120–22
Progressive Citizens of America (PCA), 105
prohibition, opposition to, 15
Proposition 14 (Calif.), 125
prostitution: after hours clubs and, 134; increase in, 14–15; role of, 33, 123; in shipyards, 69–70
Pullman Coach Company: as employer, 14; land development by, 7; recruitment by, 44; wages at, 19–20; wartime production of, 72

quilts, fig. 9

race: awareness of, 60–61, 111, 118; as obstacle, 79–80, 93; unemployment and, 95, *96*
racial interaction: coalitions based in, 106–8; in demobilization, 101–2; in leisure activities, 33, 145; in wartime boom, 77–80; white patronizing in, 109–11
racial solidarity: attitudes toward, 105; in baseball, 145–46; in demobilization, 101–2; on education issues, 103–4; on

employment and housing issues, 83–84, 111; entrepreneurialism and, 120; role of, 3–4, 111. *See also* political action; voluntary racial congregation
racism: geographic effects of, 81–82; increase of, 25. *See also* discrimination; segregation
Ramsey, Eleanor Mason, 155n27
Randolph, Edmund, 153–54n7
RCCU (Richmond Council on Civic Unity), 95, 107, 187n36
RCIR (Richmond Council on Intergroup Relations), 107–9, 187n36
real estate development: beginnings of, 7–9; housing authority and, 179n42; restrictive covenants in, 23–24, 88, 115; segregation enforced in, 88, 98, 116, 121; urban renewal and, 100. *See also* home ownership; housing
recreation center, 32, 60, 115–16
Red Robin (club), 74
Red Rock fish cannery, 21, 44
Reid, Beryl Gwendolyn, 21, 38, 81, 89, 128
Reid, Charles, 39, 82, 145
Reid family: church of, 26, 29; newcomers and, 89
restaurants: black-owned, 123; blues clubs as, 132–33; discrimination by, 82–83, 105
restrictive covenants, 23–24, 88, 115
Rheems Manufacturing Company, 72
rhythm and blues music, development of, 138–39
Richardson, Louis: council candidacy of, 111–13; as NAACP officer, 91, 181n59; as political radical, 90
Richmond: "Black Crescent" area of, 111, *112;* context of, 149–50; image of, 7, 147–48, 199–200n4; incorporation of, 9; industrial development in, 7–9; map of, *10–11;* name of, 153–54n7; newcomers' role in, 62, 63–64, 77; overview of, 1–5; population of, 7, 8, 9, *12,* 12–13, 24, 36, 41, 52, 101, 138, 147, 151n1; riots in, 126, 149; "ruling council" of, 13; sources on, 5–6; South compared to, 82–83. *See also* boomtown; churches; community development; employment; housing; North Richmond; schools
Richmond Better Government Committee, 107
Richmond Cafe, fig. 18, 22
Richmond City Council: discrimination

by businesses and, 105; elections for, 13, 111–13, 114, 124–26, 181n59, 191n84; ordinances passed by, 107–9, 187n38; petitions to, 34, 37, 86–87, 88, 98, 115; urban renewal and, 98–100
Richmond City Planning Commission, 100
Richmond Commission on Human Relations, 125
Richmond Council on Civic Unity (RCCU), 95, 107, 187n36
Richmond Council on Intergroup Relations (RCIR), 107–9, 187n36
Richmond Guide (newspaper): description of, 195n19; location of, 134; publisher of, 50, 91
Richmond Harbor, 41
Richmond Housing Authority: assistance from, 66; creation of, 84; evictions by, 87, 99; patronage in, 179n42; red-baiting by, 105; segregation by, 84–87
Richmond Independent (newspaper): on business climate, 41, 163n128; on candidates, 112; on crime and race, 77–78; on housing authority, 84; on KKK, 25; on NAACP, 91–92; on prostitution, 14; publisher of, 154n12; on tolerance, 79
Richmond Industrial Commission, 13–14
Richmond Record (newspaper), on white employment, 15
Richmond Redevelopment Agency, 97–98
Richmond Self Improvement Club, 31
Richmond Shipyard Railway, 75
Richmond Union High School: boundaries for, 103; grades in, 102; riot in, 149; shop class in, fig. 5; trustees of, 154n12; wartime problems in, 78–79
riots: alleged cause of, 78; context of, 126, 149, 201n14; in southern shipyards, 49
Roberts, Chick, 77–78
Robinson, Jackie, 146
Robinson, L. C., "Good Rocking," 132
Robinson, Paul T., 90, 109, 121, 188n40
Robinson, Rosa, 27
Robinson, Virginia, 90
rock and roll music, development of, 140
Rogers, Samuel C., 22, 31
Rollingwood district: cemetery in, 198n48; integration of, 117–18
Rollingwood Improvement Association, 117
Roosevelt, Franklin D., 58

Ross, Malcolm, 53
Ruck, Rob, 144
Rumford Fair Housing Act, 125

Safeway supermarket chain, site for, 99
St. Landry's Parish Club, 144
saloons. See taverns
San Diego, restrictive covenants in, 158n63
San Francisco Bay area: black-owned businesses in, 22–23; blacks in, 2, 82, 119; as center of black life, 16; domestics in, 20; gender ratio of migration to, 50; health care in, 193n2; interracial coalitions in, 106–8; newcomers in, 81; wartime commuters from, 75
San Francisco Chronicle (newspaper), on layoffs, 95
San Joaquin Railroad, 153–54n7
San Pablo Avenue: businesses on, 105; funeral procession on, 198n48; residents of, 13
San Pablo Elementary School, 102–3, 115
Santa Fe Railroad: employees of, fig. 2, 14, 15–16, 19; land development by, 7, 9; migration and, 48; recruitment by, 44; wartime transport by, 72
Savoy Club, 127, 131–32, 135, 136, 139
school boards: election of, 13; grievances addressed to, 201n14; segregation and, 103, 115; whiteness of, 121
schools: curriculum in, 120; desegregation of, 123; diversity in, 24; overcrowding in, 74, 102–3; racial boundaries in, 24–25; segregation in, 102–4, 115, 149; wartime problems in, 73–74, 78–79, 83. See also education; teachers; specific schools
Scott, Mabel, 132
segregation: acceptance of, 89–90; challenges to, 60–62, 86–87, 115, 116–17, 123; hardening of, 83; in housing, 18, 23–24, 83–87, 99–101, 111, 130–31, 149; requests for, 98, 103, 186n26; in schools, 102–4
Selvin, David F., 172n61
Seneca (Ill.), as boomtown, 73
Seventh Street, farming along, 22
shebeens (Irish drinking establishments), 195–96n21
"Shinola Shines," tradition of, 25
Shipfitters and Helpers (Oakland Local 9), 57–58

ship launchings, significance of, 65–66

shipping terminal, advertisements by, 163n128

shipyards: demise of, 5; discrimination in, 52–58, 67; economic effects of, 8, 40–45, 52–53; hiring for, 54–55, 59; layoffs at, 94–97; map of, 42; number of employees of, 52, 94, 169n35; photos of, figs. 12–16; postwar future of, 72; racial conflict in, 63–64; recruitment by, 45–47; riot in southern, 49; shift change at, fig. 16, 80; supervisory positions in, 57; technological innovations at, 42–43; training for, 56, 58–59; transfers among, 67; women workers in, fig. 13, 47, 50–51, 57–58; work culture in, 66–70; worker services in, 64–65. See also boomtown; discrimination; housing; wages; workers

Shipyard Workers against Discrimination: goals of, 60–61; leader of, 91; meetings of, 135; significance of, 62

Simmons, Mary, 116

Sixth Street, housing on, 24

Skip to My Lou (Camp), 78

Slaughter, Irene, 190n61

Sledge, Chlora Hayes, 30

Slocum, Jessie, 30

Slocum, Mildred Hudson: on black accomplishments, 147; on churches, 140; home ownership of, 35; marriage of, 30; migration of, 17–18, 20; occupation of, 44; on status, 26

Slocum family, photo of, fig. 7

Smith, William B., 60

Sneddon, Winifred, 109

socioeconomic class: churches labeled by, 142; emergence of middle and professional, 119, 120–22; race vs., 118; residency length vs., 25–26; similarities among, 5; status and, 25–26, 51, 55–56, 82, 119; structure in, 13. See also entrepreneurial class; upward mobility; working class

soul music, development of, 139–40

Soul Stirrers (group), 141

South: black migration from, 3, 16–17, 29, 40–41, 47–50, 63–64, 130; cultural patterns from, 127–28, 141, 143–44, 146; racial discrimination in, 3, 82–83; women entrepreneurs from, 135–36; work patterns in, 68, 174n89

South Carolina, migration from, 18

Southern Pacific Railroad Company, 14, 48

Spanish American War, 16

Spiderettes (baseball team), fig. 25, 145

sports teams: function of, 144–46; shipyard-sponsored, 64

S. S. Fisk Victory, 65

S. S. George Washington Carver, fig. 14, 65–66

Standard Oil Refinery, 7, 14, 45, 72, 96

Standard Sanitary Company, 18

Starks, Margaret H.: on accomplishments, 1, 149; on blues clubs, 131, 132, 134, 136, 137; on churches, 141, 143; on demobilization, 97; on elections, 125–26; on fair employment ordinance, 109; on health care, 129; on housing, 86–87, 118; on leadership, 111; migration of, 47; NAACP and, 86, 91, 93, 135, 181n59; occupations of, 50–51, 131, 132, 134, 136; as political conservative, 90; on racial solidarity, 102, 119; on R&B, 139; on social class, 142; on urban renewal, 100; on work hours, 68; on working women, 122–23

state clubs, function of, 143–44

State Street, housing on, 99

Steamfitters' Union (Local 590), 54–55

Stephenson, Edwin "Red," 110–11

stereotypes: crime linked to, 77–78; manipulation of, 83; unemployment linked to, 95; wages influenced by, 19–20

Strickland, Billye, 136

Strickland, Lawrence C., 31, 136

strikes, lock outs during, 19–20

Subway Bar, 82

Sundays, working on, 68

Sunset Cemetery, 24, 82

Swingshift (Fabry), 53, 63

Tappers Inn, fig. 22, 131, 132, 134–36, 137

taverns: discrimination by, 82; increase in, 14–15, 74–75; role of, 32–33, 123; women restricted in, 135, 195–96n21. See also after hours clubs; blues clubs

tax revenues, 73, 77

Taylor, Quinard, 3, 200n8

teachers: blacks as, 121; emergency certification of, 74

Terrace housing project, 98, 99

Texas: migration from, 3, 16, 18, 48, 51, 54, 135; shipyard recruitment in, 45

Third Street, housing on, 23
Thirty-third Street, NAACP on, 91
Thompson, Ray, 90, 91
Thompson, Wayne, 98, 148
341 (club), 131
Thurston, Bill: on housing, 85; on leisure activities, 131, 143–44, 145; migration of, 47–48; on union consciousness, 60
Thurston, Charles Henry: on California life, 146; on churches, 141–42; migration of, 47–48; occupation of, 55–56
Tobin, George P., 97–98
Tolan Committee, 53
tolerance committee, goal of, 79
transportation: electric trolley as, 14; limitations of, 19; for shipyard workers, 46; wartime problems with, 44, 75
Triangle Court (housing), 85, 179n42, 184n11
Trotter, Joe William, Jr., 55

UNA (United Negroes of America), 58, 61, 71, 86, 87
unemployment: benefits for, 95; minorities affected by, 36–37; political action and, 37–38; racial and gender differences in, 95, 96, 122–23, 199–200n4; warning of, 42
UNIA (Universal Negro Improvement Association), 34
United Negroes of America (UNA), 58, 61, 71, 86, 87
United Negro Labor Council (UNLC), 61, 62, 65
United States Employment Service (USES): on absenteeism, 67–68; congested areas and, 72; hiring practices and, 54–55; job recruitment and, 46
Universal Negro Improvement Association (UNIA), 34
Universal Non-Partisan League, 113–14
University of California, shipyard worker study by, 51, 55, 95
UNLC (United Negro Labor Council), 61, 62, 65
upward mobility: denied for blacks, 72; hopes for, 50, 52–53, 70; of newcomers, 64; notion of, 15
urban renewal: demolitions in, 99–100, 184–85n17; racial motives in, 97, 100–101; strategy for, 98–99
U.S. Army, 61, 67

U.S. Congress, 40–41
USES. See United States Employment Service (USES)
U.S. Maritime Commission, 43, 73, 75, 84
U.S. Supreme Court: on housing discrimination, 125; on labor union auxiliaries, 61–62; on separate but equal, 123, 138

Varlick, Orilla, 20
Vaughn, Hattie Griffin, 22–23
Verde Elementary School, 103
Vernon Street, housing on, 34–35
voluntary organizations: aid from, 38–39; on civil rights, 34; interracial, 106–8; meeting places for, 135; role of, 26, 30–32; state clubs as, 143–44. See also specific organizations
voluntary racial congregation, role of, 3–4, 118–19. See also political action; racial solidarity
voter registration, 124. See also elections

wages: for cannery workers, 21; cuts in, 55, 95, 96; discrimination in, 19–20, 52, 56; for domestics, 20–21; gender and, 57; as migration factor, 50; in shipyards, 43, 44, 56, 57, 64; significance for blacks, 66
Walker, Aaron "T-Bone," 139
Ward, Clara, 141
War Manpower Commission: on discrimination, 56, 57; on shipyard workers, 45, 46, 54
Warren, Earl, 117
wartime mobilization: industries in, 72; resources strained by, 73–74; union's demise in, 38. See also boomtown; demobilization; shipyards
Washington, Booker T., 120
Washington, Lonnie, 121
Washington Avenue, business on, 22
Watkins, F. W., 28
Watts riot, 126
Weeks, Samuel, 121
Welders Union Local, 56–57
West Contra Costa Community Welfare Council, 103
Western Appeal (newspaper), on churches, 27–28
Western Pipe and Steel Company, 14
Wheat, Vesper: on child care, 68–69; on health care, 128; housing of, 85, 116; migration of, 48, 147; on sports teams, 64

Wheat, Wilbur: church of, 140; housing of, 85, 116; integration and, 116–17, 149; migration of, 48; on newcomers, 83; occupation of, 56; on paychecks, 66; on transfers, 67; on white workers, 63–64

Wheeler, Juanita, 86, 91, 181n59

Wheeler, LeRoy, 91

White, Sylvester, 56–57

White, Walter, 62, 94–95

whites: after hours clubs for, 134; blues club women's relations with, 136–37; in housing projects, 84; job opportunities for, 95–96; in NAACP, 90; patronization by, 109–11; positive images of, 80; prejudices of, 63–64, 77–79, 98; public offices held by, 13, 15; racist organizations of, 25; upward mobility of, 15. *See also* discrimination; labor unions; segregation

Widow's Mite Fund (Masonic), 32, 38–39

Williams, Charmie Jones, 21, 26

Williams, Frank H., 117–18

Williams, Guthrie John, 113–14

Williams, Harry, 23, 26, 33, 38, 155n30

Williams, Harry, Jr., 26

Williams, Marguerite, 44, 69, 75

Williams, Neitha, 98, 99

Wilson, John Louis, 196n26

Wilson, Olly, 130

Wilson, Rosa Lewis, 193n3

Witherspoon, Jimmy, 132

women: baseball teams for, 145; as culture bearers, 130–31, 152n4; discrimination against, 4, 57–59, 122; as employment ambassadors, 21; as entrepreneurs, 123, 132–33, 135–37; occupations of, 4, 20–21, 157n50; organizations of, 14, 30–32, 124, 194n8; as referral agents for employment, 136. *See also* women workers

Women's Christian Temperance Union, 14–15

Women's Improvement Club, 14

Women's Progressive Club, 30–31

women workers: absenteeism of, 68–69; assistance for, 60; discrimination against, 4, 57–59, 122; negative images of, 80; opportunities for, 50–51, 122; as professionals, 122; recruitment of, 44–45, 46; in shipyards, fig. 13, 47, 50–51, 57–58; training for, 123; work culture of, 66–70

"Wonder City," Richmond as, 7

Woodson, Carter, 51

workers: absenteeism of, 64, 67–69; assistance for, 60; auxiliary unions for, 56–57, 59–62, 172n61; layoffs of, 94–95; negative images of, 80; postwar job opportunities for, 95–96; recruitment of, 44–47; reports on, 51, 53–54, 55; skills of, 54–56; specialized, 13, 43; training for, 43, 47, 56, 58–59, 123; transformed to urban laborers, 130; "union consciousness" of, 60–62; work culture of, 66–70; work patterns of, 68, 174n89. *See also* discrimination; employment; industrial development; unemployment; wages; women workers

Workers Alliance of America, 37–38

working class: culture and, 2, 140; declining status of, 4–5; political participation of, 13, 37–38; stigmatization of, 1–2. *See also* employment; wages; workers

Works Progress Administration (WPA), 36, 37, 194n8

World War II: segregation in, 24, 104; transformation during, 1–2; women's opportunities in, 4; worker recruitment during, 44–45. *See also* boomtown; defense industries; wartime mobilization

WPA (Works Progress Administration), 36, 37, 194n8

zoot suiters, 78

Text:	10/13 Galliard
Display:	Galliard
Composition:	G & S Typesetters, Inc.
Printing and Binding:	Thomson-Shore, Inc.